WHEN ECHOES SPEAK

a memoir

DAG SCHEER

TIPAZA

ISBN 978-1-7367196-0-2 (paperback)
ISBN 978-1-7367196-1-9 (epub)
ISBN 978-1-7367196-2-6 (mobi)

Cover design: Nayon Cho
Cover photo: Stuart Scheer
Editing: Elizabeth Barrett

TIPAZA

For Stuart, Jen, and Nick

CONTENTS

My mother in Riga, 1932.

PROLOGUE

FROZEN LANDSCAPES

MEMOIR IS PERHAPS not the right word for what my father wrote before he died at the age of eighty-eight in 1997. Thirty-six single-spaced pages in Latvian describe the major events in his life. His story is mine as well, for what happened to my family before I was born shaped my life as profoundly as my own experience. The events that defined the family have defined me.

Wars propel our stories because times of peace in Latvia have never lasted long. Most people have not heard of this nation, smaller than the state of Maine, nor could they place it on a map. The land is not one of dramatic contrasts or spectacular views. Rather, the landscape is of a gentle loveliness. Calm rivers flow toward the sea through stretches of fertile plains, through silent forests carpeted by pine needles. On hills among birch groves, oak trees provide moist shade for lush growths of ferns. Moss marshes and peat bogs surround clusters of lakes. In the spring, meadows form a tapestry of fragrant grasses and cornflowers.

It is not for its picturesque countryside but for its ice-free ports on the Baltic Sea that Latvia has been coveted and conquered by aggressive neighboring countries over the centuries. As a crossroad between East and West Europe, it has strategic importance.

At first, I didn't understand why, at the beginning of his memoir, my father wrote about a young French soldier in Napoleon's Grand Army. From history books, I knew how the 1812 invasion of Russia ended—catastrophically. Defeated, Napoleon's Army had to retreat, and starving soldiers marched across Russia's frozen countryside in the dead of winter. But what about this soldier?

In a nightmarish hallucination, I saw the ominous terrain. A Tolstoyan scene. For a moment, I had the strange sensation that I had accessed the memory of the young man. Visions appeared as if they had been stored in an atavistic memory bank.

A frigid whiteness stretched to the horizon. Ice-encrusted birch tree branches bent low, frozen to the ground. I shivered as if from a sudden arctic blast.

The soldier was one of an endless line of French troops trudging through blinding storms. Emaciated, they struggled over crunching snowdrifts, their hoar-frosted faces like gray marble, their legs gone numb. Some had collapsed and lay like bulging sacks.

Emerging from the trancelike realm of this harrowing scene, I reread my father's words.

From half a million soldiers of that campaign, only some twenty thousand endured the ordeal and arrived back in Vilnius from where they had set out. One of the surviving soldiers didn't remain in Lithuania, nor did he return to France, but settled in neighboring Latvia. He was Constantin Emanuel Le Rondon—my great-grandfather.

My father, Konstantīns, was named in honor of his great-grandfather, the French soldier.

∽

Frozen landscapes recurred in our family history, and wars continued to disrupt lives.

At the beginning of World War I, both my father and mother left their childhood homes in Riga. Along with half a million Latvians, their families fled to Russia to escape the German Army. In absurd historic symmetry, three decades later, during World War II, my family, along with, again, half a million Latvians, fled Latvia the opposite way, this time to Germany fleeing Stalin's Soviet Army.

My father was seven at the time of that first migration to Russia. His family settled in Moscow, where his father set up a printing business. One of my father's earliest memories is the distressing scene on a winter evening when his father came home, covered with snow, and didn't take off his coat. Nor did he pull off his heavy boots that left a slurry of melting ice on the floor. He sat down at the dining room table, gray and shrunken, silent for a while. Then he slammed the table with his fist.

"Those bloody Bolshevik bastards, they've taken everything," he said. Trying to control his anger in front of his wife and two young sons, he folded his arms across his chest. "Everything—all the presses gone. For what? To print their hideous propaganda posters."

Even though he was still a child, my father understood that the loss of his father's printing business was a devastating blow to the family. They moved to a small wooden house with no running water and no heat on the outskirts of the city. In winter, the family plodded through snowdrifts to cut firewood in Sokolniki Forest. My father helped carry logs on his sled and was sent to bring water from a pump quite a distance down the road. In the severe cold, water in the pump froze.

Their situation worsened when railway strikes in the country disrupted the flow of farm goods. Father remembered going to buy food with his mother and finding shelves in the market bare except for rotting potatoes and frozen cabbage. Sometimes, for a treat, his mother bought him a *leposka*—a sort of a cookie made from coffee grounds, its gritty texture hardly a treat.

My father (right) with his parents and older brother Rihards in Moscow, 1919.

In the Russian school, the kids taunted my father, pelting him with stones.

"*Bezenci, bezenci.*" Outsider.

Once they hurled a burning log, barely missing him. He tried to ignore their meanness and concentrated on his studies. A gifted student, he became fluent in Russian and excelled in mathematics.

Six years later, when my father was thirteen and it was finally thought safe to return to Latvia, the family packed up their modest belongings and got on the train to Riga. Near Velikiye Luki, about a hundred miles from the Latvian border, the train lurched to a stop. Soviet soldiers marched into the compartment and pointed a gun at his father.

Terrified, he watched his struggling father being dragged out of the compartment. As the train started to move, in a panic, he, along with his mother and older brother Rihards, leapt off the train. To break their fall, they rolled into a ditch. Brushing dust off their clothes, they walked along the tracks with no idea where they were going or what they were going to do. In a deserted part of the railway yard, where the unused tracks, littered with broken glass and metal scraps, disappeared in clumps of weeds, they climbed into an abandoned freight car. There they waited, even though they didn't know what they were waiting for. Days went by, and they had eaten the hard-boiled eggs and salted herring from the satchel, brought along from home, that his mother had grabbed as they dashed out of the train compartment. Hunger provided the courage to venture out to a nearby collective bakery for bread. Nibbling on bread crusts, they continued to wait, the unthinkable becoming more real each day. What if he didn't return?

It is strange, maybe remarkable, that my father didn't write about the fear he must have felt hiding in the derelict freight car, not knowing what was going to happen. Instead, he wrote:

Day after day I wandered along the tracks. There were these huge ancient Kolomna locomotives, abandoned there, and what made the long wait bearable was studying the wheel configurations, trying to figure out how those steam engines worked.

It is possible that my father was already developing the ability to cope in difficult situations, to deflect fear by finding distractions, engaging his curiosity and intellect.

A long six weeks later, his father suddenly appeared at the station. My father didn't write about the reason his father had been arrested or what happened to him in captivity. Perhaps he never found out. The reunited family continued their journey to Riga.

For two brief decades between the two world wars, Latvia was independent, occupied by neither Germans nor Soviets. My father's father became director of printing at Valters & Rapa, the foremost publishing house in Latvia. On the outskirts of Riga, across the Daugava River, on a quiet tree-lined street, he bought property and built a house. Years later, he built another one for my father and his brother, Rihards, and their young families—a substantial brick house surrounded by gardens.

Our family home in Riga, 1944.

My father often raved about the fruit trees they planted, the raspberry and currant bushes, and the vegetable patch at the back of the property. The fertile soil was rich in peat; their garden thrived. The taste of the frozen cabbage they subsisted on during their Moscow days may have lingered for years, but now they grew their own fresh heads of cabbage and put up sauerkraut in large wooden barrels. In autumn, the family scoured the nearby coniferous forest for the prized boletus mushrooms. The ones not eaten that evening, sautéed in butter, were put up in brine. I remember the glass jars of mushrooms, saved for the winter, lined up on pantry shelves.

Those peaceful years may have been my father's happiest. During that time, he earned a master's degree from the University of Latvia and—no doubt because he was tall and muscular, as well as a fine athlete—he was selected for the prestigious Latvian Gymnast's League.

In 1935, he married Eiženija. When I think of my mother, I see the gray hair pulled back in a sort of a bun, her blue-green eyes, the pale skin, never touched by even a smidgen of lipstick or blush.

"Maybe when I'm eighty," she once said, "I'll put on some lipstick."

Of course, she never did. I don't know much about how my parents met or what their lives were like before the war changed everything. I often pull out the photo album, the edges of the leather cover worn from the countless times I have flipped through its pages, searching for clues to fill in what I don't know.

When I look at the series of portraits my father took of my mother around the time they were married, I am struck by how beautiful she was. Yet I never thought her beautiful when I was growing up. There is a freshness, a bloom in her face, and even though these are black and white photos, she seems to glow. Was she looking at the camera? I rather think it was my father behind the camera that held her gaze. That soft, serene look on her face. An instant distilled by time. I can almost feel the chemistry between them. Maybe what I see is deep happiness.

My mother in Riga, 1935.

◆

My father wrote that even more than half a century later, he could still hear the metallic clanking of the Soviet tanks rolling down the streets of Riga in 1940. From the second-floor window of the Gutenberg Photoengraving Company, of which he was director, he watched Soviet soldiers pushing a cannon. Moments later, it fired, and all around him windows shattered.

A few days later, soldiers barged into his office and pulled him out of the chair. I can imagine that at that moment, he must have relived the nightmarish scene of his father being dragged out of the train compartment. In a state of dread, he let the Russians lead him to their headquarters, where they made ludicrous charges, accusing him of having made derogatory remarks about the Soviet flag.

"I'm sick of these filthy red rags everywhere," someone reported they had heard him exclaim. My father had no idea what they were talking about and sat silently, hoping it was nothing more than an attempt at harassment. After some warnings, he was released, but the strange episode left him fearful that anything could happen.

It took just three days for the Soviet Army to cross the eastern border and overrun Latvia. A quarter of a million troops marched throughout the country. The Communists confiscated private property, took over publishing houses and censored radio broadcasts. Local farm products were sent to Moscow, and each day it became more difficult to buy food.

Many government leaders were executed, others deported. The worst night of all was on June 14, 1941, one of the saddest days in the country's history. A day still commemorated. During that one night alone, 15,424 Latvians, among them women, children, even infants, were crowded into cattle cars and sent to labor camps in Siberia.

No one in our family was deported, but it was a difficult year. Like most Latvians, my father couldn't imagine anything worse happening than what they had just endured under the Soviets. He was wrong.

In June of 1941, German tanks crossed Latvia's western border and forced the Soviet Army out. In just two weeks, all of Latvia was under new occupation, this time Nazi occupation.

In downtown Riga, Father watched the steeple of St. Peter's burst into flames. The distinctive landmark of the city's skyline, the church where he had been married, where his daughters had been baptized, crumbled into a pile of smoldering embers.

The year under the Soviets had been of such terror and deprivations that when the Nazis invaded, many Latvians thought it might be a good thing. Some Latvians even fantasized that after driving out the Russians, the Nazi regime would restore Latvia's independence. It was said, though it was hard to believe, that there were Latvians who greeted the Nazi troops with armfuls of flowers.

~

In the old album, I search for a particular photo that must have been taken in 1943, the last one of the whole family still together. Everyone has gathered in front of the house on that spring day, with lilacs in full bloom. My father must be behind the camera because he is not in the photo. Aunt Lily and the two grandmothers stand in the back. My sister Maija and I, in identical dresses with lace collars and glass buttons, kneel in front of my mother who is holding Livija. Valija has not been born yet. I have a white bow in my hair, and I'm looking down at the glass buttons on the front of my dress. For a fleeting instant, as if a memory vault has suddenly opened, I am transported back to that spring day. I hear the click of the camera and see my buttons glint in the sun. From the contented and smiling faces, it is clear that no one was aware of what lay ahead.

My older sister Maija takes me around our garden in Riga, 1943

PART ONE

LEAVING

"*AK DIEVIŅ, AK dieviņ. Mums jāsteidzas.*" We've got to hurry.

The voices woke me.

I threw off the blanket and ran to find my mother. In her room, open suitcases gaped on the unmade bed. How pale Mother looked with a rolled-up green scarf tied around her forehead. She must have a headache. From the armoire, she pulled out her blue Sunday dress and folded it. Aunt Lily, still in her flowery robe, hurried in with a pile of sheets on her arm. Her long braid, usually twisted around her head, hung down in the back.

"We can't take them—there's no room." Aunt Lily snatched packets of photos from the suitcase. "Silver. Valuable things. That's what we should take," she said.

My mother sighed and tucked the photos back into the corners of the already full suitcase. Running to the kitchen, I listened for the glug-glug of porridge bubbling in the black pot. The stove had not been lit. The pot was gone.

Hair disheveled, Grandmother shuffled from pantry to table, piling up strawberry jam jars, potatoes and carrots with bits of moist earth still clinging to them. She added a slab of butter in parchment and a round loaf of dark bread. Muttering that the butter would go bad, she tied the four corners of the tablecloth to make a bundle.

My sister Maija, barefoot with blond pigtails in messy tangles, appeared in the doorway. Chubby toddler Livija, wiping a runny nose on her pajama sleeve, waddled up. Somewhere in the house, baby sister Valija was crying. No one seemed to notice. No one rushed to pick her up. Something was happening, but I didn't know what it was.

That afternoon, a horse-drawn wagon arrived in front of the house. In a frantic rush, suitcases and the bulging food bundle were hoisted up. The driver jumped down from his perch behind the horse to help lift in Grandmother. The coarse weave of his shirt scratched my cheek as he scooped me up and set me on top of a suitcase. Aunt Lily pulled Livija on her lap and hugged Maija alongside. Mother hurried up, carrying Valija cradled in a large wicker basket. I peered down at the baby, swaddled in pink flannel with only her tiny face and ruffle of lace cap visible. Mother lifted the basket then stood there, one foot propped against the wagon wheel, as if the effort to climb in was too much for her. As if she was not yet ready to leave.

"*Nāc tač u. Kāp iekšā!*" Come. Get in, Grandmother urged her.

The driver leapt down again to help her.

My other grandmother, my father's mother, stood next to the wagon, pressing a handkerchief against her mouth to stop from crying. She was not coming with us. In a wrenching moment of stifled sobs, we waved good-bye to her and to the empty house behind her.

With a clatter of wheels, the rickety wagon set off, creaking and tilting. The horse clomped on unevenly rounded cobblestones, and with a swish of its tail swept off the flies settling on its rump. Warm barn smells wafted. I wrapped my arm around the side slat of the wagon to keep from sliding off the suitcase, the edge of it sharp against my legs. All around us wagons, as loaded as ours, crowded the road. All heading toward the harbor.

At last the dull gray metal of the ship loomed, blurred in a salty mist that smelled of fish. On the pier, frenzied families unloaded wagons, rushed and scrambled to board. Up the ramp they hauled suitcases and rolls of bedding.

I was scared to go up the steep ramp. It rocked, my knees wobbled. "*Dod roku,*" I said. Hold my hand.

No one had a free hand to help me. With halting steps, I edged up the incline, gripping the swaying rope that served for a handrail. Nothing to hold me from tumbling off into the churning gray water far below. The impatient crowd pushed me along.

⁓

I was not yet five years old that day, on the cusp of memory, the delicate balance of my earliest years splintered by a historic worldwide cataclysm I was too young to understand. What did I leave behind when the ship left the pier? What was it that came with me?

It was August of 1944. My father had been gone more than a year, and there had been no news from him for months. Should we stay in Riga or leave? Never before had my mother faced such a tough decision. And my father was not there to give advice. All over the city, friends and relatives were packing up their most precious belongings. Many had already left. Aunt Lily, always practical, persuaded my mother that our family must also leave. Quickly. The Soviet Army had already crossed the border and was heading toward Riga.

I sometimes try to imagine what our life would have been like if we had not left that day. Two months later, we would have heard

Soviet tanks rumbling down the city's boulevards. We would have seen the dreaded hammer and sickle flutter above buildings, and jubilant Russian soldiers parading through the streets.

But we were on the ship, packed with hundreds of others fleeing Latvia. Distraught families crowded on the deck, shouting farewells to relatives left behind. The women, weeping and waving white handkerchiefs, jostled for a desperate last glimpse of faces they might never see again. Amid the crush, I squeezed in next to my mother.

As the ship pulled away from the pier, it started to drizzle, and everyone rushed for cover. The shoreline receded, and my mother stood by the railing. Alone. Watching the church steeples of Riga's skyline fade into the mist, she must have wondered whether she would ever see her beloved city again.

She would not.

༈

From the harbor in Hamburg, we made our way in horse-drawn wagons to the Thuringian town of Staitz, not far from Germany's eastern border where, on the map, Czechoslovakia bulges into Germany like a giant breast. We may have traveled from the coast, halfway down Germany to this rural area, because Mother thought, or hoped, my father might still be in Czechoslovakia.

On a farm, my mother rented a makeshift loft in a barn. The two small rooms in the barn were a drastic change from our home in Riga. My mother must have hoped that our stay would be a short one, for she was not used to such dismal surroundings.

"Mēs dzīvojam kūtī. Kā govis un cūkas." We've been reduced to living in a barn, like cows and pigs, she complained to Grandmother. She hated being awakened at daybreak by the rooster and other early-morning farm sounds. She worried about Valija, who was pale and not chubby like her other babies had been.

Dressing quickly, Maija and I would escape every morning from the cramped rooms and the grumbling. While my mother was unhappy with our new lodgings, for Maija and me the farm was rich with new sounds and smells. Unlike our garden in Riga where we had no animals, not even a dog or a cat, this farm was fully inhabited. We would dash down the narrow staircase into the barn below, filled with sweet-smelling bales of hay, where we stroked the resident cat before it scampered away. Outside in the barnyard, we played with the two black dogs that lazed in a sunny patch. Holding our breath, we hurried past the chicken coop and the steaming mound of manure behind the barn. There, the farmer's flock of white geese wandered freely, and I, being only goose-sized myself, was terrified when, honking and wings flapping, they chased me. To get away, we ran to the paddock and straddled the fence to watch the horses graze.

Often in the middle of the night, Mother would shake me awake. I heard sirens. We had to hurry to the bomb shelter. She wrapped my baby sister in a blanket, then helped me get dressed. Pleading tearfully that the steep staircase down from the loft was too hard for her, Grandmother would refuse to go. No time to argue. No time to try to persuade her. Mother and Aunt Lily had no choice but to leave Grandmother behind.

Shivering in the cold night air, I tried to keep up as everyone hurried out of the barnyard and down the street to the designated shelter. Uneven steps led into the dark, crowded cellar where, between sacks of potatoes and farm tools, we huddled against damp stone walls. From the beam of someone's flashlight, I glimpsed looming shadows and a corner where, layered with grime, cobwebs drooped.

"*Licht aus! Ausschalten! Kein Licht!*" Angry shouts to turn off the flashlight.

I heard a low rumble. Then a penetrating engine noise, louder and louder until it became an ear-piercing screech. Squeezing my eyes shut, I held my hands over my ears and tried not to breathe. The house shook and the wall behind me vibrated. The plane passed, and I heard whispers of relief. "*Gott sei Dank! Gott sei Dank!*" A moment later, another distant rumble. More aircraft thundered down and the horrible screech overhead. Then a creepy silence that hurt my ears.

"*Wir gehen?*" someone would ask hopefully.

"*Noch nicht, noch nicht!*" Not yet, others replied. We waited in the dark. My hands and feet numb from the cold.

Those were American or British aircraft bombing us. The Allied planes targeted military and industrial sites. They destroyed railways and harbors and, it is difficult to believe now, the planes bombed civilian areas as well. To crush the German people's morale, it was said.

On the way to buy bread in the village one morning, we passed a house that had been hit. The entire side of it was gone, the yard strewn with rubble. Walls had collapsed, and we could see inside the rooms. An upstairs one had pretty wallpaper—pink and yellow flowers.

"Was that someone's bedroom?" I asked my mother. "What happened to the people?"

She didn't answer.

⁓

When Germany surrendered to the Allies in the spring of 1945, millions of uprooted people, like us, were living in a state of limbo, scattered in villages all over Germany. Along with Latvians were Poles, Ukrainians, Yugoslavs, and other Eastern Europeans who could no longer return to their homes. Their countries, now occupied by the Soviet Army, had changed forever. The Allied governments divided defeated Germany into zones and began establishing displaced persons camps to provide shelter for families like ours.

When my mother learned about the camps, we left our refuge in the barn and traveled to the nearest one in Fürth. A few days later, we were transported to one in Nuremberg. It was a bleak and much sadder place than the farm had been. The cold autumn air seeped through broken windowpanes of the wooden barracks where we had been allotted a corner of the large room shared with other families. Wrapped in army-issue olive green blankets, we slept on canvas cots.

Like a shadow, my mother walked up and down the room, rocking Valija to stop her from crying. She worried that her baby was not gaining weight. Valija's cry was feeble and she was frail.

Another fear must have worried her. The possibility she might never see my father again. She withdrew into a world of silence and turned inward, away from us. It could be that she believed the worst that could happen had already happened.

Time hung heavy in the camp with nothing to do and nowhere to go. One day blurred into the next. Endless days of waiting. Waiting for something to happen—anything. Anything at all, for that would mean that life could finally move forward.

There was no news from Father. But how could there have been? He didn't know where we were.

IN HITLER'S ARMY

ABOUT A YEAR before we left Riga, on July 17 of 1943, my father received an official notice to report for duty. He had been "drafted" into Hitler's army. He was shocked. There must be a mistake, he thought. As a Latvian citizen, how could he be drafted into the German Army? No. Not possible.

But the German commanders had figured out a way. The Nazi war machine needed fresh manpower, and so they created the *Lettische SS-Freiwilligen Legion,* the Latvian SS Volunteer Legion. The "volunteer" part was absurd. My father would never have willingly joined Hitler's army. But he had no choice. Reporting for duty, he was forced to sign a document stating that he had joined the German Army of his own free will. The alternative was being sent to a Nazi slave labor camp or, worse yet, to the infamous Salaspils concentration camp in Latvia. Several days later, my father was gone.

At first, along with the other "recruits," Father hoped they would remain in Latvia and help prevent another brutal Soviet Army takeover of the country, like the one in 1940. They may have even rationalized that perhaps they could somehow help regain their country's independence. But to my father's horror, he was ordered to board the ship that would take him to the Fifteenth Waffen-Grenadier Division of the SS Headquarters near Danzig, East Prussia.

From there, because of his university education, he was sent for officer training in Czechoslovakia. Disrupting the bucolic farmlands and tranquil towns of the Central Bohemian Region, the Nazis had established the *SS-Truppenübungsplatz Böhmen,* a military training site near Benešov, about forty kilometers south of Prague. The people of Benešov and the surrounding towns and farms had been driven out. Konopiště Castle, with its four imposing red-roofed towers, became the headquarters. On military maneuvers, across sun-dappled fields, the troops' black boots trampled the wheat and barley the farmers hadn't been able to harvest before abandoning their farms. The grapevine-covered hills echoed with the hostile litany of the commander's battle orders.

With poor military rations, my father began to lose weight. One morning his gold wedding band was gone, had slipped off his finger. In a letter my mother received from him before we left Riga, he wrote:

> *There it was, lying at the bottom of the metal locker—among the hand grenades and machine gun ammunition. You can't imagine how appalled I was to see my ring next to all that horrid war stuff. I could have cried.*

In another letter, carefully worded to pass military censors, he wrote about officer instruction courses. In German, along with German soldiers, he was taught *kriegspiel,* logistics, battle tactics, military matters—five hours in a class setting and four of maneuvers in the countryside, sometimes at night. The worst part, he cryptically complained, was listening to the twisted propaganda lectures about the superiority of the Germanic race and the repellent ethnic cleansing theories. In his fine handwriting, in more detail and to add a cheerful tone to his letter, he described the exquisite scenery of the region.

… even rows of vineyards on terraced slopes with clusters of ripe grapes still on the vines. The wide view from the top of a hill—more hills in the distance, contoured one behind the other shrouded in gray mists …

∽

The fact that Latvian men had been forced to serve in Hitler's army is now an almost forgotten and still misunderstood part of World War II history. In his memoir, my father described the ordeal. It was a part of his life about which he had never spoken to us. Why did he write it? The heartbreaking story is as painful to read as it must have been for my father to write. Sometimes I thought if he were alive, I would ask him many questions. But then again, perhaps I wouldn't.

After officer training, my father's unit was deployed to the eastern front. They were to hold back the rapidly advancing Red Army, which had just launched the Vistula-Oder Offensive in Poland and East Prussia.

As the soldiers set out across fields of snow, the Latvian units were dismayed to discover that the German Army treated them like prisoners. Unlike the thick wool coats and sturdy leather boots of the German soldiers, the Latvian Legion men had been issued lightweight uniforms, and their boots were flimsy. In the bitter cold, marching within view of the Russian encampment, they took up battle positions. On their right, a German unit with machine guns was protected by tanks. Equipped only with rifles and hand grenades, the Latvian soldiers had no tanks protecting them.

The brutal force of the monstrous Nazi military machine had sucked my father, along with thousands of other Latvian men, into the tangled mess of what they knew was an immoral war. The absurd reality was that the Latvian Legion men did not hate the Germans any less than they hated the Russians. They loathed both. Badly equipped, exposed to gunfire, forced to provide cover for German soldiers, they realized they were being exploited. They felt betrayed.

At night, deafened by the ripping sound of exploding shells, my father watched bursts of gunfire and detonating grenades light up the sky. With heavy tanks and machine guns, the much better equipped Red Army closed in on them. The Latvian men, white winter camouflage slipped over their helmets and uniforms, faced the relentless Russian tanks.

Week after week, each bloody skirmish was followed by the German Army's chaotic retreat. In Father's unit, columns dispersed, and wounded soldiers remained behind on the battlefield. Some retreating soldiers got separated from their units, others simply deserted. Vastly outnumbered, the only option for the German Army and its Latvian conscripts was to retreat and keep retreating.

Reading my father's battle descriptions, I can see it—soldiers crossing the frozen terrain on foot, shoulders crushed by heavy backpacks, metal canteens jangling against rifles. He wrote that as they retreated at night, they found quarters in abandoned schools, cowsheds, or the occasional hayloft. With their combat rations used up, they ate whatever they could find—a sack of potatoes stored in the cellar of an empty house, jars of preserves in a pantry, a stash of kohlrabi in a barn. They found frozen heads of cabbage that had been left in a field—the farmers had fled before harvesting them. The pains of hunger became more acute. When they hadn't eaten for days, a slab of bacon and a sack of sugar were a lucky find. They pulled off chunks of raw bacon, dipped them in sugar, and pronounced the combination "deliriously delicious." Once, they slaughtered a stray pig and cooked it on a fire made by burning the wood of a fallen-down fence along the road. Some of the soldiers became jaundiced and were overwhelmed by nausea. Their dark urine confirmed hepatitis. During the day, they continued their march. At night, tormented by lice that infested their clothing, they were awakened by hideous combat nightmares. Disoriented from lack of sleep, they marched on.

More gnawing than hunger was my father's fear for his family. He guessed that by then we had escaped from Latvia and were probably somewhere in Germany. He was afraid of what might have happened to his widowed mother, knowing she would not have wanted to leave her home in Riga.

At one point, it looked as if my father's unit had left the Russian Army behind. Hoping to reorganize and gather strength, the soldiers took shelter in a deserted village. They were wrong. The Russian Army had advanced. Their tanks, massing from all directions, surrounded the village.

Father's unit was captured and herded into a clearing in the forest, enclosed by barbed wire. At night they huddled on the frozen ground. At first, a wagon of provisions came along, but with those food supplies used up, they were left to starve. In desperation, they killed the regiment's horse to make soup.

It's not clear from my father's narrative whether the captured men knew that by then the German Army had already been defeated in Europe. Canadian troops eventually arrived and rounded up the German and Latvian troops held captive. They were taken by train to the Fallingbostel camps, the notorious former Nazi stalag camps where some 90,000 Allied prisoners of war had been imprisoned. In April of 1945, after the Allied prisoners were released, it was used to imprison captured soldiers—German and Latvian soldiers alike, including my father's unit.

My father's description of the events at this camp is wrenching. He confessed that all along, the Latvian Legion men had secretly hoped to surrender or be captured by the American or Canadian soldiers. They erroneously believed that the truth about their forced conscription into the SS would be known and recognized. They expected they would be treated well. Some thought they might even be welcomed by the Allies and quickly released.

As they arrived at the Fallingbostel camp, a shock awaited them. Seeing the Latvian soldiers' German uniforms, the enraged Canadian soldiers kicked them viciously. The Brits attacked with clubs. Assuming the Latvian soldiers had truly volunteered, they showed even greater contempt for them than for the regular German soldiers. The truth of the Latvian Legion soldiers being coerced into fighting with the German Army didn't become known until the 1945-1946 Nuremberg trials.

Along with 7,000 Germans and 3,000 other Latvians, my father was held as a prisoner of war behind a heavily guarded, double barbed-wire fence. After being so badly treated by the Germans, the Latvian men were now treated by the Allies even worse than the German soldiers were. They learned what it felt like to be despised.

The food portions—a couple of pieces of hardtack, a small can of corned beef to be shared by five men, and an occasional watery soup—were barely enough to keep the prisoners alive. They lost weight. Many died of starvation and disease.

After what seemed like an eternity, a vague rumor circulated that they might soon be released. The rumor turned out to be true, but not as they had hoped. The Latvian men watched as, incredibly, the German prisoners were set free first. The Latvian soldiers, still hopeful, awaited their turn. To their disbelief, instead of being released, they were crammed into trucks in a long convoy, guarded by tanks. Crowded side by side, the soldiers sat, disillusioned once again by this nightmarish turn of events. Unarmed, weakened by malnutrition and mistreatment, they must have wondered why they were still considered dangerous. They lost all hope of being released and had no idea what would happen to them. They now expected the worst.

The convoy headed north through miles of pine forests, past villages of timber-framed houses, past meadows and farmlands. Gazing out from the trucks, the soldiers saw hills covered with tall grasses and heather. The road led past orchards in bloom. The soft spring breeze that ruffled their hair was a tease, and they must have wondered whether this lovely spring could very well be their last.

෪

Their destination was another camp in northern Germany, not as heavily guarded. Once in a while, their rations were even supplemented by loaves of coarse dark bread that my father found more delicious than any cake he had ever eaten.

From time to time, a Latvian minister was given permission to visit and hold church services at the prison camp. Eventually, through the minister, Latvian communities scattered in displaced person camps throughout Germany learned of the whereabouts of the imprisoned Latvian Legion's soldiers.

The minister warned that the prisoners were not going to be released anytime soon and circulated a list of their names. In Berlin's DP camp, my father's older brother, Rihards, spotted my father's name on the long list.

Rihards told an actor friend about the minister's visits to the POW camp and that his brother was held prisoner there.

In a light-hearted manner, he added, "If they let the minister in for church services, perhaps they'll let you perform a play there. You could smuggle my brother out."

"Sure, I'll get some friends together and do a play," the actor replied, also in jest.

But the more Rihards thought about it, the more obsessed he became with the possibilities of such a plan. At first, it seemed like an impossible and crazy idea, but as he discussed it with his friends, the rescue strategy became more and more real. They began to believe they could actually pull it off. Over the next few weeks, they concocted a scheme that was not without considerable risk, for they knew they could all end up behind barbed wire.

They chose a play for the simplicity of its two sets. One took place in a room in a farmhouse, the other in a bar. Both could easily be improvised with just a few props. The five acts of the classic nineteenth-century Latvian morality play *The Lost Son* would be reduced to three, and the roles played by a handful of friends. They dared not take women along; men would play their parts. The biggest obstacle was finding a vehicle large enough for all the props, the "actors," and hopefully my father on the return trip.

As they drove up to the camp and saw the sinister-looking watchtowers, they must have wondered whether what they were attempting wasn't a huge mistake. Would they all end up being arrested? They hadn't expected the forbidding grimness of the camp, its high wall with barbed wire, the tall poles with security lights beaming down. At the gate, their resolve was replaced by a sense of dread. They were seriously tempted to turn back. No one spoke, but the feeling that this might end badly was palpable.

Suspicious of the actor's permission letter, armed guards at the front gate refused to let the troupe enter. They waited in gloomy silence until an official arrived to verify its authenticity.

The huge mess hall was ready for the performance—tables moved against the walls, chairs in orderly rows, and a makeshift platform erected that would serve for the stage. As the props for the farmhouse scene were set up, prisoners crowded into the hall until there wasn't even standing room left. Any bit of diversion in the camp was a welcome relief. As the play began, Rihards, on the sidelines tending to the props, scanned the hall for my father. The thin men in rumpled prison garb with haggard faces and sunken cheeks all looked alike. He realized my father wouldn't look any different from the other gaunt, ashen-faced prisoners.

Sitting on one of the tables in the back of the hall, squeezed in between his cellmates, my father likewise didn't recognize his brother working next to the stage platform.

By the end of the second act, Rihards still hadn't spotted my father and began to worry that he hadn't come. An awful thought occurred to him. Perhaps he had died.

At the end of the third act, a melodramatic moment in the play was accompanied by the sound of thunder. The lost son climbs in through the open window of the farmhouse to take money from his father's desk to pay gambling debts. The old man, mistaking the intruder for a burglar, shoots him—his own son. Another roll of thunder ends the play. Looking over to where the thunder sound was being produced, Father recognized the figure in the shadows. It was his brother banging out a drum roll on the seat of a chair.

Rihards? Is that Rihards? What's he doing here? My father thought he must be imagining it.

While the actors took their bows, my father pushed his way through the crowd. Recognizing his brother at last, Rihards put his arm around Father's bony shoulders and dragged him out to the waiting van. Safely inside, he changed into civilian clothes that lay on the back seat.

⌁

Left off in Hamburg, Father started his search for us by catching rides on freight trains, the only transportation left in war-torn Germany. Sitting on top of coal-filled wagons, his face blackened by coal dust and soot, breathing fumes from the locomotives, he crisscrossed Germany. From one displaced persons camp to another, he searched across the country. In Wildflecken, he was told that we may have been there but had already departed.

"Try Eichstätt," they said.

He didn't find us in Eichstätt. We might be in a camp in Fürth, it was suggested. We had been in Fürth, but by the time he arrived, we had been transported to the displaced persons camp in Nuremberg.

There, behind barbed wire fencing in a low wooden barracks, Father found us.

The athletic and muscular man that my father had been when forced into the German Army was a skeletal figure now. The blond curly hair was mostly gone; his attempt at a smile revealed missing teeth. Behind wire-rimmed glasses, his pale blue eyes had a distant look.

I think that my mother, at first, didn't believe it could be my father. Then her relief when she recognized him must have been marred by the shock of his appearance. Father, too, must have been alarmed when he first saw my mother. The suffering she had endured had lined her face. In her drab clothing, she hardly resembled the elegant wife he had left behind in Riga.

What should have been a joyful reunion was a subdued one. Father looked at his daughters, one by one, with a strange expression on his face, as if he didn't quite recognize us. Perhaps he didn't. We had grown since he last saw us.

No one spoke. How could Father begin to tell what he had gone through? He knew there was the awful possibility that he might be taken prisoner again. Nor did my mother want to talk about living in a barn with the constant threat of air raids. In silence, as if numbed by their experiences, the family sat on cots, wondering what life in a DP camp would be like.

From the camp in Nuremburg, we were taken to one in Ansbach, where we spent the next five years.

With my sisters. I'm in the back (left) with Maija.
In front are Livija (left) and Valija.

QUIET CHILD

MEMORY, ANISH KAPOOR'S installation at the Guggenheim Museum, captured for me the dilemma of articulating memories. The twenty-four-ton steel megasculpture, weathering over time, had acquired a rust patina. Despite the rigidity of the industrial material, steel tiles welded together formed an oddly irregular, swollen form that suggested something organic, biomorphic. Squeezed into a space too small for it, the massive bulging piece appeared to press against the walls, as if trying to free itself from confinement.

At the museum, I viewed the work from various points, but it was always only partially visible. Sections of it remained maddeningly obstructed, so that the entire work could only be imagined. Through a small aperture in the sculpture's side, I peered into its vast interior, a black hole of time and space deformed, spiraling inward. The more I contemplated the installation, the more elusive its meaning became, similar to memory itself.

As I dredged up details of long-ago events, I faced the problem examined in Kapoor's installation, of reconstructing the whole from its parts. The years in the Ansbach DP camp have acquired a foggy remoteness, but memory can trick one into summoning up what was thought to be long forgotten.

The fragments that follow describe life in the camp as seen

through the eyes of a child, my eyes. There is the urge to coax a pattern from these early recollections, hoping they might provide clues for what followed later in life.

∽

Rain streaked the window in dirty rivulets. From the second floor of the grim brick building, I looked out at the puddled dirt field and rows of wooden barracks. Although I couldn't see it, I knew that behind the barracks, barbed wire fencing enclosed the camp.

Our two small rooms were bare except for beds, a rickety table or two, and an iron stove in the corner. I slept in the smaller of the rooms with a bed for my grandmother and three beds stacked on top of each other, bunkbed style. Maija, my older sister, had the bottom bed; I the one above hers; and on top was Aunt Lily's. To get into bed, I stepped on the small table placed next to it.

A piece of colorful fabric tacked to the wall or a mirror could have brightened the rooms, made them more like home. But my mother made no effort to lessen their dreariness. To her, this was just a temporary place, but temporary lasted five years. It's not that I remember the absence of a mirror; rather that if there had been one, I would have known what I looked like.

On that rainy day, Aunt Lily had left her hand mirror on the table beside its matching silver-handled hairbrush, treasures from Riga. I ran my thumb on the grooves of the monogrammed LL on the tarnished silver on the back of the mirror, then picked it up. Eyes stared back at me. Eyes of palest blue. Too pale, as if the blue had been washed out the way the water in the basin tinged blue when I rinsed out my white ink-stained hanky. The eyes in the mirror were not like Maija's, or Livija's, or even Valija's. Theirs were darker, a more greenish-blue. I lowered the mirror to the rest of my face, dismayed to discover the pale skin of my nose and cheeks spattered with tiny light brown spots. Freckles. I quickly put down the mirror.

When the sun came out, to escape the two crowded rooms, I ran outside to join my friend Maruta, already drawing hopscotch squares in the dirt with a stick. Tired of jumping, we took turns on the swings. I clambered up on the rough plank, rigged to tall poles by a cable made of twisted wires. Higher and higher, long pigtails flying, wind scouring my face. When Maruta took her turn on the swings, I searched for bits of glass strewn in the dirt, green and brown shards from broken bottles. The sun sparkled off a shiny red chip from the smashed taillight of a military truck. I would make a necklace.

❧

School started. Classrooms were set up in a low wooden building near the camp entrance, teachers recruited from among Latvian refugees. On school mornings, I put on my dark-green dress, black stockings, black apron, and a little white collar, the only thing that got washed each week. Having a clean collar gave me a feeling of freshness and order. My mother brushed my curly hair and braided it tight so that my scalp tingled. From the way she yanked at the tangles, I felt her impatience, her unhappiness.

I was ready for breakfast—hot chicory coffee in my tin cup and a slice of dense dark bread slathered with lard. At school there was lumpy barley porridge. The teacher walked up and down the rows of desks, spooning out dollops of the tepid mass from a big pot.

Once in a while, to relieve the tedium of long division or copying paragraphs from the blackboard, the teacher let us draw. I liked to sketch a crude profile of Stalin with his curled-up mustache and black hair, oiled and combed back. The mustache was fun to do. All the kids drew profiles of Stalin. We didn't know much about him, except that he was evil and the reason we were in the camp. We had heard the names of other evil people—Molotov, Vyshinsky—but we didn't know what they looked like.

In the afternoon came the dreaded cod liver oil. A glass bottle with the sickening yellowish contents was brought in and set down on the teacher's desk. The class lined up for a revolting spoonful. I struggled to swallow it, the spoon warm from all the mouths of the children in front of me in the line. The oily, fishy taste lingered.

In the evenings, Mother brought soup from the communal kitchen—powdered pea soup or something not easily identified. Rarely, a piece of pork with congealed white fat floated on top, which my parents ate but made me gag. We had to finish our soup before we could leave the table.

A simple thing, an orange—an unusual treat. One day, Aunt Lily brought one for us. At first, we stared at the bright orange of it. Not a color found in our drab surroundings, like a bit of sunlight. It was peeled and partitioned into neat segments, one for each of us. As I bit into it, the tangy sweet juice sparkled on my palate.

Years later, when we were living in Ohio, at lunchtime in the school cafeteria too many choices dazzled—slices of meatloaf, silky gravy, mashed potatoes, sweet kernels of corn, baked beans, plump fragrant hot dogs. And for dessert: quivering cubes of red, yellow, or green Jell-O. The wafting smells, the splendid display, all the giddying options. So much food! How could I choose? I would remember the thin powdered pea soup meals we had in the DP camp. Overwhelmed by such abundance in front of me, sometimes I would leave the school cafeteria line with an empty tray and go hungry the rest of the day.

Two of my sisters had defective teeth because we rarely had milk and no cheese in the camp. When Maija lost her baby teeth, the enamel of the permanent ones didn't form properly. Seeing the brownish stubs that marred her smile, I felt sorry for her.

One evening my father came home carrying a big cardboard box under his arm. He set it on the table with exaggerated ceremony. The capital letters on the box spelled out CARE. With his pocket knife, he slit open the top. I elbowed myself up to the table, jostling my sisters to get as close as possible. Slowly, making this special moment last, he pulled out one precious item after another. Packets of flour, sugar, and powdered milk were lined up. A can of corned beef. Then a jar of something that puzzled him. He unscrewed the lid and passed it around for us to sniff. We shook our heads and wrinkled our noses.

"Doesn't smell good." My sisters and I agreed.

Father set aside the peanut butter. Next came powdered eggs and a small box of raisins.

"Can we have some?" I asked. Father started to open the box, but Mother put her hand on his arm.

"No, wait. Let's save the raisins. I'll make a cake." The CARE package contained all the ingredients she needed.

Father set down the raisins and fished out a can of coffee, more corned beef, and a can of pineapple juice. I was afraid the box was now empty and wished we could eat some raisins. Father reached in again, fumbled in the bottom of the box, and came up with a bar of chocolate wrapped in silver foil.

The next day, he unwrapped the chocolate and divided it up in squares. There was a piece for me and another that I was to take to Maija. I ran outside to find her. Admiring my square for a moment, I popped it into my mouth and felt the corners of it with my tongue as it dissolved. The dark sweetness disappeared down my throat too quickly. I looked for Maija. The other little piece, the one for her, was beginning to melt in my hand. Without thinking, I put that one in my mouth also. As soon as I swallowed it, I was sorry. I didn't know the word *guilt*, but the feeling of it stayed with me for a long time.

After dinner we got to taste the pineapple juice. We had heard that someone had once opened the can after drinking the juice and found a whole slice of pineapple at the bottom. We asked Father to pry open the can with his pocket knife, hoping there would be that bonus slice inside. There wasn't.

Dressing up.

✧

When we still lived in Riga, my mother sang "Un Bel Di" while kneading bread. She had a beautiful, clear soprano voice. In the camp, she no longer sang, and I only heard her lovely voice again many years later, when she sang that same song and I recognized the aria from Puccini's opera *Madama Butterfly*. In her youth, she had studied violin and piano, but had abandoned lessons after getting married. Now that she had four daughters, her musical ambitions were focused on them. In particular, she had hopes for me.

At age three, I sat at the piano in our dining room in Riga for long stretches at a time and picked out simple melodies. Hitting two or three keys together, I discovered chords and harmonies. My mother interpreted my inventive approach to the piano at such an early age as a sign of talent. In the camp, her plans for my musical training seemed better forgotten. However, she was tenacious. How to continue musical training for her daughters when living without even the most basic necessities? She would find a way.

To start with, on a long piece of cardboard, she drew a few octaves of the piano keyboard, shaded in the black keys, and laid the mock keyboard on a table in front of me. Trying to rekindle my interest in the piano, she wanted me to practice playing on the cardboard. The stiff, mute keyboard produced no melodies, no harmonies. I quickly lost interest.

My mother didn't give up. One morning, furniture being moved in the other room woke me. Beds, as well as the table where we ate, had been rearranged and a space cleared against the wall. Later in the day, incredibly, an upright piano was brought in. Our family lacked proper food, clothing, and most other essentials. The piano was a bizarre acquisition. To rent it, Mother must have traded silver or some of her jewelry brought from Riga. Borrowing sheet music from a musician who had taught piano in Latvia, she copied by hand pieces she wanted us to learn.

My eighth birthday seemed an ordinary day, and I thought everyone had forgotten. Our dinner was the usual watery soup that tasted stale, like dust. I dawdled, not wanting to eat it. Mother insisted.

"Then," she said, "you can have your birthday present. It's hidden under the covers of your bed."

I quickly gulped down my soup. Was it a doll? I really wanted one. I ran and pulled back the covers.

"What's that?" I asked.

"A violin bow," my mother said.

I didn't have a violin, but I had a bow. I struggled to hide my disappointment.

∽

One Sunday morning, carrying Valija on his shoulders, Father took us across the large bare-dirt quadrangle that separated our building and the camp's entrance. Stepping aside as military trucks passed, I tried not to breathe in the fumes and clouds of dust. At the entrance barrier, guards pored over our identification cards before letting us pass. Leaving behind the gray misery of the camp was like stepping from a sepia world into one of exploding color. Outside the gates, the narrow cobblestone streets were lined with neatly painted houses and fenced-in gardens with flowers in bloom. Under ceramic toadstools, grinning elves seemed to wink at me. Every window had white lace curtains and pots of bright red geraniums on the sills. What would it be like to live in one of those houses? I imagined the warm cushiony couch, the soft carpet, a table set with porcelain dishes and shiny silver.

Leaving the small village behind, we hiked up a grassy incline to the woods. I skipped ahead into the dappled green world of mosses that muffled footsteps. Ferns, damp with dew, brushed against my bare legs. It seemed a hushed world, but by listening closely I heard countless tiny sounds—the swish of leaves, an insect drone, warbling from up high in the branches. In a sun-soaked clearing among tall grasses, my sisters and I picked buttercups. A decaying log bridged a brook. Wading in the cool clear water, we collected smooth pebbles.

My father with Livija (left) and Valija.

My father carrying Valija.

On the way back, we passed an orchard where ripe plums had fallen and lay scattered on the ground. We picked them up until our aprons bulged, and that evening Grandmother lit the little wood stove in the corner of the room and cooked the plums, filling the room with sweetness. We each got a spoonful of the sticky mass in our tin cups, and giggling, my sisters and I let the syrupy fruit run down our chins. It had been a long time since we had tasted anything so delicious.

෯

Looking out the window one day, I saw Maruta riding a shiny red bicycle. Oh, if I could do that I would be so happy, I thought.

"Could we rent one too? In the village?" I asked my father.

He shook his head and said he didn't have time. Father taught math and was principal of the camp school. As a photographer, he also worked in the darkroom at night, developing photos for the refugees' immigration documents.

"Besides," he said, "you don't know how to ride a bicycle, and they won't rent one unless you do. You know how the Germans are about their rules."

Father, so thin now, looked tired. He rarely smiled, I think because of his gold teeth. Disappointed, I turned away.

Then I thought, how difficult could it be to ride a bicycle? Maruta was riding one. You just sit and push the pedals around. Not giving up, I blurted out that I already knew how to ride a bicycle. Father looked surprised, but then said he would take us when he had time.

It amazed me that Father had agreed so readily, and I felt uneasy about saying I knew how to ride a bicycle. He believed me.

When my father was finally able to arrange some free time, he took my sisters and me to the bicycle shop. The shopkeeper sized me up and brought out a small bike. I was supposed to take a spin around the courtyard to show him how well I could ride. My sisters stood aside and watched while my father held the bike as I got on. I grabbed the handlebars and started to push the pedals. Father let go. Without realizing what was happening, I, of course, immediately fell over, bike and all. I picked myself up.

Father returned the bike to the shop. The shopkeeper dusted it off and shook his head, muttering, "*Nein, nein, es geht nicht.*"

Father was angry, and I was ashamed. We walked back to the

camp without saying a word. He didn't need to scold me. I felt awful. Then, as I thought about it later, I began to blame him. In a pathetic attempt of self-justification, I asked myself, "How did my father think I had learned to ride a bike anyway? Where? When?"

My father relented and came back one day with a bicycle. In the flat area near our building, he patiently held the bicycle as my sisters and I took turns. When he left to work on his backlog of ID photos, we stayed with the bicycle. My sisters and I helped each other try to get the hang of it. They quickly got bored and left.

I stayed and kept struggling on my own—falling over, picking myself up, trying again. I even once got going and was pedaling away when I realized I couldn't stop. I jumped off the moving bike and heard it crash. Limping, I walked the bicycle back to our building. A day or two later, while undressing, I noticed black and blue blotches on my thighs from the fall. Mother would be angry. She hadn't wanted my father to rent the bicycle.

Saturday was our day at the bathhouse, and I would have to undress. My bruises would be seen, and I would be scolded and punished. I hated the Saturday baths. Women in the morning, men in the afternoon. Our hair was inspected for lice. Ilga, a classmate of mine with long blond pigtails, had to have her head shaved. She wore a scarf until stubble grew back in. My sisters and I had not had the lice treatment, but there was always that fear. In the steamy room, I hated the smell of bodies and wet wood. I kept my head lowered to not look at the women's fleshy bodies, their sagging breasts and bellies.

At the Saturday baths, no one noticed my bruises.

∽

On a freezing winter morning, as I walked to school, camouflaged military trucks rumbled past me. I shivered in my thin coat.

Inside the classroom, I sat at my ink-splotched desk in the second row without taking off my coat. My cold, numbed fingers could barely hold the pencil as I copied the multiplication exercises from the blackboard. Wearing a shabby beige coat belted around her waist, the teacher entered. The class stood up and waited until she motioned for us to sit. The boys in the back made the usual unnecessary loud scraping noises with their shoes. Ignoring them for the moment, the teacher smoothed back her graying hair, piled up on top of her head in a messy bun, and struck a match to light kindling in the iron stove in the front of the room. As the pieces of wood caught fire, she left to get coal. Except for the annoying whispers and pencil tapping of the rowdy boys, the class worked quietly and waited for the stove to generate some heat.

On a compelling impulse, my heart pounding, I jumped up from my desk and ran to the front of the classroom. I unlatched the door of the stove, picked up a flaming piece of wood, and darted around the classroom, swinging the burning wood above my head. Everyone screamed.

The teacher returned, dropped the pail of coal, and ran after me. She grabbed the burning stick and put it back into the stove.

"You crazy girl. What are you doing?"

She lowered her angry red face to mine, and I felt her warm breath on my cheeks. Raising her hand, grimy with coal dust, she glared at me. I thought she was going to hit me. She shook her head, and her bun came undone, loose strands of hair falling down about her face.

"You stupid child!" she screamed. "You could've burned down the entire school. The wooden desks, the wooden floor, the whole wooden building."

I stared back at her. I had no idea why I had done it. I stood there in silence.

My parents were troubled when they found out. To them, this potentially dangerous behavior didn't make sense, for I was a quiet, obedient child. I didn't understand it myself. I had not thought about doing it at all. I had just done it.

How to explain such an outburst? I can't retrace what was inside my head at that moment. Perhaps it was because, night after night, as I huddled under the thin blanket in my bed, I caught muffled fragments of grownups' conversations from the other room.

"What's going to happen to us?" my grandmother would moan tearfully. "The girls need fruit, they need milk. How thin and pale ..."

My mother would sigh. "To think of what we left in our garden. Apples and pears ripening, tomatoes ready to be picked, potatoes still in the ground."

In hushed murmurs, they talked about Stalin. Thousands of Latvians, even children, transported in the middle of the night in cattle cars to slave labor camps in Siberia.

"I'm tired of waiting," my mother would complain. "We don't even know what we're waiting for."

"Things could be worse," Aunt Lily would comfort her.

"How could they be worse?"

"We could be in Siberia," my father would say, his voice full of weariness.

They were sick with worry about my other grandmother, my father's mother, who had remained in Riga. Would they ever see her again?

"… thousands of refugees, like us, driven from our homes, families separated."

"Where will we end up? America, Australia, Canada, Brazil? All so far away."

"… trapped in this miserable place."

"… life passing us by …"

They whispered that they didn't know what was going to happen next, that we might not be able to leave. Then what?

For the most part, I couldn't make out what they were saying in the other room, but I heard the sadness and helplessness in their voices. The long silences, the sighs. The words would buzz around in my head like pesky black flies until I finally dozed off.

❦

That cold winter day in the classroom, an uncontrollable rage had surfaced with an overpowering impulse to act. To do something, anything, to protest the miserable reality in which we were living.

I often think that meager years, the ones filled with loss, doubt, and disappointment, remain etched in our psyche like the annual rings in the trunk of a tree. Years of abundant rain and sunlight grow wide rings, narrow ones suggest drought, or an insect infestation.

A deformed ring may result from frequent storms on a windswept hill, a dark smudge from a forest fire.

Once grown, the tree's rings can't be undone, nor the impact of bleak and stressful years in us. They remain embedded.

GETTYSBURG, OHIO

LIVING IN THE camp was a dead time for my parents, when life seemed to have lost meaning. They grieved my father's mother, left behind in Riga, now behind the Iron Curtain, and with whom they could no longer communicate.

The wait to leave the camp was interminable. Lacking just about everything, my parents made do with only the basics and learned to improvise. A tin can with a wire handle served to carry soup from the communal kitchen. Summer sandals for my sisters and me were made from cut-up discarded tires of military trucks. Worn-out clothing was mended and mended again. A toothbrush, soap, and most toiletries were luxury items, unavailable.

Whatever economic or academic advantages they had once enjoyed were now gone. DPs were all equal in status and lived in the same humble circumstances. Worse than that, they had lost control of their lives. An arbitrary bureaucratic process would decide their fate.

Formed by the Allied governments, the United Nations Relief and Rehabilitation Administration, and later the International Refugee Organization, searched for sponsors and employment for displaced persons. Governments in the United States, Canada, Australia, and England were beginning to recognize DPs as a valuable pool of labor for hard-to-fill low-level jobs. Still, the cumbersome immigration process took years.

Finally, one spring day, my father had good news. We would be leaving the camp and going to Ohio.

"It's in America!" he said.

Even though *Ohio* was such a strange word, especially the way my father pronounced it, for my sisters and me, America seemed a magical place. Not that we knew anything about it. America meant Coca Cola and sunny California, where oranges grew. On a map, Ohio was near the very blue Lake Erie. We would go swimming.

⮜

In Bremerhaven, my family, along with other refugees, grim-faced and gaunt, carrying their belongings, hurried toward the *USS General R. M. Blatchford*, the decommissioned U.S. Navy ship built to transport thousands of troops. I was ten years old, Maija twelve, Livija eight, and Valija had just turned six. We each carried a small cardboard suitcase. Mine contained a change of clothes and the doll from my ninth birthday. We followed our mother as she struggled up the steep ramp with a suitcase bulging with practical necessities and bundles of deckle-edged black-and-white photos from Riga. Snapshots of family and friends gathered for christenings and family outings. Dear faces that had disappeared from her life. Photos of our lovely home in Riga and the summer garden in bloom. Forty-five years of her life condensed into a precious repository of captured moments, ensuring that the past not fade into oblivion. Proof of an active life—a privileged one.

I often think of what this journey must have been for my parents. They, along with the other refugees, had lost everything— their property, their family network, their social status—and had undergone a cruel leveling process. With the disintegration of their cultural framework, professional achievements and academic degrees were irrelevant. They had become a subculture that would start at the bottom of the economic ladder somewhere in the United States. They were just ID numbers now, part of a herd of immigrants being transported to faraway destinations.

Going through my mother's papers after she died, I came across a yellowing sheet. The International Refugee Organization had issued a No Return Travel Request Order for me and for every member of our family.

Dagnija Miske ID No. 789827
Date of Travel: 5 May 1950
Purpose: Processing & Final Shipment to USA

Awaiting the immigrants on the new continent would be the most menial jobs that no American worker wanted and, most likely, substandard housing. My refined and clever aunt, who had studied economics at the University of Latvia and spoke four languages, had written on her immigration application that she was seeking employment as a gardener. When the ship docked, the refugees would disperse and travel to different parts of the country, to be greeted by sponsors whose primary consideration may have been cheap labor.

The crossing was rough. The roiling ocean, metallic gray like the corroding hull of the ship, rolled the vessel in a sickening seesaw. A heavy cloud cover, dense and dark, released freezing squalls and never once lifted during our journey. Rusting metal, vibrating rumble—engine fumes hovered with the smell of vomit. Nauseated, I struggled over the heaving floors of narrow corridors.

Our crowded quarters were filled with countless three-tiered bunk beds—the bed a net of rope attached to a metal frame. At night, I, in the topmost bunk, clung to the cold metal, afraid the swaying and lurching would send me to the steel floor. During the day, wrapped in damp blankets, we huddled on the deck, ducking cold, briny spray. The lingering taste of bile on my tongue robbed my appetite. In the mess hall at a long table, crowded on a narrow bench, I tasted my first American food—slices of soft white bread that stuck to the roof of my mouth. What I wanted was coarse dark bread with lard. When a strange soup arrived, I pushed it aside. It was quickly eaten by someone else.

Gulls swirling and soaring above signaled the approaching shore. A dark sliver on the horizon gradually expanded and promised firm terrain. Apprehension etched on their faces, the passengers gazed at the approaching land. I listened to the gulls' plaintive calls and would have answered but for the stranglehold of a frozen knot in my throat.

Arriving in the United States, May 1950. The four sisters with Aunt Lily.

With the ID tag No. 789827 affixed to the lapel of my coat, I set foot on American soil.

Finished with the tedious bureaucratic processing of our immigration papers, my family made its way to the Greyhound bus station in Boston. After the swaying deck of the ship, my footing on the city sidewalks felt solid and reassuring. I breathed the crisp evening air of early spring. Nothing in the relentless grimness of the DP camp had prepared me for the mega-experience that is a big city at night. It made me dizzy. Out of the initial swirling merry-go-round blur emerged the cosmic proportions of the glittering light-defined skyline. The scale of what I saw was like nothing I had seen before or could have fantasized. Surrounded by the city rumble of honking cars, screeching brakes, the far-distant wail of a siren, jostling crowds streamed past, faces frozen and expressionless, hurrying as if frantic to reach urgent destinations. Unable to filter out the sensory overload from the chaos around me, I absorbed its frenzied energy.

I stared at the brightly lit store windows displaying lifelike but rigid mannequins with strangely contorted limbs. One, draped in a white dress with big purple flowers, gazed back at me with a haughty look. A shoe store—men's shoes, women's shoes, children's shoes. Among the masses and masses of shoes, a bright-red patent leather pair looked about my size. Smooth and glossy. I wanted them. They would replace the awkward rubber sandals.

Sitting next to the window on the Greyhound bus, I conjured up the new life awaiting me in that strange place called Ohio. The excess of what I had just seen sparked my greedy imagination. I visualized my family living in a huge house where I could run from room to countless room. I would have seven pairs of patent leather shoes—a different color for each day of the week. My doll's hair was just painted on its plastic head. My new dolls would have long curly hair that I would comb, eyes that opened and closed, ruffled, lace-trimmed taffeta dresses with glass buttons.

When I woke up, the skyscrapers were gone. Outside the rain-streaked bus window, through a bleak drizzly dawn, flat fields stretched as far as I could see. Field after endless flat field growing I didn't know what. Here and there, we passed modest wooden houses with red barns nearby. Next to the barns, mysterious tall round structures loomed, for which I would later learn the word—silos.

✑

The bus took us to Gettysburg, Ohio, population 532. It had only one significant business—the Petersime Incubator Company, the largest poultry incubator factory in the world. Ray M. Petersime had sponsored our immigration to the United States. My father would work in his factory for seventy-five cents an hour.

My parents and the four daughters with Aunt Lily (right).

We settled into a small white frame house separated from the main road by a couple of hydrangea bushes. In the middle of the tiny lawn was a well with an iron pump. Vigorous pumping produced only dark, strong-smelling rusty water that we couldn't use for drinking or washing. We carried pails of water from the house across the road. In the back of the yard, filled with layers of drooping cobwebs and menacing wasps, was the outhouse.

In the fall, my sisters and I enrolled in school. The kind townspeople of Gettysburg donated boxes of clothes, nice clothes their children had outgrown. I entered sixth grade but could speak only a few words of English. My classmates must have wondered why I had inexplicably appeared among them—wearing a blouse, a skirt, or a sweater they had once worn. These sixth graders had known each other since first grade, their little groups and friendships long established. While they weren't mean or unfriendly in any way, they were not sure how to treat me or incorporate me into their games.

During the daily multiplication and division exercises, I learned that I was way ahead of the rest of the class, but the other subjects were a muddle. On written tests, not understanding even the vocabulary of the question, in desperation, I devised a crude and dubious device. I studied the words that appeared in the question, then rearranged them in a way that, I hoped, might represent an answer.

I dreaded recess. I stood alone in the shade of the giant sycamore tree beside the baseball field and watched the groups of kids jumping rope and playing ball. I wished I could join them.

My long curly hair was in tightly braided scalp-tingling pigtails that reached to my waist. I asked my mother to cut my hair. To my surprise, she agreed. Perhaps she had gotten tired of the daily early-morning braiding sessions. My new short hair felt light, blew in the breeze, curled loosely around my face. I looked like the other girls in my class.

In the spring, I found a baby robin that must have fallen out of its nest. My sisters and I had never had a pet and were thrilled by this gift of nature. I cupped my hands to pick up the tiny bird, felt its soft, warm quivering. We put the robin in a cardboard box, fed it water and bread crumbs, and gave it a name. Unable to fly, the robin perched on an outstretched finger, fluttered to a shoulder, and tried to hop in the grass.

One morning, running to refill the water dish, I found the robin stretched out in the box, its feathers ruffled, lying in a pool of a strange dark ooze.

"No, no," I cried, not believing what I saw. "My poor baby bird." The robin was dead. Tearfully, my sisters and I buried it under bushes next to the fence in the backyard. I was sorry for the sweet little creature.

For a long time, when I thought about the robin, I sensed a strange emptiness, like hunger that persisted even after I ate. One day I had picked up the plump bird, noticed the feathers in its front starting to turn orange, and the next day it lay motionless at the bottom of the box, cold and stiff when I touched it.

I would remember how it opened its yellow beak wide for a bread crumb, the funny way it cocked its head. How, like a tiny black bead, its eye stared at me. I had watched its attempts to hop on the ground, making soft chirps I could barely hear. And then it died.

It is curious that I remember the robin's death so vividly. Perhaps because it was a tangible loss. I had held it in my hands and cared for it, yet suddenly it was gone, and I could no longer hold it. In my eleven-year-old mind, it was inexcusable and unjust that this adorable thing must die. It could be I felt it so acutely was because the loss of the robin represented other losses of a more abstract nature, losses experienced by my parents and others around me that I had absorbed but barricaded from my mind. I hadn't grieved them because I couldn't name or define them, as I could the loss of the helpless hatchling's warm feathery body tickling the palms of my hands.

In the evenings, my father came home tired. He would sit outside near the iron pump and smoke a cigarette. The heavy labor in the incubator factory, carrying cinder blocks for a construction project, was wearing him down. The war years had depleted his strength. When he was hospitalized for an emergency hernia operation, he realized he had to find a different job. He needed a better paying job, so he could begin to pay back Ray Petersime for the costs incurred to bring our family to Gettysburg.

Aunt Lily no longer lived with us. Despite her university degree and excellent qualifications, she worked as a live-in maid for a wealthy family in another town. Since there were no better job opportunities for either of them in the area, my father and Aunt Lily decided to go to Cleveland to search for employment. Perhaps the large Latvian community there could help them.

THE LETTER

But I believe above all that I wanted to build the
palace of my memory, because my memory is my
only home.

Anselm Kiefer

MY FATHER ACCEPTED a job at a photoengraving company in
Cleveland and rented a furnished house for us on the west side of
the city. The dark brick semidetached home on Franklin Avenue
was not only furnished, but every drawer, every closet overflowed
with things left by the owners. Vases, candlesticks, ashtrays, salt
and pepper shakers filled the corner cupboard of the dining room.
My sisters and I poked around, amazed at such an accumulation
of objects. Water glasses, pitchers, wineglasses, tiny liqueur glasses
lined kitchen shelves. Under the counter, frying pans and pots were
stacked up. We rummaged around the musty drawers jammed with
linens and towels. We had never seen so much stuff.

Despite our delight in finding the other family's possessions, my
mother was not happy with the house.

"Such silly, useless things," she said, dusting the porcelain fig-
urines. All these fussy objects were someone else's gaudy taste, not

hers. The ruffled pink curtains, chenille bedspreads, and painted wicker furniture in the bedrooms were not her style. For years she had managed to get by with the barest minimum of possessions, had gotten used to having only the essentials. All these belongings, this excess, overwhelmed her and perhaps even offended her.

After a year, we moved to another house, this time unfurnished. The rent must have been more reasonable, for while most houses by then had oil or gas heating, ours had a coal-burning furnace. My sisters and I changed schools again, but we didn't care because we had not made any friends yet.

The white clapboard house at 2028R Corning Avenue was hidden behind the main house. Instead of the front entrance, we used the more convenient kitchen door that opened off an alley. On my way home from school, turning into the narrow treeless passage between the backyards of houses embarrassed me. Rather than a proper street, we lived in a shabby alley.

Scouring secondhand stores, my parents found an ancient pedestal oak table for the dining room, a glass-front bookcase with carved columns and brass trim for the living room, mismatched wood beds and nightstands for the bedrooms. The old furniture had a lovely worn look and gleamed from use and polish. I would try to imagine the other families that had sat around the table, the ancient books that had once filled the bookcase.

Later, when there was more money, my parents no longer bought used furniture. My mother wanted new furniture, modern pieces, not things used by other people. The burnished farmhouse table was replaced by a Formica and chrome "dinette." The bedrooms got factory-slick blond veneered bedroom suites.

Aunt Lily lived with us. She had given up her independence and merged into our family, as was the custom for unmarried Latvian women. Her small room on the first floor lacked a door. For privacy, she hung a piece of heavy fabric on a curtain rod to separate it from the dining room. In the evenings, we heard the clicking of her adding machine as she practiced tallying columns of figures for her bookkeeping class. She cut off the long braid, pinned around her head like a crown, and wore her graying hair in a modern cut. After she got a job, she helped pay the rent.

Saturday mornings, Father went out early and returned with a white box from the Polish bakery. We would scramble around the kitchen table and watch him lift out baked goods, one by one—a different assortment each time. Slices of babka, jelly doughnuts, poppy seed rolls, squares of sponge cake, apple racuchys, pecan rolls. My sisters and I would eye the cakes, deciding which to choose first. I would take a bite of a jelly doughnut, leaving the oozing jelly part for last. Next, I might grab a piece of sponge cake with a white icing so sweet, it made my teeth hurt.

My father would watch us devour the cakes, and his face would soften.

"To spoil my girls a bit," he would say.

Like a curtain, for a moment, his usual sternness would lift. He revealed a tenderness toward us that we rarely saw. But his gentleness made us squirm, and we felt awkward because we were not used to it. We preferred it when he was strict with us. We even preferred his anger because we understood it and were used to it.

When I think about it now, the Saturday cakes must have been his attempt to make up for all the years when we had no cakes, no sweets, no candy. It was his way of expressing his affection for us— not directly, but through a box of cakes.

On those mornings, I would reach for a third piece, maybe a sticky pecan roll, but would leave it half eaten on my plate. It was too much. I was not used to eating sweets, and a queasy feeling would set in.

∽

To a child who has never seen a library, entering even the smallest local branch for the first time can be overwhelming. Shelves and shelves of books. All these books filled with stories, I remember thinking, and I wanted to read them all.

I had started eighth grade and was a good reader, but after school when I went to the library, I would hurry to the children's book section, squeeze into the tiny chairs set out for toddlers, and leaf through big picture books. Page after page of gorgeous drawings in bright colors. The books we had read in the camp had only an occasional dull black ink drawing. I had never seen such stunning illustrations. I would run my fingers over the thick glossy pages, transported into the magical world of the splendid images. Then I would wander into the other room, to the shelf that held the row of Nancy Drew mysteries with gripping titles: *The Secret in the Old Attic, The Clue in the Jewel Box,* or *The Sign of the Twisted Candles.* It was hard to choose just two, the library's limit for the week. Later I discovered Thomas Hardy and immersed myself in his gloomy heaths, identifying with the brooding characters of a faraway time and place that fed my fantasies.

Upon returning from school one day, a surprise awaited my sisters and me. Against the wall in the living room stood an upright piano with an antique swivel stool with legs that ended in quaint, carved bird claws clasping glass balls.

Music lessons for my sisters and me was a dream my mother had never given up. To her, music symbolized culture. The love of arts was something the traumas of war could never take away or crush. She believed music would elevate us and set us apart. That we would discover its beauty and it would define our lives.

Music lesson.

After school, twice a week, I walked many blocks to lessons
with a Latvian pianist, Mrs. Gaiķēns. I trudged up the narrow staircase that smelled of garlic and something I couldn't identify, maybe
dead mice. Her husband, who didn't seem to have a job, would lead
me into the living room to wait. I cringed at the horrible mistakes
of even the simplest pieces that came from the music room. When it
was my turn for the lesson, upon entering the room, I caught a whiff
of the cloying cosmetic scent that emanated from Mrs. Gaiķēns, a
large and imposing woman, with a heavily powdered face as smooth
as a baby's and hair lacquered into a complicated upsweep. Her
ample bottom spilled over the edges of her chair. When she played
a particularly difficult section for me, I marveled how her plump
hands and fat fingers could execute such intricate passages. Her

relentless insistence on scales and arpeggios improved my technique. At the conservatory of music in Latvia, she had learned to love the showy pieces by Rachmaninoff and Chopin, which she chose for me to play.

∽

One rainy autumn day after my lesson, when it was already getting dark, I hurried up the alley. In the kitchen, my mother sat peeling potatoes. In a glass bowl, cucumbers steeped in sweetened vinegar and dill. Something mouthwatering roasted in the oven. Maija was setting the table. As I placed my music books on the piano, I heard Father's heavy steps and went to the dining room where he stood holding a letter. He eased his tall frame into a chair at the table, and from his grim face, I could tell the letter had brought bad news. He put the envelope down. It looked tattered, as if it had come from far away and taken a long time to arrive. The stamp was strange.

Wiping her hands on a dishtowel, Mother came in and picked up the envelope.

"*No Latvijas,*" she said. The letter was from Latvia.

Maija set down the pile of dishes she was holding. We waited for Father to speak. Only the patter of rain against the windowpanes interrupted the sudden hush in the room. I tried to imagine what the strange letter revealed. Father sat there not saying anything, as if it was too much of an effort to speak. Maybe it was as if telling us would make real whatever was in the letter.

"*Māte nomira,*" he finally said in a hollow voice.

Father's mother had died in Riga. I had never seen my father look so distraught, so lost. I stood there not knowing what to say, how to comfort him. Over the years, silence and resignation had become our family's default emotional reaction.

The letter didn't explain when and how she had passed away. I tried to remember what Grandmother looked like, her pulled-back white hair, the steel-rimmed glasses, the dark dress with lace collar and brooch. How she had stood the day the wagon took us away, sad and alone, wiping her eyes. But her face was a blur. I couldn't imagine it, and I would never see her again.

⌑

Thinking back to that day, I am reminded of what the French writer Marcel Pagnol discovered when writing his childhood memories. In the foreword to *La Gloire de Mon Père*, he wrote:

> *It is not about me that I write, rather about the child that I no longer am—a small being that I once knew but who has dissolved in timelessness, in the manner of sparrows vanishing without a trace. The subject in my writing is not the child. The child is only a witness to the events.*

The twelve-year-old that I was then was a witness to that sad scene in the dining room. I saw Father's pale face and Mother standing behind him kneading the damp dishtowel in her hands. I understood the heartbreaking news in the letter, but it is only now that I see its deeper significance and how it brought about a fundamental change for my family.

After the sorrow and shock of his mother's death started to diminish, my father must have been relieved that she no longer suffered. He knew how difficult it must have been to live in a country that had changed forever. With no family left in Riga, how lonely she must have been.

She had been our last bond with Latvia. That bond, like a taproot, that strong root that grows straight down into the soil, had served as an anchor. With it severed, my parents probably understood they would not be going back to Latvia. It would be necessary to grow new roots, lateral roots, here in Cleveland. It was now their home.

By then, we had been in the United States for two years. For social reasons, not religious ones, my parents joined the Latvian Lutheran Church, a meeting place to observe holidays and national days. Even if Latvia was no longer theirs, no one could take away their language, their folk songs, the way they prepared their food, the way they celebrated holidays. The church was a place for us, Latvian teenagers, to interact; a place where in Sunday school we learned Latvia's literature, geography, and history. We became part of the Latvian community. The family was beginning to feel settled.

Most importantly, my parents now had control of their lives. The family's future depended on them alone. After four years in the house on Corning Avenue, my parents and Aunt Lily had saved up enough money for a down payment on a house.

CLEVELAND

IT HAD ONCE been the grandest house on Clinton Avenue. Wide front porch, bay windows, even a turret. Through a solid oak door, inset with beveled glass, you entered high-ceilinged rooms. Carved woodwork and parquet floors gleamed. Columns and green tiles decorated fireplace mantels. An imposing staircase led past a stained-glass window to four bedrooms upstairs.

But our house didn't retain its Victorian character. Pink linoleum hid the lovely ornate floor in the dining room. My parents installed gray wall-to-wall carpeting that concealed the contrasting wood pattern in the living room. Fuchsia-colored sofas and a glass coffee table created a fifties look.

Perhaps this clash of styles reflected the disruption of my parents' lives, caught in a painful pull between the past and the present.

In the evenings, while my family watched TV in the living room, I secluded myself behind the sliding doors of the only room that kept its Victorian charm, where the inlaid wood floor remained exposed. Seated at the Steinway grand in the bay window, I practiced Chopin polonaises and Rachmaninoff preludes, drowning out Liberace and Lawrence Welk.

My father was able to buy this gracious home because the west side of Cleveland was no longer what it had once been. Middle-class families had moved to Parma and Lakewood, the new suburbs. With their decaying infrastructure, the older areas became affordable to less affluent immigrants like us. My father had a well-paying job at the photoengraving company. With a master's degree from the University of Latvia, he could have pursued a career in the academic world, but with a large family to support, he had given up the idea.

Cleveland's blue-collar jobs in factories and steel mills attracted immigrant communities. At the turn of the century, Czechs, Poles, and Russians settled in neighborhoods next to the city's industrial zone. Over the years, they built churches and halls for meetings and social events, imitating the architecture that reminded them of home. In a gritty working-class neighborhood of huddled houses with lawns behind chain-link fences, St. Theodosios, the Russian Orthodox Cathedral, rose incongruously, its splendid copper onion domes in lurid collision with the bleak surroundings.

The Estonians, Lithuanians, and Latvians arriving after World War II organized congregations, schools, veteran organizations, and credit unions. But it would take years before they could acquire their own churches and halls. The Latvians rented the second floor in the paint-peeling National Bohemian Hall. On Sunday after-noons, Latvian teenagers gathered there to socialize and dance.

To get there, my friend Biruta and I could have taken a bus across the more than a mile-long Clark Avenue Bridge that spanned an inferno-like complex of steel mills. But as if drawn by the night-marish place, we walked. A brownish smog blocked out the sun, its thickness almost palpable, its chemical stench like something you shouldn't breathe in. It infiltrated our hair and clothing. Eyes stinging, we would stop at the railing, riveted by the monstrous, begrimed structures and tall cranes, a confusion of towers and pre-carious catwalks. Coal and ore, in enormous mounds, was heaped along the railway tracks. Flowing molten metal from the blast furnaces shot up flames and sparks. Black clouds from the smokestacks layered the nearby asphalt-shingled houses with soot. A shroud of pinkish haze hovered.

At the Bohemian Hall, someone banged out tunes on the out-of-tune piano for our folk dances, and later switched to ballroom music.

Edvins, a quiet and skinny kid with dark slicked-back hair, often dragged me onto the dance floor with a firm hand on my waist. When the music started, as if transformed by it, he squared his shoulders and lifted his head high. He spun me around, and I too was transformed. Swept up, light-headed, gay. We whirled and twirled around and around until we were breathless and dizzy. At a time when most teenagers were listening to pop music on the radio and doing the jitterbug, we waltzed and mastered the more demanding steps of the tango.

Sitting at the Formica kitchen table one Sunday, eating not the usual weekday soup but my mother's pork chops fried in butter, my sisters and I chattered on in English.

"*Runājiet latviski.*" My mother had to keep reminding us to speak Latvian. "*Pa latviski.*"

"It's bad enough the four of you are beginning to look like American teenagers," my father complained.

"Good. I want to look like an American kid," I replied, insolence creeping into my voice. "And I want to wear jeans."

From my father's icy stare, I knew he didn't approve.

Hoping to delay the inevitable loss of the Latvian language, my parents insisted my sisters and I join the Latvian Girl Scouts, attend Latvian school on Sunday mornings, and participate in Latvian community activities. We grudgingly obeyed. But at Lincoln High School, I had American friends. The two sets of friends stayed separate. My two worlds never intersected. I was beginning to lead a double life.

∿

When I was sixteen, to earn money for college, I got a job at the Ohio Bell Telephone Company as a switchboard operator. During the summer and holidays, I sat on a high stool in front of the black console with rows of jacks and cables. No job could have been more boring. To relieve the tedium, I listened in on people's conversations. It didn't relieve the tedium, though. What trivial stuff people talked about. At times there were long moments of silence on both ends, as if they had nothing to say to each other. I sensed that life could be filled with the boring and the ordinary.

From time to time, I signed up for the six p.m. to midnight shift. For the same pay, I worked only six hours instead of eight. The problem was the trip home. Leaving the Ohio Bell building after midnight, I hurried across the deserted downtown area to catch the bus. Store windows, tall buildings, all pitch black. Lampposts cast strange, oblique shadows. Gusts of wind swirled bits of newspaper, candy wrappers, and dirt. No sound but my echoing footsteps. Imagining I heard someone behind me, I would run all the way to the bus stop.

With just a couple of passengers, the bus made its way along the urban blight of Detroit Avenue. Abandoned storefronts next to shuttered thrift stores. The few bars still open flashed neon beer signs in dirty windows. Sometimes a lone figure staggered along the dimly lit street.

From the bus stop, I took the shortcut through the Fisher Foods parking lot. With pounding heart, I sprinted across the empty lot and dashed up the steps to the little chain-link gate that led into our backyard. In the warm, brightly lit kitchen, with everyone asleep upstairs, I made a cup of tea and sipped it with only the hum of the refrigerator for company. I tiptoed up the back staircase that led from the kitchen to the second floor. Years ago, this gloomy, narrow back staircase had been used by maids to get to their rooms in the attic. Perhaps the house too, like my family, had a complicated past, had witnessed better times.

~

By the time I went to Miami University in Oxford, Ohio, I had learned to wear pleated plaid skirts, matching sweater sets with the obligatory strand of pearls, bobby sox, and white canvas Keds. On Friday nights, I drank beer at the local pub with other freshmen. Deftly navigating through insipid conversations about Miles Davis, Johnny Mathis, DKE fraternity house parties, and football, I started to resemble my new friends.

In my sophomore year, two good friends, both in the Delta Zeta sorority, persuaded me to participate in rush week—a week of parties for sororities to meet and socialize with prospective members.

I was uneasy about joining a sorority, remembering what my father had said. After a Sunday dinner the previous summer, my sisters and I stood around the dining room table as my father brought out an old photo album, its black matte sheets separated by crinkly transparent paper. Leafing through the album, he pointed out the black-and-white photos from his youth. Grainy pictures of him as a toddler with curly blond hair, another taken in Moscow, where he is wearing the school uniform with brass buttons.

"Can you find me in this photo?" Father asked.

We stared at the rows and rows of students in the group photo of his university graduation class.

"In the second row." Maija was the first to spot him.

I noticed that most of the men in the picture wore a cap and a wide striped ribbon across the chest.

"How come you're not wearing a cap, Father?" I asked.

"Those are for men who belonged to *Talavija* or *Lettonia*. Fraternities."

"You didn't belong?"

"No."

"How come?" I persisted.

"I never wanted to join a fraternity," he told us. "Everyone can't join. You have to be invited. I didn't like that their activities were secret." He shook his head. "It's not right. I don't approve of organizations that exclude people."

Despite what my father said that day, when asked to join, I pledged the Delta Zeta sorority, found out about its symbolic secret rituals, went through absurd initiation rites, and wore the tiny diamond-adorned Roman lamp pin above my heart.

The following semester during rush week, I took part in choosing new freshmen for Delta Zeta. At one of the parties, in the roomful of cheerful flutter of pastel-colored shirtwaists, I saw her. White blouse and narrow black skirt, dark hair pulled back, palest pink lipstick, hands folded in her lap, sitting apart. Others had clustered in frivolous chatting groups.

Joining her, I introduced myself and asked the standard opening question: "What are you majoring in?"

"Political science," Bernardine replied.

As strange an answer to me then as if she had said she wanted to become an acrobat. My friends and I were English majors, education majors, studying liberal arts, other vague disciplines—stop-gap endeavors until we got married.

"Political science," I echoed.

After her degree, she thought she might study law. Amazed, I listened as she told me about her interest in juvenile justice. With surprising intensity, she admitted that her idealism was probably unrealistic, but she wanted to make a contribution to society.

Wow, I thought.

As the party broke up, I knew the one recruit I wanted for Delta Zeta was Bernardine.

To discuss and vote on the freshman candidates, the sorority suite was set up with rows of folding chairs and a long table in the front. The president and secretary shuffled through lists and would call out a name and summarize the candidate's academic standing, activities, and interests. Then came comments from members who had met her at one of the parties.

I waited impatiently for Bernardine's name. In my head I went over what I had prepared to say. When Bernardine's name came up, the president skipped to the next.

"What about Bernardine?" I asked. I heard murmurs all around, but no one spoke up.

Someone whispered, "She's Jewish."

As they started to discuss the next pledge, anger surged up in me. I stood. My temples throbbed. I tried to control my shaking hands

"Bernardine's ... smart, ambitious ... committed to good causes ..." My throat tightened. I couldn't go on. Silence settled in the room.

I blurted out, "What does her being Jewish have to do with it?"

I scanned the room for someone to answer, to agree with me, but all I saw was smug, tight-lipped faces.

It suddenly occurred to me that I hated the pointless secrecy, the silly rituals. The unfair criteria used to select some, exclude others. My father had been right. The hollowness of it all. I didn't want to be there.

I didn't belong in Delta Zeta.

⇜

What I didn't know back then was that Bernardine Dohrn would one day be on the FBI's Ten Most Wanted list.

More than a decade later, on a sweltering day, I sat out on the stone patio of our house in Rio de Janeiro. Clinking the ice in my drink, I pressed the cool glass to my sweaty forehead. On the wrought iron table in front of me lay a days-old issue of the *New York Times*. I unfolded it and absentmindedly scanned the front page. The name *Bernardine Dohrn* popped out in an article. What a coincidence, I thought. But no. The name was too unusual for there to be someone else with it. The article continued on another page, and there was a photo. It was Bernardine. The same long dark hair parted in the middle, the same pretty face.

I read the article. Bernardine was the most charismatic, articulate, and fanatic member of the militant Weather Underground.

Outrageous, flamboyant in her thigh-high boots and leather mini-skirts, Bernardine had become the most famous face of the militant revolutionaries who wanted to overthrow the U.S. government. Theirs had been the most radical wing of the Students for a Democratic Society in Chicago in 1969, which split off to form the Weathermen and later became the Weather Underground.

Why? How did this happen? Astonished, I read on.

Members of the group were enraged by U.S. military involvement in Vietnam, illegal and immoral, they said. They abhorred the racism in the United States. In their "Days of Rage," they overturned cars and smashed windows with lead pipes.

I reread the article and tried to reconcile the freshman Bernardine at Miami University with this new description of her. I couldn't.

Yet thinking back, I remembered her intensity, her optimism. She had talked about wanting to do something about all the injustices that existed. About making a contribution to society. Her earnestness had been striking.

Somehow, her idealism had escalated into violence. What was the pivotal moment? Was it an accumulation of disappointments? At what point had her commitment become fanaticism? How did she get there?

I put aside the newspaper and breathed in the caramelized-almond smell wafting from the frangipani tree. The question, as if rebounding off the crumbling wall at the end of the garden, bounced back to me. How did I get *here*? What decisions and events led me to sit in this lush tropical garden with twisting vines and strange large-leafed foliage? As if the garden held an answer, I went and picked up the creamy blossoms fallen from the tree. From a branch hung an old bird cage that had once held a macaw. It now stood empty, except for a few stray red and blue feathers.

᷈

After the sorority meeting that rejected Bernardine, I quit Delta Zeta. My father was pleased when I told him.

Each time I came home from college, our house in Cleveland seemed more and more cluttered. An organized clutter—more an accumulation of things saved for the future. The DP camp had taught my mother not to waste anything. Not out of thrift. She was not particularly thrifty. If she wanted something for her daughters, she didn't worry about the price. The piano, violins, a cello, music lessons. To her, not luxuries, but necessities.

The clutter increased because my mother was incapable of throwing anything away. The weekly Latvian newspapers, tied in bundles, stacked up in the basement. Empty Maxwell House instant-coffee jars became receptacles for sugar, flour, and her home-made plum preserves. In the attic, garment bags protected all the dresses and shoes my sisters and I had ever worn. The glass-front bookcase was crammed with books—Latvian books. My parents spoke German and Russian fluently and English quite well, although with an accent. Father read every page of each issue of *Scientific American*, yet I don't remember that either one of them ever read a book in English.

᷈

On Saturday mornings, my father did the grocery shopping, not at the supermarket just past our back gate, but at the West Side Market, an imposing brick structure with a tall clock tower. The hundred or so vendors in the enormous concourse sold not only the freshest fruits and vegetables, but also old-world delicacies— smoked eel, salted herring, loaves of dense dark bread, sauerkraut, and pickles in barrels. Nowhere was the fish as fresh. Father bought meat, not packaged in plastic, but directly from a butcher who would cut the pork roast just the way he preferred.

I looked forward to the warm glow of our family dinners on Sundays and holidays, especially festive when Latvian friends were invited. My father extended the round dining room table and added more chairs. I set the table with a freshly ironed tablecloth, our best blue and white china, and the good silver. When the candles were lit, a little wine was served in liqueur glasses—Mother's assurance that no one would drink too much. Through the swinging pantry doors, her faced flushed from the hot oven, she carried in the crisped pork roast that had filled the house with its aroma all day, the braised sauerkraut that only she knew how to prepare. Potatoes and dilled cucumbers. Simple fare. Finally, the many-layered Latvian buttercream torte—the only extravagant part of the meal.

"In the old country" is how, at some point during the dinner, my father would begin a sentence. The festive atmosphere would shift. The conversation turned to the often repeated comparisons of life as it had been in Latvia and how it was in Cleveland. Without bitterness. As if the two parts of my parents' torn lives had to be continually examined and verbalized. In my father's memory, those earlier prewar years, compressed by time, had become idealized. It may have been that the present needed to be filtered through a curtain of the lost past to eventually weave the two together.

It could be what my parents missed was that in Latvia, life was still full of promise. Was it their youth they missed? Or Riga's historic Jugendstil buildings and narrow cobblestone streets, where they had once strolled on their way to organ concerts at the cathedral? It could be they were saddened remembering how they gathered mushrooms in the nearby pine forest. Ours had been a different life then. On the large property on the outskirts of Riga, four generations of family had lived in comfortable homes surrounded by gardens that they planted with white lilacs, fruit trees, raspberry and currant bushes. A strawberry patch and thriving vegetable gardens produced more than the family could use.

During the war, it all came to an end. Trauma accumulated upon trauma. Warm bonds were broken, the family dispersed.

Uprooted more than once, my parents didn't find it easy to put down roots in a new place, although they tried. Cleveland to them was, in many ways, an alien place. They were in their fifties now, and their life had settled into a routine of patient resignation.

Their focus was on us, their four daughters. Our futures were more important than their own. They hoped we would achieve what they could no longer expect. I felt the burden of representing their hope.

My parents' lives could never be made whole again, but mine had not yet frozen to exclude the future. I didn't want to wait for happiness and meaning. I would go out and find them.

The unknown can be frightening, but it presents possibilities.

PART TWO

STRANGLER FIG TREE

ONCE AGAIN, I was crossing the Atlantic, this time on Cunard's luxurious *Saxonia*. With my black steamer trunk in the ship's hold, I was on my way to England.

"But you have no experience teaching young children," my parents had argued, trying to persuade me not to go. They were right, of course. My classroom experience consisted of one semester of student-teaching high school biology. Knowing how impractical and self-absorbed I was, they would have preferred that I find a job in Cleveland, somewhere nearby. But I needed to flee from advice and the predictable. I was twenty-one.

On the ship with nothing but the leisurely routine of multi-course meals, I lounged on the wooden deck chairs, a warm blanket at my feet. At midmorning, attentive stewards brought scalding cups of bouillon and, in the afternoon, tea and scones. Too distracted to read the book on my lap, I stared at the horizon where the choppy green water dissolved into a metallic sheen, like that of the August skies. The ocean's swells rolled the ship, and cold spray stung my cheeks. I breathed the purifying salt air.

I was headed for Smethwick, a small village in the Midlands, on the outskirts of Birmingham, the manufacturing hub of England's Industrial Revolution.

Birmingham had been bombed during World War II. In 1961, it was still more grim and gritty than I had imagined, and famous for its pea-soupers, the dense greenish-yellow smog from factory coal fires that blanketed the city. Even more grim was the town of Smethwick, its narrow, treeless streets lined with identical dark-brick row houses, dreary working-class neighborhoods where many Punjabi immigrants had settled for the factory jobs.

I soon found out that the overcrowded Smethwick schools had a reputation for dismal teaching conditions and discipline problems. Finding qualified teachers, always a difficult problem, had led the school district to advertise in American newspapers, hoping to attract applicants from a wider pool of candidates.

That first day, facing my class of thirty-four unruly eight- and nine-year-olds with runny noses and chapped cheeks, I had serious second thoughts about my decision to come here. The Crockett Lane Primary School lacked even the most basic textbooks and supplies. My indispensable teaching tool would be the blackboard. I remembered how in the DP camp in Ansbach, the teachers, also without books, had relied on the blackboard for presenting lessons. I knew it could be done. Considering the school's unstructured curriculum, I could create my own teaching program.

On a salary of five hundred pounds a year, my options for living accommodations were no less bleak. The Townsend Club, recommended by the school, provided lodging for single women. A room and breakfast could be had for two shillings a week. But living under the vigilant eye of the "warden" and breakfasts of beans on toast were too austere, even for my reduced circumstances.

For rent of substantially more than two shillings a week and with a much longer commute to the school, I rented two rooms in a lovely house in King's Heath owned by Miss Long, a violinist. Each elegant room had its own fireplace, the only source of heat in the house. But getting a coal fire to burn is a tedious and messy task that I seldom attempted, except on a rare weekend.

Drizzly fall mornings, I waited for the bus in the numbing cold. Not a bitter cold, but an aching dampness that settled in and permeated. A soot-smudged cloud cover trapped layers of sulfurous fog, and fumes from the coal fires irritated the throat. In the street, leaves lay clumped in sodden heaps. Amidst a wet-wool smell, I rode on the upper level of the red double-decker bus. Rain-streaked windows blurred the color-leached streets. Slick sidewalks reflected trunks of bare trees. A constant drip drip of rain.

On these sloppy rainy days, the kids sloshed through puddles and arrived shivering in damp clothing to sit in the classroom with barely any heat. I devised a game to warm them up. Lined up in teams, the kids raced up to the blackboard, one by one, to fill in the blanks of the multiplication exercises on the board. A devious way to warm them up and hopefully improve their math skills.

For a geography lesson, I borrowed a globe and asked my class to locate England on it. Some pointed to the large land mass of Africa, others picked out the intriguing shape of South America. I showed them the little slip of land that was England. They laughed and refused to believe me.

They listened to the stories I read, always begging for more. In their poor households, parents didn't have the luxury of time to read to their children. As afternoons dragged on, I sometimes took the class to the assembly room where the school's morning prayers were held. Sitting on the floor around the piano, they listened as I played a Mozart piece or two. Afterward, we sang cheerful songs.

In the spring, they brought me little fistfuls of flowers.

෴

Midmorning and late afternoon, the teachers gathered for tea break. The strong black tea was served in delicate cups with pink roses. It had steeped in a matching porcelain teapot, and a maroon tea cozy that one of the teachers had knit kept it warm. In England, women were always knitting—on the bus, in train stations, everywhere there was the click of needles. I saw sagging sweaters, woolen vests for husbands to wear under tweed blazers, knee socks with argyle patterns, striped scarves. Patterns that didn't make them any less drab.

Knitting was also part of the teachers' teatime ritual. From their baskets, the women teachers took out their works in progress, picking up where they had left off the day before. As predictable as the knitting was the monotonous repetition of the same topics of conversation—the weather, football, school matters. From time to time, we stopped to listen to the racket of the games and quarrels on the playground just outside the window, where the children played during recess, even in the rain.

Harris, the headmaster, often came in late. One day he announced that an older boy had needed disciplining again, had to be caned.

"The lad exposed himself to the girls ..." he explained.

I had seen those canings. Red in the face, distended veins in his temples, Harris brought the cane down with a sharp swish across the upturned palms of the poor troublemaker. Teatime and recess were over when Mr. Harris blew his whistle.

෴

Sears, a teacher at the school, didn't join us for tea. Reginald (Rex) Sears was, as his name implied, an imposing presence. But we didn't use first names in school. His BBC English had been honed by parts in Shakespeare plays. Tall with graying hair, a convincing Othello he must have been. An athlete, he had played cricket in British Guiana. When the rest of us gathered for tea, he remained writing at his desk. Having finished a novel, he was writing a play.

It was just as well he didn't join us. Upon entering a room, he altered its dynamics. There was tension between him and the rest of the staff, who viewed him as an outsider. In this school setting, Sears, a superbly educated black man, aware that he would never be fully accepted, embraced his isolation.

Gradually, through the kinship of our outsider-ship, Sears became my mentor. He took it upon himself to interpret England for me and to shape my experience—imperceptibly driving a wedge between the other teachers and me.

After school, boarding the bus to Birmingham together, I listened as Sears vented his frustration.

"Look at what Harris has to do to maintain discipline! The kids have no respect for him. He has to resort to caning to ensure obedience."

Other afternoons, the focus of criticism was on the other teachers. "The whole stodgy lot of them are totally ignorant of anything outside their own rigid and narrow worlds."

Often his complaints were of a more general nature. "Ah, the awful uneventfulness of middle-class English life is a bad thing for someone like me. This dull manner of living could almost be called vicious were it not for the fact that *vicious* at least suggests some action."

To continue our discussions, we would wander along Birmingham's streets. His anger would gradually subside. The conversation would turn to literature.

Sears had just read Henry Miller's *Tropic of Cancer* and quoted,

"'I felt the misery grind itself out with pestle and mortar ...' But Miller is not a great writer!"

Another day, Sears launched into a professorial lecture about the book.

"It has no shape and a claustrophobic atmosphere. Miller doesn't evoke, simply records, and then not even vividly. Now, *Colossus of Maroussi* is a much better book about Miller's travels in Greece—none of the four-letter words. He writes like a man purged and purified."

Trying to insert myself in the conversation, I asked Sears how he had enjoyed the record of Prokofiev's *Alexander Nevsky* I had lent him.

"At first hearing, I objected to its bombastic banging and booming the Russians seem to adore, but listening to it again and again, the piece no longer assaulted my ear. Oh, there's that Russian oversentimentalizing and ponderousness, and yet, the damn thing gets you—can still thrill."

Sears liked to tell me what I should read.

"Read *Christ Recrucified* by Nikos Kazantzakis," he told me. "So generous with emotions, much like Dostoevsky, but because the subject is Greece instead of the Russian gloom, there is LIGHT. His *Freedom and Death* is less successful. Although the characters drink and fight and make love, action aplenty, they just don't HIT you or develop or move or grow in stature or complexity. They're just there, that's all."

Sometimes, there was no stopping Sears. When in an expansive mood, he overwhelmed me with his literary monologue.

"And Hemingway's *The Old Man and the Sea*—an understatement of calm flow. So unpretentious, so PURE." He encouraged me to read Durrell "for his sense of touch—what one might call the texture of locality. And Baldwin's *Another Country*, gently sad.

Baldwin trying to dislodge from his frail shoulders the various chips he inherited."

"When will I stop telling you what to read?" Sears laughed.

Absorbed in animated conversation, to the passerby on the street, a strange couple we must have appeared.

Some afternoons to get out of the rain, we stopped at San-Sheng's for egg drop soup. In a nostalgic mood one day, Sears spoke about British Guiana.

"Whites, blacks, mulattos, East Indians, aboriginal Indians—a rich mix. Ah, I miss the warmth of that place. No, actually, it's bloody hot and humid there. But, my dear, there is color."

With a faraway look, as if transported back to an earlier time, he continued, "Yes, there is color in my country. Scarlet macaws so bright, like a piece of rainbow in flight. Muddy rivers flow through rainforests. Inaccessible, never been explored. Trees and birds … all manner of life. Vines like thick ropes loop from tree to tree."

To illustrate twisting vines, Sears made a spiraling motion in the air. After a moment, he went on.

"Mists drift through treetops … warm moisture clouds. High up on moss-covered trunks … orchids. From branches, hanging like green fringe are … whatever those damn things are."

The waiter brought a pot of jasmine tea, and I poured. We sat in silence for a bit, and I realized that he must miss his country.

In between sips, Sears went on. "In that year-round hothouse climate, trees just grow and grow, get too tall for their shallow roots and topple over. On the bark, there's an EXPLOSION of new growth. All sorts of ferns and things shoot up from the decomposing trunk."

I poured more tea. A dimming light filtered through the restaurant's window. Outside in the cold drizzle, shapeless forms in gray, brown, dark-green coats hurried past. Faces behind black umbrellas.

A dirge-like monologue of colors. I looked back at Sears and stifled a laugh. The only burst of color was his tie—cobalt blue with large white dots.

I held the cup of tea in both hands and felt its warmth. But perhaps the warmth came from being transported to a lush tropical forest, if for just a moment.

⁂

Having spent all afternoon in the city, in the evening we often made our way to a nearby pub. The fog formed fuzzy gold halos around lamplights. Wet sidewalks glistened. Finding a place at the long oak table by the fireplace, we watched the glowing logs, the intermittent sparks. Over a pint of unchilled pale ale, Sears told me his play was finally taking shape. He was pleased with its rhythm, the sharp dialogue that had bite, the vigorous writing that he hoped to sustain to the end.

"What is it about?" I asked.

"All the issues of mankind, all the fundamental human problems. Love, adultery, incest, jealousy, even murder. In the play, nothing is resolved, because nothing ever IS. Plain ordinary people living plain ordinary orderly lives. Mostly by default. Lives and action shaped by fears. Then suddenly, something happens to disrupt the equilibrium of that day-to-day existence. And, oh, how EASILY respectable, acceptable behavior reverts to the laws of the jungle."

After a long and unusual silence, Sears said, "Chérie, I want you to know that this play is dedicated to you."

I stared down into my nearly empty glass of ale to hide my confusion. He had never addressed me like that before. It surprised me, and the familiarity made me uncomfortable.

༶

One Saturday evening, Sears and I met in town to attend a Shosta-kovich concert. Enjoying the sound of his own voice, he recited as we walked.

Poetry is like mining radium.
For every gram you work a year,
For the sake of every word
A thousand tons of verbal ore ...

He knew I had been reading Vladimir Mayakovsky. The raw-ness of his poetry appealed to both of us. Like Sears, I had started to analyze everything I read. I was puzzled that the poet had com-mitted suicide, and asked Sears about it.

"Perhaps," Sears conjectured, "he couldn't reconcile the sti-fling life he was leading with the more vibrant one he'd imagined for himself. Maybe some vital thing missing? The reason probably resides in one of his last lines. 'Love's boat has smashed against the daily grind.'"

"It's curious, Chérie, this attachment you seem to have for all things Russian." Sears laughed and changed the subject.

The line of the poem reverberated in my head. I pondered whether Sears too had imagined a more vibrant life for himself than the one he was leading. As in his play, did he find his days had become plain, orderly, and ordinary? A life led by default.

༶

There was no spring in England that year. In June, I still wore my winter coat. In July, with only three weeks left of school, I had already booked my passage home. My one-year contract was over. I wasn't coming back.

One evening before I left, Sears and I lingered over a pub meal, and he told me that his main aim was not to read what others had said but to say something of his own—and to say it well and memorably. Only writing seemed to offer him a chance of escape, to build his own tragic and comic world.

"The bosh we say to appear thoughtful and original." He laughed at his own seriousness.

I asked about his play.

"Sometimes it reads like so much tripe, other times it seems almost magnificent. I have found a title for it." He paused for a moment. "*So Near the Jungle.*"

∽

The return Atlantic crossing was no less an escape than the previous one had been. This time, from an ambiguous and untenable friendship. Sears had become a complicating event in my life. In the role of mentor, he had turned on me a focus so intense that I had been strangely captivated. Like a moth circling around a source of light, dizzy from vertiginous loops, I had been distracted from my own course.

Thirty-seven letters from Sears followed me after I returned to Cleveland. The long letters, in fine handwriting that often filled six closely spaced pages, were a continuation of our conversations about literature, concerts, and plays, detailed descriptions of little dramas at the school. There was also a new element—us.

The salutations on the letters at first flattered, then troubled me.

Chérie

My beloved

Dearest
Some letters began with all the above.

He wrote:

... so depressed after you left—our relationship was not of insipidity. I miss you very much, very wisely, very foolishly, but how I miss you. And even you, who try to be so blasé, must feel this emotional turmoil.

Emotional turmoil? Our friendship had been transformed into a relationship. I crumpled the letter as if to efface the idea. In the next letter:

The dead leaves of autumn lie brown and curled, so different from last year's when they squelched and oozed as we walked.

Then he wrote about celebrating his forty-eighth birthday. For the first time and with a shock, I realized he was close to my father's age.

You have been not only a means of rejuvenation, that's not the word I want for I never really felt old. You are that force which made me retain my youth. My inner self gleams again.

Entangled and trapped in Sears's verbal web, I had missed clues about his feelings for me. He had cast a powerful spell over me, but this was not how I had imagined our friendship.

Have you found a charming international man? I hope not. What woman would be content with second best after having known me? Chérie, why have I not heard from you?

I didn't know what to think and stopped writing to him. His letters continued to arrive.

But it seems to me that I can now view you semi-detachedly, never fully, the very essence, the quintessence of your being, has taken a form which I can hardly describe. Please write, Chérie!

The quintessence of my being? The overdramatization annoyed me. I began to doubt his sincerity. Then he wrote about a dream he had.

You are put in a blazing fire—you shrink but are not scorched—and you step out smaller, firmer and yet even softer, with that elfin smile I remember so well. Your sudden laughter and equally sudden gleam of anger in your eyes so different from mine which is vast and cataclysmic and oh, so childish. You do not write, Chérie.

I was becoming a histrionic protagonist in a play. His play. In the next letter:

Why the silence? You will not believe that you are growing dearer to me every minute. Let your hair grow. Let it hang down your back.

The letters became frantic.

I think you like to run all manner of risks with men in love with you, apparently in the conviction they will just talk and go away when they find it's no use trying to get you to change your mind. I don't think I will be satisfied with a no.

As the letters continued, I dreaded opening them. But out of an obsessive compulsion, I read them.

Your silence gives rise to many imaginary scenes and you are right in withholding your telephone number from me. Why is it that I am so often misunderstanding you? So often I get you wrong.

Still, I did not write back.

No man accepts rejection, even I do not. Chérie, and not a word from you. Shall we go visit Greece? Come with me to that light-pervaded land of heroes. Then there won't be any chance of forgetting, there will be no difficulty in remembering.

I began to suspect that rather than love, these letters were about salvaging pride and ego. By his warmth and intellect, I had been drawn into Sears's magnetic field, but now his complex hold on me had become threatening, like a volcano that might somehow erupt and disrupt. The way he wanted to take over my life reminded me of a strange tree, the strangler fig tree, found only in the deepest, most remote rainforests. Its tiny, sticky seed gets lodged high in the crook of a branch of another tree, its host. There, in the humid, protected crevice, the seed sprouts, grows slowly, sending thin rootlets that dangle from the host's branches, eventually descending to the ground where they anchor in the soil. Then the growth becomes rampant. New networks of roots quickly form and wrap around the host tree. They grow and thicken and fuse together. Squeezing the trunk, they choke off the flow of nutrients. Slowly, the host tree dies. A hollow center is all that remains of it. With its umbrella-shaped canopy of thick waxy leaves, the strangler fig stands on its own.

I was suffocating from Sears's dominating hold on me. I knew he would choke off my personality, my will. I was like that host tree. Eventually, I would be hollowed out.

I needed to break free.

GLIMPSE OF THE SEA

AFTER I RETURNED to Cleveland, the big event in late August was Maija's wedding. My father, solemn and standing tall, escorted his oldest daughter down the aisle. The three younger sisters, Livija, Valija, and I, her bridesmaids in coral-pink taffeta dresses and dyed-to-match linen pumps, followed behind. Conrad, the groom, had agreed to have the wedding ceremony in the Latvian Lutheran Church even though he was Catholic.

Maija was the first daughter to wed. So, a special event. A milestone celebration for my parents who, after the church service, beamed as they greeted family and friends at the rented hall. Seated at long tables, guests piled their plates with *pīrāgi* (savory bacon and onion pastries), *galerts* (pork aspic with horseradish), pink-tinted herring and beet salads, mushrooms in a dilled sour cream sauce, and *rupjmaize* (dark grainy rye bread). Bottles of wine and liquor lined up within reach on each table.

A live band with an accordion churned out the steady beats of polkas and waltzes. The newlyweds, faces flushed from wine, danced in the humid late-summer heat. Across the room, my mother watched as the couple whirled by. Head tilted, she touched her hair from time to time, as if to check her new style. For the occasion, she had gone to a beauty salon, something she never did. My father had joined the men smoking in a corner of the hall. It occurred to me that I had never seen my parents on a dance floor.

❧

Maija emptied drawers and her side of the closet in the room we shared and moved into the apartment Conrad rented for them in Lakewood. Her bed was carried down to the basement and a table brought up to serve as my desk.

In September, Livija and Valija went back to college, and I started work at Tremont Elementary School, two long bus rides away. Getting off the bus, I hurried along the cracked sidewalks, past unkempt lawns and modest houses of the neighborhood where my second graders lived. Some came from the Projects, low-income housing near the steel mills.

A dog tied to a chain-link fence barked as I approached yards with banged-up trash cans and abandoned clutter. A loose gutter dangled from an asphalt-shingled house; a broken baby stroller stood propped up by a pile of old tires. Across the street, rusted bedsprings and a bicycle missing its front wheel leaned against a sagging porch—once useful things, now discarded and taking up space in narrow yards. The startling image of blood-red plastic geraniums poking out of a window box next to a front door painted flamingo-pink stayed with me as I entered the school.

Thirty-eight squirmy kids jostled each other into the classroom each morning. Boys with scraped knees and scuffed shoes. I learned the children's names. Philomena, the girl who scampered about in a flimsy cotton dress. Gyula, the boy whose family fled Hungary in the 1956 revolution and spoke only a few words of English. Patty, whose glass eye didn't quite match the color of her good one and didn't fit properly. I wanted to know what happened to her right eye, but was reluctant to ask. Tracy, Jill, Penny, and Sue came in an orderly cluster and didn't compete for my attention like the noisy ones who jabbed and annoyed one another.

Negative energy permeated the room as I stood in front of the class, trying to summon the sternest look I could manage, trying not to inhale too deeply the stale mix of chalk dust, unwashed socks, and the overripe banana forgotten in someone's desk. The snickering and fidgeting eventually stopped, and the children settled down. Where to start? A question I asked myself daily. These kids were not reading at grade level. Most of them were behind in their number skills. There was a lot of work ahead in the coming school year.

✦

On Sundays, in a windowless room in the Latvian church basement, I taught a dozen eight- to twelve-year-olds whose parents were, for the most part, both Latvian and wanted their children to learn about their country.

In 1962, it had been only a dozen or so years since Latvians settled in Cleveland, the DP-camp experience still fresh in their minds. Some of them, rather unrealistically, hoped for the improbable collapse of the USSR so they could return to their towns, their homes, and find them as they were before their departure. They imagined stepping back into their old lives, which had been irreparably disrupted by the war.

But the Soviet Union would not break apart, nor Latvia and the other Soviet-controlled nations regain their independence, for almost another thirty years. An independent Latvia in 1991 came too late for those who fled the country in 1944. They had been gone too long, and most of them didn't return. By then they had rebuilt their lives and become established in their adopted homes in the States, England, Canada, Australia, and elsewhere.

The Latvians who did return found a landscape dominated by

shoddy Soviet-era high-rise apartment complexes. Riga, after so many years of Soviet neglect, was not the city they remembered. The medieval and turn-of-the century Art Nouveau buildings, the famed architectural gems, stood in disrepair. As they walked down Riga's streets, the banter they heard around them was in Russian. When they overheard snippets in Latvian, they discovered that their language had been corrupted by Russification. Over decades of Soviet occupation, the intonation and pronunciation had changed. Their own mother tongue sounded strange to them.

≈

Arriving at the church for my class that first Sunday, I retrieved an old rolled-up map of Latvia from the supply closet. As I unfolded it, I saw it was the same one that had been used when I attended these classes. On the map, the country, recognizable by the deep notch carved out at the top that looks like someone took a big bite out of the country, floated on a white background.

What lay beyond the country's borders was not labeled. As if what surrounded the nation was of no consequence. From the map, you wouldn't know that to the east, Latvia shared a long border with the USSR. As if the mapmaker wanted to avoid any reference to that unfortunate proximity and how it had dominated the country's turbulent history.

I thought back to when I was a kid sitting in this same room. We didn't learn about the economic and strategic importance of the country's ports and the decisive role the Baltic Sea played in the country's past, that its sought-after geographical position led to recurring clashes with neighboring nations over centuries. We didn't talk about the Soviet Union's takeover of Latvia, nor that large numbers of the population had fled, become refugees, forced to restart lives in foreign places all over the world. Instead, on Sundays, we had learned the country's geography.

The kids needed to learn about Latvia's tragic history. Didn't they? Seeing their fresh and eager faces in front of me, I hesitated. I would tackle the difficult and painful topics later in the year. They would learn what lay beyond Latvia's borders and its wars soon enough. I tacked the map up in front of the room. Like the teachers before me, I handed out sheets of paper with the outline of the country drawn and asked the children to trace the courses of the Daugava, Gauja, Lielupe, and Venta, the major rivers that snake through the land, to place big dots for Riga, Daugavpils, Jelgava, Ventspils, and Liepāja, the principal cities, to mark the location of Gaiziņkalns, the highest mountain. Not a big mountain, just over a thousand feet high.

The children worked on their maps, and I thought about Torilds. His strange name—like a character from a Wagnerian opera.

Torilds had a gorgeous voice. He had been invited to perform selections from Schubert's *Winterreise* song cycle at the Latvian Baptist Church, where his father was minister. He asked me to accompany him on the piano. Tall, with an Ivy-League crewneck-sweater look, his hair longer than men wore at the time, and clutching a dog-eared sheaf of music, he arrived at my house to practice. I sat down at the piano, intimidated. He was older, in his late twenties, and a bit starched, I thought.

The song cycle was a challenge for the singer as well as for me, the accompanist. Not that the score was technically difficult, but its abrupt switches of tempo and mood were complex. The music, gloomy and sad, was composed when Schubert suffered from depression and illness. The twenty-four songs portray a young man's anguished psychological journey, and perhaps the composer's deep melancholy had seeped into the music.

The melodies change from major to minor harmonies and back again to evoke nuances and shifting textures. In the third stanza of "Frühlingstraum," Torilds's voice suddenly acquired a tremulous legato, and a sadness crept in. Trying to understand, I interrupted my playing.

"What's so sad here?" I asked. "Can you translate?"

He leaned against the fireplace mantel. "I don't need to translate," he said. "I know the words in English but prefer to sing in German. Anyway, in English, the lyrics sound rather mundane.

Who drew those leafy flowers
Upon the window pane?
Why do you mock the dreamer
Whose garden blooms in winter?

As I played, I saw ice-flower patterns on wintry windows. Not mundane at all. At times, Torilds's rendering would suddenly become animated, and he would gesture with energy. I would stop playing again.

"What's the story here?" I would ask. It helped when I could visualize the drama of the song. Irritated that I had stopped midphrase, he recited the stanza dutifully, mechanically.

A storm has ripped
The gray robe of sky
The clouds fly apart
In wild disorder.

"The words are lovely, even in English," I said.

We continued, and I immersed myself in the tragedy of the song, the young man's despair as he makes his way across a winter landscape. I listened to Torilds as he sang and breathed when he breathed, softened my touch on the keys when he mellowed his intonation, slowed down and accelerated when he did. I was overcome by the atmospheric outpouring and passion of the story. I felt the aching sostenutos in Torilds's inflection, its tenderness. As the melody soared and throbbed, it penetrated me. Glancing up, I saw that he was looking at me, and the warmth of his voice enveloped me.

There were still many practice sessions before the concert. Torilds asked me out several times. After dinner at a restaurant, he would invite me to his apartment. We drank red wine and listened to his LP collection of Mahler symphonies, Verdi operas, and Bach cantatas. During those evenings, I found him withdrawn, almost distant. When not listening to records, we sat in long, awkward silences.

My mother was pleased I was seeing Torilds. He would encourage me to continue my musical training, she thought. She liked that he was Latvian and a minister's son, as if that would confer piety upon him.

❧

At Tremont School, the kids had left for the day. As usual, the afternoon had been tiring. Sitting at my desk, I had leaned back and closed my eyes when I heard someone enter. It was Mrs. Alexander, the principal. I stood up.

"Excuse me for interrupting," she said. "I've come to talk to you about Kevin."

I didn't understand. There was no Kevin in my class.

"Kevin Galeffi," she said. "I'm going to switch him from Eleanor Gallo's class to yours."

With her sleek silver hair and crisp white blouse, Mrs. Alexander looked as though she belonged in an exclusive girls' school rather than in this poor-neighborhood one. Despite her soft and modulated voice, she exuded authority.

"Yes, of course," I said. "But why?"

"When I walk past your classroom, I see learning is taking place."

What? She must have come by on a good day. Most of the time, I still had trouble keeping the kids in their seats and focused. She explained that Eleanor, the teacher of the other second grade class, was threatening to quit, to go into early retirement. She could no longer deal with one child continually disrupting the class.

"Yes," Mrs. Alexander said. "That child is Kevin."

The following day, as I sat in the middle of the reading group at the front of the class, Mrs. Alexander came in. She had brought Kevin. He looked like an ordinary second grader. Perhaps bigger. I don't know why that surprised me or what I had expected him to look like. His hair, in a crewcut, was shorn practically to the scalp. Under a plaid flannel shirt, a once-white T-shirt peeked out at the neck. Maybe I noticed something a little odd about the firm line of his mouth, the way he jutted out his chin.

I thanked Mrs. Alexander, guided Kevin to his desk, and handed him the worksheet the class was completing. I wanted to spend a few minutes with him but couldn't interrupt the reading lesson.

"When you finish, you can color in the pictures," I said. I grabbed a handful of crayons from a plastic container on the windowsill and put them on his desk.

Back with my readers, I glanced at Kevin from time to time. The class had become quiet, as if Kevin had created tension. Perhaps they knew about him or had encountered him on the playground.

When I next looked up, he was fiddling with something—a grimy pencil stub attached to a thick rubber band. As long as he fussed with that thing and keeps quiet I was going to ignore him.

I turned back to my group. I was particularly troubled about this group's reading, worried they wouldn't catch up by the end of the year. Philomena and some of the others still struggled with the simplest words. I almost gasped as it dawned on me. He could use that thing as a slingshot. I thought of Patty's eye and jumped up.

"Kevin, give it to me."

He twisted the rubber band around the pencil stub with grubby fingers.

"Let me have it."

He shook his head.

"Let me have it," I repeated. "Now!"

"No," he said without looking up.

"Hand it over." I held out my hand.

The class stopped working, pencils in midair. The reading group looked up from the books in their laps and waited in thick silence. I waited.

"It's not yours," he said. His rudeness startled me. He wasn't going to give it to me. If I persisted, it could become a disruptive confrontation. And it hadn't even been fifteen minutes since he arrived in my class.

I returned to my readers and the class went back to their worksheets. When I looked over a moment later, the rubber-band thing was gone. Kevin had crumpled his worksheet into a ball and sat with his head between his hands.

With Kevin's arrival, the atmosphere in the classroom changed. I could never predict when he would suddenly erupt over some misconceived slight and upset the order I was trying to cultivate. At times, for no reason I could guess, he would run up and grab the blackboard erasers or the container of crayons and hurl them across the room, or snatch someone's snack bag, throw it on the floor and crush the contents with his foot. Shoving and kicking, he could be aggressive with the other kids. Once when I tried to pull him away, I felt the strength in his arms and muscled shoulders. It was as if a rage welled up in him, and he couldn't control the impulse to do something destructive.

I had thirty-eight other needy children, yet I kept having to focus on Kevin's inappropriate behavior. It affected the other kids, who were confused by his outbursts and afraid of him.

Eleanor Gallo was an older teacher who had taught at Tremont for thirty years and looked forward to retiring after a couple more. I went to see her one day after the students had gone home. She was clearing off her desk and getting ready to leave. Seeing me, she sank her heavy form into her chair and sighed. It must have been a difficult day for her too. She looked as drained as I felt.

"I'm sorry," she said. "No teacher should have to put up with him."

"Maybe you can give me some advice," I said.

"The kid's a mess. That's all I can tell you." She rolled her eyes in exasperation. "I tried everything. Nothing worked."

"What about the parents? Have you met with them?" I asked.

"You don't know?" She looked surprised. "Father's in jail."

Eleanor shuffled through a pile of papers on the desk, then looked at me. "I haven't seen her, the mother. But she's got some weird ... deformity. I don't know, something wrong with her arms."

I left Eleanor's room feeling sick, my heart aching for Kevin. I thought about his harsh world and the heavy weight on his young shoulders, but I had no idea how this disturbing information would help me.

One March evening when I returned home from school, I found a light-blue aerogram in the mailbox. From Libya. It was from Nancy, a friend I had known in college who had gone to teach English at the Oil Companies School in Tripoli. In the brief note, she wrote that she loved teaching there and wanted to let me know that the school was expanding and the superintendent would be hiring more teachers. She urged me to apply. One of the two teachers with whom she shared a villa was leaving at the end of the school year. Maybe, if I got hired, I could take her place in the villa.

A villa, I thought. What did a villa in Libya look like? Nancy didn't describe the villa, but at the end of the letter, she added, "From the bedroom window, when I stand on my tiptoes, I can glimpse the Mediterranean Sea."

I had been back in Cleveland less than a year. The teaching at Tremont was tough, but I was making progress with my second graders and feeling a sense of accomplishment. Under their boisterous rowdiness, the kids were sweet, and I had grown attached to them. Kevin's outbursts had become more predictable, and I was usually able to avert them. He was smart and could do the work. There was not much I could do for him except make sure he left with grade-level skills. The rest he would have to figure out for himself.

And what about Torilds? I had to admit that my friendship with him was odd. When he sang Schubert's poignant composition, a powerful connection drew me to him. We shared something deeply moving. But when he stopped, that emotional closeness was severed, as if a light had been switched off. He became someone else—once again aloof, the minister's son. I was no longer attracted to him the way I had been a moment earlier.

It could be that, when Torilds sang, he became in my mind the tormented wanderer of the song cycle, a figment of my imagination. The young man I conjured up evoked my emotional reaction, not Torilds. I had been seduced by his honeyed voice, not the man himself. I knew that after the concert, I would not be seeing Torilds again.

⋘

One late winter day, the class worked quietly, and for the moment even Kevin was focused on the assignment. From the windows at the back of the room, I looked out at the mud browns of the empty playground and the vacant lot next to it, overgrown by weeds and strewn with construction debris. A brick building, once a warehouse, stood defunct, its windows boarded up with vertical slats, warped and weather-stained. Along the road, rows of trees appeared black, bare except for the crinkled, bronze-colored leaves still clinging to an oak's gnarled branches. Snow had been plowed into dirty mounds. I felt the endlessness of the afternoon, as if time had slowed to a sluggish drip. A dormant, frozen world gripped by an oppressive torpor. An emptiness and desperation that settled and penetrated like dampness.

As I stood there, I thought of Eleanor. From her classroom windows, day after day, she had looked out at this same cheerless scene for thirty years.

I decided to apply for the teaching job in Libya.

SABRATHA

Like water, the world ripples across you,
and for a while, lends you its colors.

Nicolas Bouvier

AT MIDMORNING, THE sky darkened. Sand hissed and blew against the school building, a primitive one-story structure with classrooms strung out like a train, accessed from an open outside corridor. It was a *ghibli*—the dreaded storm, when desiccating winds swept in dust-laden clouds from the desert. Fine dust coated roads, trees, and penetrated houses. It seeped into clothing and made the air unbreathable. A reddish haze hovered for days.

I hurried out to the playground to bring in my second graders. Serious gusts whipped my dress; swirling sand stung bare arms and legs. Following me, the children scrambled back to the classroom. Wooden shutters banged against the outside wall. Struggling against the wind, I grappled with the ill-fitting closures. The children emptied sand from their sneakers. I turned on the fluorescent ceiling lights.

"My teeth feel gritty," someone said.

"Mine too," I told them.

Most of the kids, like me, hadn't experienced a *ghibli* before.

With no glass panes in the windows, sand sifted through the slats of the shutters and formed small piles on the floor. The wind wailed. Without their usual bounce, the kids sat subdued, too distracted for lessons. I was too. I handed out drawing paper.

It was my first week of school. I had just arrived in Tripoli, Libya, for my new teaching job at the Oil Companies School. The fathers of these second graders, American and British geologists and geophysical engineers, worked for oil companies and drilling services here. The lucrative jobs allowed them to bring their families.

With the shutters closed, the heat in the room was oppressive. The kids worked on their drawings. Sad little scrunched-up faces bent over their papers, foreheads damp with perspiration. The shutters rattled. Pencils scratched on rough paper.

"That's Scruffy, my dog." Ian came up to show me his drawing. "He's back home in England."

I walked around the class.

"Our house in Texas," Gary said. "I'm just doing the green part for the grass where we play catch."

I couldn't quite make out Melanie's drawing. A round pink mass in the middle of the page.

"It's my shell. I found it on the beach in Florida," she said.

Going from desk to desk, I looked at what they were drawing. Like an inventory of what was inside their heads, the sketches hinted at what the kids had on their minds. Their scrawly attempts conjured up little scenes from home. To them, Libya had not yet become home. Their pictures revealed what they were too young to verbalize, happy moments in the past. With the sandstorm raging outside, they may have been wondering why they were here and wished they were back home with their friends in England or the States.

❧

Downtown Tripoli, 1963.

The Oil Companies School recruited teachers from the United States and England—mostly young single women. Rumor had it that the superintendent hired only attractive teachers. We used to laugh about it, but now as I look at the school yearbook and see the radiant faces of the thirty or so teachers, I think it might have been true.

The school provided housing for us. In twos or threes, the teachers shared spacious villas that had sprung up in the sand in Giorgimpopoli, a few miles outside Tripoli. Enclosed by walls, the modern villas lined sandy lanes that had no names and where sheep wandered.

The young female teachers were a magnet for the single geologists and geophysicists who worked for Esso, Gulf, Mobil, Schlumberger, Halliburton, and other companies. With no phones in our villas, no excuse was necessary for the young men to come by and visit in the evenings. We saw them on the weekends at the British Underwater Club, where we swam, snorkeled, and stayed for the evening curry buffet.

The men impressed us with their talk about complex technologies of assessing rock formations, seismic refractions to map subsurface layers, deep drilling of wells. They flew out to the desert to locate this hidden "black gold" that was transforming the world. After its discovery, Libya had become wealthy overnight. It was high-quality oil, low in sulfur content. "Sweet crude," it was called, more like the name for a harlot. The exotic aura surrounding the geologists' work fascinated us.

We also got to know the fighter pilots who came to Wheelus, the American Air Force Base outside Tripoli. The pilots, stationed in Bitburg and Ramstein Air Force Bases in Germany, came to fly the supersonic bomber jets, the F-100s, capable of sound-barrier-breaking speeds. The pilots were married, but with their wives and families far away, they came to our parties. After training missions, they arrived with a tired swagger and bottles of booze from the base commissary. By mid-thirty, their faces had already lost the freshness of youth. Gravity's downward pull at takeoff, I thought. With arrogant bravado, they sometimes buzzed the school. They exuded glamour, talked about flying and death. I hadn't met this breed of men before.

෴

Soon after arriving in Libya, I bought a used powder-blue MGB with a black leather interior. Perhaps a little extravagant for a first car. An oil company pilot had just finished his tour and, needing to sell it, didn't charge much.

"It never rains in Libya," he said. "You can leave the top down all year."

The MGB turned out to be an unwise choice.

On my first trip out of the city, I set out to visit Sabratha, some thirty miles west of Tripoli. Wearing a light-blue sleeveless dress with a long white chiffon scarf streaming behind in the breeze, I drove along the coastal road past a tuna canning factory and citrus orchards. On both sides of the road, rows of tall palms bore huge clusters of dates. Then came ancient olive groves with silvery foliage and thick trunks gnarled and twisted into tormented silhouettes. In villages, goats scampered across the road, and I had to slow down. At a rusty sign, I turned onto an unpaved road lined with tall cypresses, the obelisk shapes dark green against the dusty landscape. At the end of the road, I looked for what remained of the ancient Roman port city. I could see no entrance gate, no one here besides me.

In Italy, jostled by crowds of tourists, I had visited ancient Roman monuments, gray from the grit and grime of modern city pollution—the fine details of columns and statues etched by acid rain, eroded away.

Here, the ruins of Sabratha, of a lovely, warm roseate stone, were untouched by pollution. I wandered along the silent streets, laid down in a grid, paved with large, uneven stones, worn down, grooved from the wheels of horse-drawn chariots that once rode here.

A few columns stood here and there—a spare skeleton of the once-splendid city. A row of six columns of more impressive proportions might have been the façade of a forum or a temple. Scattered segments with fluting lay near rubble of shattered Corinthian capitals, acanthus leaf fragments hidden in the weeds.

As I walked near the shore, I came upon a floor mosaic that might have been a communal bath. I thought of someone kneeling in the hot sun, arranging tiny chips of marble to form patterns as graceful as an Oriental carpet. Inserting bits of translucent glass in blues, greens, and ochres. Tableaux, which could be quite elaborate, of long-ago moments frozen in time. Hunters with spears on the trail of a boar, a fisherman in a boat harpooning an octopus with a trident, nets brimming with the day's catch.

Entering through the archways of the amphitheater, I could

almost hear the voices of the noisy spectators who had once passed through this same passage, rushing in to see some ancient spectacle.

A pale, camouflaged lizard scuttled to safety as I sat down on a sunbaked stone seat. Laid out, row upon row in a semicircle, the seating faced the stage with a stunning backdrop of three stories of columns. Through the arches, two shades of blue met at the horizon—the lighter of the sky and the darker of the sea. Not the slightest breeze rippled its surface. The architect, in his genius, had positioned the theater so that the entire audience could look out upon the sea and feel its cooling and soothing effect.

The beauty here was astounding. Beauty had mattered here.

I sat in the amphitheater as if suspended for the moment, between my past and a future full of optimistic expectations. Freed from relationships that tugged and pulled and tried to keep me in place. A tabula rasa. I felt that right then was the beginning of something new and significant.

Roman amphitheater in Sabratha.

The droning whir of cicadas broke the silence. At midday, the sun beat down unbearably. Lightheaded and feverish from thirst, I returned to the car. The scarf I had left on the front seat was no longer there. I had the eerie thought that I hadn't been alone. I had been watched.

On the road back, I passed the now-familiar landmarks. A tall minaret meant I was approaching a village, color washed out by the glare of the sun, white walls almost blinding. Here and there, sheep grazed in barren fields with not a patch of shade nor blade of grass. Goats in the road again. Near olive groves, an unpleasant fermenting sourness emanated from towering mounds of pulpy olive residue.

A bit off the road, a building appeared that looked like it might be a school. Barefoot boys wearing the traditional white cotton cap ran about outside. They looked to be eight or nine years old, about the age of my second graders, but thin and wiry. I drove down the narrow dirt road to the schoolyard.

Near the simple low school building, partly enclosed by a wall of prickly pear cactus, the boys kicked a ball, raising dust on the field of bare earth. They shouted, laughed, and pushed each other. A taller boy, a bit older, stood nearby. He too was barefoot, tan shorts and a grimy shirt open at the neck, with a maroon felt cap perched on the back of his shaved head.

Pointing to me, he shouted something. The game stopped. The ball rolled away and with a soft thud bounced against the wall, coming to rest in the dust. In surprise or curiosity, the boys stared at me, shifting from foot to foot in silence. I smiled and waved.

The tall boy stooped down and picked up something. I realized what was happening when the stone bounced off my windshield. As if following an order, the rest of the boys picked up stones and began pelting the car. The staccato, guttural sounds of their Arabic were no longer playful. They were angry. Stunned and frightened,

I tried to shift into reverse. Stones hurtled past me, one grazed my ear. The boys were not adept and mostly missed their target, me. I backed down the road in a cloud of dust.

As I got back on the main road, my initial rush of fear was replaced by outrage. For a moment, I had been afraid. Now I was furious that I had been humiliated by a pack of scruffy kids.

My anger subsided, and I realized it was my fault. I had been insensitive to the complexity of life in this country. It hadn't occurred to me that I was not invisible as I drove around the countryside.

In this Muslim country, women out in the street wore a heavy white garment that covered them from head to toe, the cloth draped carefully and firmly around the head, leaving only a small opening for one eye.

The unexpected sight of me in their schoolyard, bareheaded in an open sports car, must have been shocking, even offensive to the boys. They had probably never seen a woman not veiled and must have felt threatened, perhaps even afraid. What had happened was inevitable. As an American, I had assumed that the strict dress code of Libyan women didn't apply to me. Now I wondered whether it did.

≼

Images of Sabratha's sunlit stone, its marble columns, reconstructed arches, and pristine shoreline stayed with me. I imagined the bustling port of millennia ago where Roman triremes once moored to receive goods from lands of coastal North Africa. Huge palm leaf baskets mounded with lemons, figs, and dates carried aboard; sacks of wheat and giant amphorae of olive oil and wine stacked in the hold. I visualized the frantic commotion at the arrival of the long-awaited camel caravans that had trudged across the Sahara, laden with riches that Rome coveted and only Africa could supply. Elephant tusks hoisted onto the deck, along with caged lions and leopards, hunted and captured for gladiator games. Ostrich feathers and rhinoceros horn collected in treacherous thickets of the unexplored wilds of a remote continent.

As I walked along the ruins of Sabratha's basilicas and squares, my sense of time had expanded. I began to view a world not defined by Europe's wars, DP camps, or the sad confines of our cities' grim concrete structures, proliferating and creeping outward, leaving behind boarded-up storefronts, asphalt shingles, and chain-link fencing. Over centuries, Sabratha had crumbled, been reduced to rubble and buried in sand. It hadn't gradually decayed the way our industrial cities sometimes did.

It could be that I started to perceive history not to be measured in decades or centuries, but rather in millennia that stretched deep into the past, into an altogether different kind of world.

ACANTHUS LEAF

ON WEEKENDS, MY two villa roommates and I went shopping in Tripoli or *Città Bianca*, as it was known when it was an Italian colony. The city dazzled with white office buildings, mosques, and hotels. Wide tree-lined boulevards led to orderly traffic circles, and along the city's curving coastline, palm trees shaded a promenade. We wandered down the arcades of colonnaded buildings to buy Italian shoes and have our hair done in a trendy beauty salon.

After Arabic, Italian was the second language spoken in Libya. Luigi, a geologist at one of the oil companies, whom I had met at a party, taught me a few words of Italian.

One Saturday, he invited me to join him for lunch at La Romagna, an Italian restaurant in downtown Tripoli. When I arrived, he was waiting on the upstairs terrace where a dozen or so tables were set with white tablecloths and vases of bougainvillea. Spotting him, I realized he was more attractive than I remembered, tall and lanky with a cascade of dark curls. He rose to greet me with a kiss on both cheeks, and with an exaggerated flourish, pulled out the chair for me to be seated. I loved his old-fashioned formality.

"Try the *vitello tonnato*, it's the specialty here." He pointed to it on the menu.

"Cold veal with tuna sauce and capers? No, I think I'll get my usual *mozzarella in carrozza.*" I was a little embarrassed that my knowledge of Italian was limited to menu items.

The popular restaurant filled up for lunch. Animated talk at adjacent tables drowned out our conversation. We leaned across the table to hear each other.

"Italians are loud," Luigi said. "But I shouldn't criticize, being Italian myself."

He told me his family's history and how they came to put down roots in Libya. After Italy invaded Libya in 1911, at the time still part of the Ottoman Empire, it became an Italian colony. His family along with a hundred thousand other countrymen settled here. Over the years, the Italians planted olive trees, citrus orchards, and vineyards and built the roads and other infrastructure in the country.

"Italians built Tripoli." Luigi gestured, making a wide arc as if to include everything around him. It made me smile the way he talked with his hands.

The waiter brought our food, and we tasted the red wine.

"So, Luigi," I asked, "having grown up here, do you still think of yourself as Italian?"

I cut into the crispy crust of the *carrozza* and watched the melted cheese ooze onto my plate.

"Well, I was born here and have lived here all my life. But I am Italian—although I'm not sure what that means anymore."

"Would you like to live in Italy someday?"

Luigi looked surprised at my question and took a sip of wine before answering.

"No, not at all. Libya is my home. You may think this strange, Dag, but I've sort of absorbed both cultures."

As we ate, I thought about his two cultures, Arabic and Italian, so different and contradictory in many ways. It must have been difficult to adapt at times when he was growing up. Maybe that's what I found fascinating about him, his complexity.

The waiter brought our dessert. We watched the crowds hurrying by on the street below.

"Finish your *crostata di ricotta*," Luigi said, "and I'll take you to the souk for some tea."

We stepped out into the hot afternoon sun. Passing through the arch of the high wall into the old city, we entered another world.

Archway leading into old city of Tripoli

In narrow tangled alleys, silversmiths fashioned filigreed hands of Fatima. Amidst clanging noise, brass sheets were hammered into trays. Blacksmiths' shops reeked of hot metal. Children from the souk neighborhoods ran about. Luigi guided me through a narrow passageway to an alley where weavers sat in front of looms. Sounds were suddenly muffled, as if absorbed by the big bolts of fabric and rolled-up carpets.

Luigi knew many of the shopkeepers and greeted them, sometimes in Arabic but usually in Italian. In the maze of alleys, we found ourselves in the leather souk—embroidered slippers, bags, and belts of badly tanned hides still reeking of gamey animal scent. To make way for a passing donkey cart, we pressed ourselves against the wall.

From food stalls, spice smells wafted. A man squatted in front of palm leaf trays filled with dates, walnuts, and almonds. Stopping to buy some almonds, Luigi chatted with the old man.

"I wish I could speak Italian," I told Luigi over tea at a side-walk café.

"I'll teach you," he said.

"Thanks, but you're always away, out in the desert."

I was determined to learn Italian. Twice a week in the evening, I drove to Wheelus Air Force Base, a sterile collection of concrete and cinder-block buildings with guards at the entrance gate. The Italian courses were offered in the high-school building on the base.

In class, I noticed him, seated a few rows behind me. Fair hair, tortoise-shell glasses, linen blazer over a striped shirt. He looked like he might be a young professor at a university. While the rest of us struggled with pronunciation, he read the phrases effortlessly. Something about him intrigued me.

"Who is he?" I asked one of my classmates, a nurse I had befriended.

"He's the new assistant chief of internal medicine here at the hospital."

"There's a hospital on the base?" I asked.

"Yes, and it's big—eighty-some beds. The base is huge. Thousands of military and their families. We've got a commissary and PX, post office, dry cleaners, movie theater, officers' club, snack bars. A self-contained little town. Some folks never venture off base."

During the break, she saw me looking over to where he was standing.

"By the way, his name is Stuart," she said.

For some weeks, he didn't come to class. Perhaps he had night duty.

When he came back, I introduced myself after class. He told me he had arrived only recently.

"It was night when I got here. Next morning when I looked out the window, I saw the Mediterranean. What a surprise. Right there in front of my quarters." He laughed.

"And mounds of washed-up seaweed on the beach," I said.

He described his two-week basic officer training at Gunter Air Force Base in Montgomery, Alabama. The routines of military life and the South were quite a change from New York City, where he was from.

"The Confederate flag flying above the Stars and Stripes on the state capitol! Doctors, dentists, nurses, optometrists, and other medical types—all there learning how to wear our newly issued uniforms. How to march in precise formation. How to salute. I had my first taste of grits."

I started to get to know Stuart—very different from the partying, hard-drinking geologists and pilots.

He had just finished a year of residency at a hospital where he worked on early stem-cell research.

He invited me to visit the base hospital.

᪣

In the hospital cafeteria, we grabbed trays and stood in line for the typical American fare: sliced roast beef, mashed potatoes, corn, franks and beans, various salads.

"Iceberg lettuce?" I asked.

"Everything here gets flown in."

We carried our trays to a couple of empty spaces at a long table by a window.

To start a conversation, I asked Stuart about the strange propellers displayed near the headquarters building I had seen as I walked to the hospital.

"Oh, those. That's quite a story," he said.

As we ate, Stuart told me they were the propellers retrieved from the *Lady Be Good*. After a bombing attack on Naples Harbor during World War II, the U.S. Air Force plane had disappeared somewhere deep in the Sahara Desert. Crashed in the sand. Only discovered fifteen years later. Almost intact.

"Did you notice how the tips of the propellers are bent from the impact?" he asked.

I hadn't noticed.

The bodies of eight of the nine crewmen were found, buried in sand but well preserved. Five of the men had walked some seventy miles in search of help. One had gone over a hundred miles before dying. They had survived for eight days without water.

Finishing the story, Stuart looked at me for a long time and then added, "I thought it a wonderful survival story."

"But they didn't survive," I said.

"Well then, a story of tenacity." He hesitated for a moment and then added, "and the will to survive."

We started on our devil's food cake when a young woman in a nurse's uniform rushed up.

"Dr. Scheer, so sorry to interrupt, but there's a patient ..."

Not waiting for her to finish, Stuart took one last bite of the cake and got up. In passing, he squeezed my shoulder and was gone.

On my way back to the car, I passed the propellers again. This time I saw what I hadn't noticed earlier. The tips of the propellers were bent. I thought about the airplane crashing in the desert and remembered the strange sadness that had crept into Stuart's voice as he spoke about the crews' tenacity and will to survive.

❧

After class the following week, Stuart invited me back to his quarters for a glass of sherry. One of his rooms had been turned into a studio. Turpentine and varnish smell. Canvases stacked against a wall. Scattered on a table, tubes of oil paints and metal cans with brushes. Tacked along the wall, small brown ink wash drawings. So, not just a scientific mind. This man had another side to him.

The other plain room had been transformed by a thick earth-toned wool Misurata carpet and goat-hair rugs on a wall. The bed, covered with a coarse Berber *burnouse* and cushions, had become a couch. A bookshelf filled with records and books. Beside an Arabic dictionary, an antique Roman glass flask from Beirut, the only delicate touch in the masculine decor.

Listening to Corelli's *Concerti Grossi*, we sipped sherry. I noticed a silver frame on a side table. It was the photo of a beautiful dark-haired woman.

"My wife, Jane."

"Your wife?"

The shock must have shown on my face. We sat in sudden silence.

"She died."

❧

Weeks passed and I didn't see him. Then one Saturday, Stuart arrived at our villa.

"Come, I want to show you something remarkable," he said.

After driving about eighty miles eastward along the coast, we turned up a sandy unpaved road toward the sea. The site wasn't marked on our map, but it had once been the most stupendous city of the ancient world—Leptis Magna.

Roman ruins in Leptis Magna.

Only our footsteps on the large paving stones broke the silence of the scorching hot afternoon. We walked down the Triumphal Way that millennia ago had teemed with crowds and horse-drawn chariots. At a four-sided arch, I sat down on a fragment of a column in the shade. Stuart stood, trying to decipher a nearly obliterated inscription.

"Septimius Severus."

As Roman emperor, he had built opulent forums, basilicas, and temples. Public baths. Carved statues had once embellished every niche. Fountains had filled the city with the cooling sounds of water.

"What happened to Leptis?" I asked.

"It's a bit complicated, if I remember correctly. First an earthquake, then invasions by Vandals, later by Berbers and other desert tribes."

What was left of Leptis was finally finished off by one last invasion, nature. The encroaching sand dunes covered the city, leaving only the tops of the tall marble columns protruding. The ancient city lay buried until excavated by Italian archeologists.

"Come, let's go." Stuart reached down to pull me up.

We walked past a row of columns still standing that must have been a basilica. Scattered nearby lay remnants of others that had toppled and crumbled long ago. Fluted column stumps. Pieces with carved lettering, the lines still crisp. Chunks of white marble.

Stuart knelt and, searching through the rubble, picked out fragments. I watched his hands, good, strong, tanned hands, as he turned each piece every which way, like pieces of a jigsaw puzzle, to try to fit them together. In the heat, sweat dripped from his forehead. On the ground, he assembled what had once adorned the capital of a column, a perfect acanthus leaf.

We climbed to the top row of the huge amphitheater, from where we could see the port and the sea, a gorgeous deep indigo that day. A long sandbar blocked the entrance into the wadi, the passage through which the triremes had once sailed. In its shallow pools, a lone heron waded.

As we drove back to Tripoli, I thought about the acanthus leaf, remembering the way Stuart had assembled the bits of marble to make it whole again. It made me think about his wife, her death. Would he be able to piece his life together after the tragedy? He had talked about her death only briefly, but I knew the impact of such a loss had to be devastating.

Stuart in Khartoum, 1963.

OASIS

AT THE BEACH, we spread our blanket where we could watch fishermen from the tuna canning factory go out for the day's catch. They came carrying a long rope, with several loops of it draped around each man's shoulder. At that moment, the muezzin call sounded from a distant mosque. They dropped the rope and, facing what I guessed was Mecca, knelt down to pray, forehead in the sand. When they rose, they attached the rope to their black boat and, chanting in unison, dragged the boat down to the sea.

A peaceful scene. Timeless. I lay in the warm sun with the muezzin call still echoing in my head and thought how sometimes Stuart and I didn't need to talk. It was enough just to be together.

The sun was setting when we drove back to Tripoli. Near the city center, on Sharia Istaklal, the traffic slowed. On sidewalks, crowds milled about. Not the usual lively street scene. Something was happening.

"A parade?" I asked.

"No idea," Stuart said.

Hostile-looking men lined the street, waving signs and yelling things in Arabic I didn't understand. With the road ahead blocked and side streets barricaded, we were trapped in an unmoving line of cars. Horns honked. Impatient drivers swerved onto the sidewalk. Angry protesters waving clenched fists converged, jostling and pushing, and spilled into the street in a chaotic crush. A sense of dread washed over me.

"Get down." Stuart shoved me down. Heart pounding, I crouched under the dashboard. Footsteps thumped on the pavement amid the deafening car horns and furious shouting. Then a new sound—stones bouncing off metal.

A dull thud and our windshield shattered. Glass fragments hailed down on my shoulders and hair. I peered up, expecting Stuart to be slumped over the steering wheel. But no, he was fine. Staring straight ahead, he changed gears and hit the gas pedal. We sped forward. Whatever blocked the street had been cleared. I eased out from under the dashboard and picked bits of glass from my clothing. I could still hear the shouts of the mob behind us.

"What was that?" I asked.

"Not sure. On the signs, I recognized the word *Benghazi*, and I think ... *killing students*."

"It was in the paper," I said. "Police killed students in Benghazi. Don't know why."

"They're protesting something. Might be about that Benghazi attack. Thank God we're out of there."

On the coastal highway, as we drove along with no protective windshield, hot gusts of air whipped my face.

"Deciphering those signs," I said. "Quite the Arabist."

"Not quite."

I thought of the firm hand on my shoulder, pushing me down to safety. How calm he had been.

෬

After long days at the hospital, Stuart was never too tired to explore Tripoli. Sometimes he suggested longer excursions.

"From the top of Jebel Nafusa, you can see the desert," he said one day. "It's a long drive, and not many people go there."

We took my car because the windshield of his had not been repaired. We headed south along the eucalyptus-lined road through the grasslands of the Gefara plains. The fertile land gave way to stunted trees, scrub brush, and esparto grass. Berbers with goatskin gourds herded thin sheep and goats. Up and up, the dusty road wound in countless spirals and hairpin turns along steep slopes and deep canyons. Abandoned stone houses of ancient Berber towns perched high on limestone cliffs—a tortured landscape of cracked soil littered with stones and the occasional thorny shrub. The terrain became more desolate and desiccated as we drove along. We stopped to share a small tin of smoked oysters and a few chunks of Libyan halvah that Stuart had brought.

"People once lived here?" I asked.

"Maybe it wasn't always this bleak."

We drove to the top of the jebel and stepped to the edge of the cliff. In front of us, as far as the eye could see, stretched the Hamada, the Red Desert. A vast copper-colored emptiness that continued for a thousand miles, perhaps more. Moon-crater country—immense and scorched. Lifeless land. Silence surrounded us, so deep, so absolute, it was almost palpable. Almost unbearable. We stood in the dry wind under the violent sun. A terrifying terrain that conjured up death. I thought of Stuart's wife.

Despite the searing heat, a chill seeped through me. I became aware of a raw and aching barrier separating Stuart from me. They had been married for less than a year when Jane, pregnant with their first child, had been killed in a car accident, just a few months ago. That was all I knew. We never talked about it. There never seemed to be the right moment to bring it up. There was too much to say and no words for it.

I was reluctant to intrude into that residue of sadness, which I knew would last a long time, if not forever. In a strange way, I still thought of him as a married man and felt I shouldn't compete with the memory of his young wife. If we continued to see each other, that tragic part of his life would become part of mine too.

I understood the Italian classes, the Arabic classes. The painting. The two sterile bachelor-quarter rooms made comfortable. The Alfa Romeo he had ordered. Sad attempts to fill the emptiness, I thought.

For me, Jane would remain forever frozen as the lovely image in the silver frame; but for Stuart, there would be the countless moments of life together to be relived again and again. The heartbreaking tragedy reverberated like an excruciating chord, each iteration more and more complex, each a reminder of the finality of death.

∽

By evening, windblown and dusty, tingling from sunburned skin, we returned through the unlit streets of the outskirts of Tripoli and stopped at Le Lanterne. Small tables had been set under trees hung with paper lanterns. A faint breeze only hinted at coolness. After some bracing grilled green peppers and briny olives, we savored the creamy silkiness of the *tagliatelli al burro*.

Between us on the table, a tiny candle flame flickered. Hair tousled over a sunburned forehead, sleeves of his white shirt rolled up over tanned arms, Stuart looked more relaxed than I had ever seen him. We sat in silence, and I watched as he swirled the bit of red wine left in his glass. Something about him was always in motion. A restlessness, an intensity, and I was drawn to that intensity. More than drawn. But I wasn't sure there was room for me in his life.

∽

The noisy gatherings with the geologists and the pilots, with their cocky banter, seemed shallow now. One of the teachers would organize a party, and the pilots arrived with bags of chips and bottles of Scotch and bourbon from the commissary. We provided a welcome diversion from the stress of their dangerous flying missions. But I no longer wanted to be a diversion.

I saw Luigi from time to time. One weekend he took me to his home in the old city, where he lived with his parents when not out in the desert. We navigated the mazelike alleys with Luigi pushing his way through the crowds. He stopped in front of a heavy nail-studded door and unlocked it. Inside the white-walled house, it was cool. Solid dark furniture glimpsed between archways and columns, and faded rugs on the marble floors lent the rooms a stark feel.

"It's so quiet in here, feels like a chapel," I said.

"A lot of history here."

We sat in the living room, and through the window, I could see the massive ancient wall that surrounded the old city. Luigi brought glasses filled with a bright red liquid—Campari and soda, bitter and astringent, a new and strange taste.

"So much history, you said, Luigi."

"This part of the city dates back over two thousand years. Its history becomes part of you, but it weighs you down, too."

"Quite different from our modern villas in Giorgimpopoli plopped down in the sand," I said.

"I like it out in the desert. Nothing there but sand. It's clean. I feel free."

Some weekends, Gordon, an Amoco geologist, invited me to join him for an evening at the glitzy Uaddan Hotel and Casino. After dinner, we watched the show—belly dancers, acrobats, or an Italian rock star—and danced late into the night.

One Saturday, Luigi came to our villa.

"Luigi, tell me about your trip," I said, leading him into the living room. "Sorry, I have no Campari, but I'll make some tea."

I was on my way to the kitchen when there was a knock at the front door. Luigi came up behind me as I opened the door.

"Stuart," Luigi said.

"Luigi?" Stuart couldn't hide his surprise. For a long and extremely awkward moment, the two men stood looking at each other. Luigi was the first to react.

"I must go," he said. The two men shook hands, and Luigi left.

"I'm taking you to Ghadames," Stuart said.

"The oasis?"

He nodded. We had not seen each other for several weeks, not since our trip to Jebel Nafusa. As he stood in the doorway, I realized how much I had missed him.

"Yes," I said.

After the small charter plane took off for Ghadames, I watched the green of the coastal area turn to subtle dust colorations, bare rock surfaces, places where the shifting sand blown by the wind gave the impression of breaking waves. Ghadames, deep in the Sahara, where the borders of Algeria, Tunisia, and Libya met, was an oasis that for thousands of years had been used as a stop for slave-trade caravans.

From my window seat, I gazed down, amazed that this unforgiving realm had once been crossed by camel caravans—the harrowing journey only made possible by oases scattered far apart.

I tried to imagine how, day after day, the caravans must have trudged on in never-ending monotony over shifting sand dunes and dreadful, dried-out, crusted salt lakes—a lifeless topography. At any moment, the sky could darken, the caravan overtaken by a driving sandstorm that obliterated landmarks. The intense heat and dryness must have seared the throat, shriveled the skin, and parched lips, making them bleed. The sun's glare creating quivering mirages on the horizon. And then, after sunset, the temperature would drop precipitously.

"What are you thinking?" Stuart pressed his shoulder against mine.

"The camel caravans. Why would anyone undertake such an ordeal?"

"Must have been lucrative."

Or had it been something else? Could it have been some practice of rigorous austerity, an ascetic way of life, a journey of spiritual purification? To survive such a journey, it could be that the body closed down, willed into a trancelike dormancy. The mind turned inward to pursue a dialogue of deepest reflection—a soliloquy. I could imagine that gradually, privation and suffering could bring a sense of detachment, a distilled state where time ceased to matter. A blissful state where the present merged with eternity. So that, at the end of the journey, when the destination—the clamorous Mediterranean port—was finally sighted, rather than relief, they might have felt a sense of regret.

"Still thinking caravans?" Stuart said. "We're almost there."

The plane circled and descended toward a patch of emerald green. Thousands of date palm groves, tiny plots of cultivated land, a jumbled huddle of cube-shaped dwellings surrounded by a wall.

We walked down the ramp of the aircraft into a burning flame of hot air, the intensity of which I could never have imagined—a heat that no breeze stirred and no rain would ever dissipate.

"How can anyone live here?" I asked.

"It's a precarious existence. Only three artesian wells. If they were to dry up, Ghadames would vanish. Quickly reclaimed by the desert."

Through the city gates, we entered a dark passageway where the cool air felt like a refreshing drink. Houses with thick walls of mud, lime, and palm trunks were connected by covered alleys and labyrinthine passageways that snaked through the town. People had figured out how to protect themselves from the unforgiving sun. The mile-long network of shaded tunnels and arcades echoed with children's laughter. Wrapped in a dark blue burnoose, a tall Tuareg strode past, his face concealed by a veil. Only the haughty black gaze of his eyes could be seen.

After settling into our room at the small inn, we strolled to a teahouse, its walls hung with brightly decorated flat baskets, wool carpets on the earthen floor. Men, sitting at low tables, waved and said something I didn't understand. Stuart returned their greetings in Arabic. The men responded with big, surprised smiles. Stuart seemed to have made a connection, for the men continued to chat in a friendly way. I was struck by the ease with which Stuart moved in a culture so different from our own. The strange hot brew served in tiny glasses revived us.

Tuareg in Ghadames, 1965.

Covered street in Ghadames.

Outside the wall, we explored the oleander-lined walkways—shaded by palm trees—that led through irrigated orchards of pomegranate trees. A cluster of camels stood around a tiny newborn one, not more than a few days old—pure white. Pure white, like our new relationship. Unmarred by any harsh words, before any disagreements.

From somewhere far away, the faint braying of a donkey could be heard.

⇜

We began to spend all our free time together, often seeking out isolated beaches along remote roads. One day we hiked across high sand dunes, sinking midcalf into hot sand, then sprinting to the cool dampness of the shore. The sea shimmered turquoise, darkening to deep violet at the horizon. With the blinding sun directly above, the immense heat seemed to press down. Its glare deformed and fragmented the palms into quivering illusions that dissolved in light and reflections. The air vibrated and left a taste of hot stone in my mouth.

We dived into the crystal-clear sea and swam far out. Sparkling ripples of water, warm at the surface, swirled with coolness around our ankles.

Side by side on the blanket, we dried in the sun—a white powdering of salt on our skin, lulled by the rhythmic swoosh of waves as they washed up and receded. Had it been possible, we would have stopped the passage of time to sink deep into the softness of that afternoon.

⇜

When the school year ended in June, I would be leaving Tripoli. In September, Stuart's tour with the Air Force would be finished.

In our shared experiences over those two years, Stuart and I had captured something, perhaps fragile, perhaps fugitive, but something essential. Being with him heightened my awareness. I felt more intensely alive. He anchored me, perhaps I anchored him. We had no dialogue of options or of logistics for what might happen next. There was no need to discuss conditions, demands, or even promises.

It was like that single elegant premise upon which the entire complex world of computers, its language and all its far-reaching applications, is based—the simple logic of binary code and its two fundamental choices, a *1* or a *0*, a switch of either *on* or *off*. Between us there had emerged a gradual and mutual realization of the inevitability that the switch would stay *on*.

Just the exquisite simplicity of *on*.

MAX AND ROSE X 2

ON THE GROUND floor of our building on East Seventy-Ninth Street, bold abstractions covered the white walls of Jill Kornblee's contemporary art gallery. Each month brought a new exhibit. On my way out, I would stop to view the Pop Art, Op Art, weird assemblages, and perplexing plexiglass sculptures that attracted the trendiest of New York's art scene in 1966. During opening receptions, the crowd spilled outside onto the front steps. Thin women wearing miniskirted Courrèges dresses sipped white wine.

We chose the rather grandiose third-floor apartment for its high ceilings, working fireplace, and floor-to-ceiling bookshelves. Our first home after getting married. Stuart started a two-year hematology fellowship at the New York Hospital—Cornell University Medical College.

We had just moved in, and the fresh paint smell still hovered in the apartment, bare except for a few essentials in the kitchen cupboards, a bed and a dresser in the bedroom, a white couch in the living room. Two crystal vases, wedding presents, on the fireplace mantle.

When the doorbell rang that morning, I knew it was the movers bringing Stuart and Jane's household goods, stored in Cooperstown, New York, during the two years he was in the Air Force in Libya.

The men inspected the tiny elevator, shook their heads, and used the stairs instead to haul up the boxes and furniture. They stacked it all in the middle of the living room.

After they left, I began to unwrap the furniture. A pine dining table with fold-down leaves, beautifully restored. Simple ladder-back chairs. An antique bentwood coat rack. Two well-worn cane-seat rocking chairs. An Albrecht Dürer woodcut print in a wide oak frame. Heavy foot-high stoneware crocks with cobalt-blue bird motifs.

I unpacked a box of white dishes with a brown woodland pattern, the kind you might find in a country cottage in England. Then a set of tiny earth-colored ceramic bowls, a different design on each one: sage, thyme, rosemary. Mixing bowls, a wooden cutting board, an assortment of useful kitchen items. A white ironstone soup tureen.

Another box held an ecru linen tablecloth and napkins. A set of fringed jute placemats. Two needlepoint throw cushions with yellow tulips. In a box of books, a slender volume of engravings of herbs. A gardening manual. An illustrated guide to American colonial furniture. Two volumes of Julia Child's *Mastering the Art of French Cooking.* I flipped through its pages. Engrossed in the detailed recipes for soufflés, quiches, and mousses, I lost track of time until I noticed that through the windows, the late-afternoon sunlight was beginning to fade. I turned on the lights and hurried to finish unpacking before Stuart got home.

From the bottom of a packing crate, I retrieved a small gray box of black and white photos. Kneeling on the floor, I spread the pictures out in front of me. With a ski lift in the background, Stuart and Jane, bundled in heavy sweaters, smile at the camera. Inside a rustic cabin, Jane, wearing the same bulky Fair Isle sweater, sprawls in front of a blazing fire. In a backyard somewhere, a pair of bright-eyed Siamese cats stare at me. In a living room, Jane sits on a sofa, cradling a cat on her lap. Next to her are the tulip needlepoint cushions I just unwrapped.

A bundle of wedding photos is secured with a rubber band. A white-spired New England church. Jane holds onto her veil, her white lace bridal gown billowing out in the back, as she walks up the steps of the church. At what looks like a wedding reception in a garden, I spot Stuart's mother among the guests. Clusters of women wearing strands of pearls and wide-brimmed hats mingle with men in linen suits. There's a snapshot of Stuart's brother Malcolm reaching for an hors d'oeuvre on a large tray. In another photo, the camera has caught the smiling newlyweds in a vintage convertible. They wave to the guests as they drive away.

As I gathered up the photos, I detected a new smell pervading the apartment. Lavender, cats, a slight mustiness, dried herbs, patchouli? I couldn't identify it, but it conjured up a home, a domestic scene. Colonial furniture, books, Siamese cats. A sense of who Jane was began to emerge. I thought of the young wife creating a home. I pictured the coziness of a winter evening—the table set with the ecru linen tablecloth and a hearty *soupe à l'oignon* in the tureen. The reality of a happy marriage began to sink in. With the force of a physical blow, the enormity of the loss struck me. With Jane's things around me, stacked up everywhere, on every available surface, the apartment no longer belonged to me.

I felt Jane's presence and, at the same time, her absence.

I unwrapped one last thing. An antique child's chair. For the baby—never born. With a stab of pain, I thought that Stuart probably never knew whether it was a boy or a girl.

≈

A few years before we moved in, Hungarian-born Olga Lengyel bought this old, elegant brick and stone mansion, squeezed in between nondescript apartment complexes. Even at sixty, her blond hair upswept in a perfect French twist, she was a beautiful woman. Only the fading blue numbers tattooed on her left arm hinted of tragedy in her past. She had survived Auschwitz.

Her book, *Five Chimneys: A Woman Survivor's True Story of Auschwitz,* described in painful detail her seven-month ordeal. I learned how upon arrival at Auschwitz, Olga's two young sons were pulled out of her arms. Chapter after chapter told of the appalling conditions in the barracks, the sadistic treatment by camp guards, and how, miraculously, Olga endured it all.

Among all the passages in the book, one in particular haunted me. The chimneys at the camp spewed forth a sweetish burnt smell. At first, the other prisoners told Olga the smell came from the camp bakery. She was sickened when she found out the real source of the "freshly baked bread" smell—the cremation ovens. Later, she learned that her sons, as well as her elderly parents, were killed in gas chambers. Her husband, a prominent surgeon, died in a slave labor camp.

I struggled to reconcile the lovely, beautifully dressed Olga, who appeared unscathed if not pampered, with the image of the Olga who almost starved and experienced inhumane treatment in the camp. The two images were of unusual disparity. Yet Olga rebuilt her life and dedicated it to making sure that Auschwitz was not forgotten. Amassing books and documentation, she created the Holocaust Memorial Library on the second floor of her mansion. We were occasionally invited to the small gatherings she hosted there for her Eastern European friends. Evenings of sad World War II stories, red Hungarian wine, and homemade goulash.

∽

Stuart had grown up in New York and was pleased that the residency at Cornell University Medical College brought him back to the city. Until he went to medical school in Boston, he had lived with his parents and older brother, Malcolm, in an apartment on Hillside Avenue in upper Manhattan. The prewar building, with an Oriental carpet in the lobby, had an old-world elegance. He remembered the shiny brass elevator doors, polished daily by the elevator man, the gilded mirrors on the walls and red velvet cushions on a marble bench. Over the years, one by one, these upscale touches disappeared.

From old photo albums, I tried to piece together Stuart's family history. The unidentified faces on the first few pages, in faded sepias mounted on thick black paper, stared back at me, unsmiling. A distinguished-looking man with a white beard, women in long dresses with cinched waists below ample bosoms, hair piled on top of the head. Dark-suited men with wing collar shirts and pins stuck through their ties.

On the next pages, pictures of little girls with hands tucked into fur muffs. A young lad with a prayer shawl and ankle-high boots holds a Bible. Through a historic glaze, I studied their faces to see what they might reveal. I wanted to record something about their lives, believing that only if the past is committed to paper does it have a chance to survive. To tell a story, to squeeze out some meaning, it is tempting to use the malleability of the past. But these nineteenth-century images, taken in forgotten interiors, in either Austria or Romania, offered no clues.

Stuart could tell me nothing about them.

"Why are there no stories?" I asked.

"Maybe Malcolm and I weren't interested when we were growing up," he said.

And now it was too late. No one left to tell us anything about these ancestors.

Perhaps the older generation didn't talk about their backgrounds. They could have been too overwhelmed with a difficult present and uncertain future to have the luxury to ponder the past. Perhaps conditions for Jews in Europe during the latter part of the nineteenth century had worsened, and they decided to seek opportunities that would lead to a better life in America.

All we have are faces on photographs and random dates—births and deaths, with nothing in between those two dates. A birth certificate, a death certificate, naturalization papers don't serve any purpose unless you breathe life into them. Nothing more than an accumulation of days, months, and years, they don't reveal anything about these early generations.

It was with the two Max and Rose couples, the two sets of Stuart's grandparents, that I began to trace the families' histories, their journeys. Max and Rose Edelstein on his mother's side, and Max and Rose Scheer on his father's. Born in the late nineteenth century, they immigrated to the United States and settled in New York.

Max Edelstein and Rose Wexler may have left Romania because, around 1875, old anti-Semitic laws were once again enforced, making life difficult for Jews and leading to a wave of their emigration on a large scale.

Stuart's mother told him that her father came to the States as a young man by way of the French Foreign Legion. She remembered the embarrassing moment at the movies one evening when she was still a child. Hearing "La Marseillaise" played in a newsreel, her father stood up respectfully and was indignant when everyone else in the theater remained seated. In New York, Max became a lawyer and opened an employment agency.

He married Rose Wexler, who had arrived in New York with

six sisters and a brother. The six sisters, great-aunts to Stuart, were a nurturing presence in his youth. Max and Rose had three children: John, the eldest; Ray, with the unusual boy's name, was Stuart's mother; and Sophie, the youngest.

John, a psychiatrist, met a woman from Scotland when he was stationed in England during World War II and married her. After the war, when John returned to New York, the family severed all ties with him because his young bride was not Jewish. I wondered about this story because, when Stuart and I married, I always felt welcomed by his family.

Max and Rose Scheer emigrated from Austria. In one photo, Max, a tailor, sits in a leather chair wearing a perfectly fitted suit, trousers crisply creased. They had five children, more doting uncles and aunts for young Stuart. Willie became a dentist, Artie a physician, and Harry, Stuart's father, a lawyer. Edna and Ruth, the two aunts, had no distinguishing careers attached to their stories. In this family, only the men had identifying professions. We don't know the dramas of the women's lives and can only imagine that their days were spent in repetitive domesticity of housework and the thankless chores of raising children.

After the two Maxes and Roses arrived in New York, they made use of the opportunities the city offered. They built successful lives for their families, and New York became their home.

Stuart often spoke about his childhood. Even though only five at the time, he could still visualize the breathtaking maze and convoluted cloverleaf highways of the fantasy city in the Futurama exhibit at the 1939 World's Fair. Every day after school, there was stickball in the street until dark with neighborhood boys.

On Saturdays, while their mother stayed home to cook, the two young sons went on outings with their father. At the Museum of Natural History, how could the life-size blue whale suspended from the ceiling not impress? In the dimly lit galleries, the boys had to be pulled away from the realistic dioramas, where they stood mesmerized, amazed at the stunning accuracy of every authentic detail. The arid terrain of an African savanna, with antelopes and wildebeest, was so convincing, Stuart imagined the clouds drifting across the sky and breathed the dust in the air.

He remembered well the hot, humid air that enveloped them when they entered the conservatory at the Bronx Botanical Garden. Enormous leaves dripped moisture as he searched out the carnivorous plants. At the Metropolitan Museum of Art, eerie African masks, spears, and ornamented shields may have sparked his curiosity about faraway cultures.

On Sundays, their father would drive the family down to Chinatown or take them to Café Brittany, where Stuart first tasted coq au vin. He still recalls the silky boeuf bourguignon and the licorice taste of endive salads. The boys were introduced to more exotic foods in Syrian and Lebanese restaurants. On special occasions, they dined at Lüchow's, the opulent, wood-paneled German restaurant where, while eating sauerbraten, Stuart heard Strauss waltzes played on the grand piano.

In the summers, for weeks at a time, the family gathered at Great-Aunt Lizzie's farmhouse in the Catskills. Stuart, Malcolm, and the other cousins chased cows in the adjoining fields and fed Lizzie's chickens. One picture shows the simple white clapboard house with an old iron pump in front, and the whole family squeezed together on the front steps of the porch. Stuart, still a small child, sits on the bottom step with a toy stethoscope around his neck.

"You had a happy childhood," I told him.

᷍

At the hematology lab at Cornell, Stuart met Ron Stark, whose strange story is impossible to reconcile with the person we knew back then in New York. Ron, a technician at the lab, was quite a character, very smart. He and Stuart had absorbing discussions on all sorts of topics. After six weeks in the lab, Stuart moved on to clinical work at the hospital, work he preferred.

Ron kept in touch.

From time to time, he came to our apartment or we would go out to dinner together. Ron seemed older, closer to middle age, although I found out later he was only in his late twenties then. Medium height, a little on the heavy side, solid. He was charming and articulate, and had done interesting things.

We hadn't seen Ron for a few months, and then one day he called and asked whether I would take care of his dog, Hamlet, for a month while he was in California. I was reluctant as we had just received news that Stuart had been accepted into the Foreign Service, and his first assignment would be to run the medical unit at the American Embassy in Sanaa, Yemen.

But I had a more compelling reason for not wanting to take care of the dog. I was eight months pregnant and busy getting ready for the baby's arrival. I had already quit my job at the Museum of Natural History since we would be leaving a month after the baby was born.

Ron could be very persuasive, though, and in the end I agreed to take Hamlet for the month he was away. When he arrived with the dog, I got a bit of a shock.

"My God, he's huge," I said.

"He's a Great Dane. Still a puppy."

"I don't know, Ron." I already regretted my decision. I noticed too how haggard Ron looked—dark circles under his eyes and wearing a rumpled shirt. By my hesitation, Ron saw I was ready to back out.

"He's a very nice dog. You'll fall in love with him. You'll see." He leaned down to pat the dog, yanking on the leash.

"Oh, and by the way," he added, "could you keep this for me while I'm gone?"

He handed me the package he had been carrying under his arm. By its shape and size, it looked like a coffee can wrapped in layers of blue plastic.

"What is it?" I asked.

"Stu knows about it. Something from the lab. Got to run now."

With a quick good-bye, Ron was gone. I was left standing in the hallway holding the container and the dog's leash. The container was easy, but the dog?

Our apartment was not suited for such a big dog. Although already fully grown, Hamlet was still an energetic puppy. In the living room, the white couch had to be covered with a blanket, rugs rolled up, and decorative objects removed from tabletops. Several times a day, Hamlet and I squeezed into the tiny elevator to go for a walk in Central Park. It was an early spring that year, with trees beginning to leaf out and forsythias in bloom. I had hurried across the park every day when I worked at the museum. Now I no longer needed to hurry. My only worry was encounters with other dogs. Once he saw them, an overexcited Hamlet ignored my commands, and I could barely control him. Instead of the park, I sometimes braved the crowds on Madison Avenue—fewer dogs, plus art galleries to browse. People stopped to admire Hamlet, a handsome dog with his brindled coat.

I showed Stuart the container, which I had put on the shelf of our coat closet.

"Oh, yes, he told me about that. Contains a mold or something. Ron thinks it might have some antibiotic properties. He said he got it from a friend at some other lab and was going to try to sell it to a pharmaceutical company."

When not out on walks with Hamlet, I knitted baby garments with the dog's warm muzzle on my knees.

I called my parents in Cleveland to tell them about Stuart's new job and that we would be leaving soon for Yemen.

"But you just got back," my mother interrupted me.

"That was, what, almost two years ago, Mother."

"Why do you need to leave again? You've been away for so long. And Yemen, I don't even know where it is. I'll have to look on a map. And what about the baby?"

My parents, especially my mother, were not happy about our plans to go to Yemen. But then they had not approved of my going to England or to Libya either. Perhaps it was a little crazy to take a baby to such a faraway country, but Stuart was a doctor, and I trusted him to keep us safe and healthy.

After a month, Ron returned as promised and took Hamlet and the container.

I had just gotten the apartment back to normal when, on May 28, Jennifer was born. Perfectly adorable with peach-colored hair and blue eyes. We were thrilled.

In the following weeks, mixed with the excitement of our baby were feelings of tension about our departure. During busy days, I tried to find free moments to read Freya Stark's book about her journeys in Yemen in the 1930s. A riveting storyteller as well as an explorer, Stark described the legendary ancient city where we would soon be living. I visualized the bare hills surrounding Sanaa and studied the pictures of the mosques and hammams of the old city, their burnt-brick towers the same ochre as the hills, except for the curious white embellishments that looked like decorative icing on a wedding cake.

Dressed as an Arab, riding a donkey, sometimes a camel, Freya Stark made her way along arid escarpments, crossed dried-out wadis, followed the ancient frankincense trade routes across unexplored lands. Trekking alone to remote villages in the desert and the mountains, she observed the daily life of the ancient and fabled cultures. Her courageous voyages kindled my imagination. What would it be like living in Sanaa?

Suddenly, our plans unraveled. The State Department notified Stuart we would not be going to Yemen after all. We had been following the news about the Six-Day War between Arabs and Israelis that broke out on June 5. Israel gobbled up the Gaza Strip, the Sinai Peninsula, West Bank, East Jerusalem, and the Golan Heights. Under pressure from the Egyptian government, Yemen broke diplomatic relations with the United States. The American Embassy in Sanaa was closed.

Gone was my dream of living in exotic Yemen. Instead, Stuart would be working at the State Department's Medical Division in Washington, DC, waiting for another overseas assignment.

While we were still in New York, Ron invited us to the Greenwich Village house he had just bought. On a warm and drizzly spring evening, we drove down to the Village. Following Ron's instructions, we spotted his historic-looking white house.

"They must have paid quite a tidy sum for the antibacterial mold," Stuart said, obviously impressed.

Ron's house, however, was bare. Everywhere in the narrow living room, canvases, framed drawings, and prints were stacked against the walls. We sat on empty packing crates. Hamlet wasn't there. I was sorry as I had looked forward to seeing him.

Ron uncorked a bottle of red wine. As he poured, he said,

"Thought you two would appreciate this." I wasn't sure whether he meant the house, the art, or the wine. One by one, he turned the artworks around for us to see, identifying each artist. As a parting gift, he gave us a thousand-dollar stock certificate as a present for our baby, Jennifer. As we left, Ron waved to us from the open doorway.

∞

Some seven months after we moved to Washington, Ron called. He told Stuart he had some business to attend to in the capital. Since we hadn't seen him in a long while, Stuart invited him for dinner. When I opened the door that evening, there was Ron, wearing a long brown djellaba and a kaffiyeh, the Arab headgear. A bit theatrical, I thought, but then Ron could be full of surprises. I realized he could easily pass for an Arab.

As I looked back to Ron's visit in Washington, nearly five decades ago, I wondered whatever happened to him. Did he really discover a cure for some disease with his antibacterial mold?

So, one day, I typed Ron's name into Google and hit enter. An image came up immediately.

I stared at the mug shot. It was Ron Stark. The receding hairline, the dark circles under the eyes, tie askew just as I remembered, but the enormous drooping mustache was new. The computer screen filled up with references to Ronald Hadley Stark, "The Man Behind the LSD Curtain."

What? I was stunned.

An entry read, "Ron Stark was, and still is, an enigma. With a clutch of different identities, he had moved like a chameleon from communes and LSD laboratories to luxury hotels and exclusive gentlemen's clubs."

I couldn't believe it. Was this the Ron Stark we knew?

I remembered taking photos of him that evening in Washington when he came for a visit. In retrospect, that was unusual, not something I generally did. I think it was because he was wearing that strange djellaba.

I dug out the old album to see if I could find the photos. There, among all the pictures of baby Jennifer, were two of Ron, dated 1968. In one, he's standing in our living room. In the background, through the floor-to-ceiling windows, you can see the city all lit up with the illuminated dome of the Capitol in the center. The other photo is of Ron talking on the kitchen phone. During dinner, he had excused himself several times to make calls.

Researching further, I discovered articles suggesting Ron might have been a deep-cover CIA agent, or a drug dealer, or may have had connections with international terrorist organizations. He had become a legend, a myth. But facts were mixed with assumptions that cross-referenced each other in a circular manner. It all seemed too incredible to be true. How to reconcile the Ron Stark we knew with this mysterious multilayered individual?

Then I came across the strange coincidence of the djellaba. I read that in August of 1969, Stark, wearing a djellaba, supposedly arrived at the California ranch of the Brotherhood of Eternal Love, a group of idealistic individuals hoping to transform the world with LSD. Since the production and possession of LSD had become illegal, their supply was running out. Stark brought a container with a kilo of pure LSD—about ten million trips. He had more, he told them, and access to unlimited supplies from his labs in Europe.

What a strange story. I mulled over what I had just learned. Unsolved mysteries are uncomfortable, and that's why the elusive Ron Stark story continues to baffle me, even though I realize that to separate the man we knew from the myth is impossible.

But there is another aspect of Ron that bothers me. Why didn't we think it bizarre that he asked us to keep that container for him?

Were we so involved with the excitement of our new baby and leaving for Yemen that we didn't realize how weird a request it was? I shudder to think how naive we were back then that we didn't ask the most obvious questions. Why did Ron think the container was not safe in his own apartment? Was he afraid his apartment might be searched? By whom? Why?

If Ron is still alive, and there are rumors that he might be, I would ask him, "Ron, that coffee can that we kept for you in our closet for a month back in 1967, was that really antibiotic mold or was it filled with a kilo of pure illegal LSD—enough for ten million trips?"

≪

Knowing we might soon be leaving for our first overseas assignment, Stuart's parents visited us in Washington. They were thrilled with their first grandchild, showering her with baby gifts and hovering in a flutter of excessive excitement. They took turns holding and fussing over Jennifer. At the dinner table, after the cheerful talk about the baby was exhausted, the conversation turned to an old and often repeated topic.

"Stuart," his mother said, "it's not too late, you can still change your mind. What about private practice in New York? Look how well Uncle Artie has done."

Over the years, Stuart had learned it wise not to engage in this discussion. He knew that counterarguments were futile and only exasperated his mother. He continued eating the lamb roast silently, waiting for the conversation to turn to a different subject.

"And Uncle Willie too," his mother said, "has a good practice. And then you wouldn't have to go away."

"And what about your baby?" Stuart's father asked.

Sensing that anything I said would only make matters worse, I stayed out of the discussion.

"You don't have to leave, you know," his mother said. "You could still cancel the contract or whatever. New York has everything you could possibly ever want."

Stuart's mother had always dreamed that one day her son would have a successful private practice in New York. She argued, and many New Yorkers would agree, that since the city had so much to offer, that it was—in essence—the center of the universe, why would anyone in their right mind want to go anywhere else. Stuart's father, sitting at the end of the table, would nod in agreement.

Of course, we loved living in New York. We were not impervious to its glitter and glamour. How could we not be affected by its feverish energy, the allure of its nighttime sizzle, its swarming humanity? With its endless attractions, the city could captivate and hold you.

That evening, we once again politely listened to Stuart's parents' advice. But opening a private practice in New York was not going to happen. We were on our way.

Stuart's parents meant well, only wanted what was best for us. We knew that. And they worried about our well-being. But often, their concern and worry seemed more like tentacles reaching out to grasp and hold us back from what we wanted to do.

After nine months in Washington, Stuart came home one evening with the news. In the living room, ten-month-old Jennifer was crawling around with her toys. In the kitchen, chopped vegetables were ready to go into the simmering beef stew. Dashing from kitchen to living room to keep an eye on the baby, I didn't hear Stuart come in the front door. His sudden appearance startled me. Setting his briefcase down, he stood there with an unusually big smile.

"What?" I asked, wooden spoon in midair.

"We're going to Rio."

We were elated. Once again, we started preparations for our departure. For me, that included reading everything I could find about Brazil.

PART THREE

HUNTING ACCIDENT

AT GALEÃO AIRPORT, we squeezed into the car waiting for us. With our huge amount of luggage, one suitcase had to go on the front seat. I hugged baby Jennifer on my lap, and Stuart got in next to me. "We made it." He sighed in relief. It had been a long flight. Cars and trucks choked the road. The driver, going too fast, passed cars on the right and swerved to avoid pedestrians. Swiveling his head back to talk to us, he kept taking his eyes off the road. I wished he wouldn't do that. We couldn't understand what he was saying anyway.

"This is insane," I said. "He's too close to the car in front. Are we going to get there in one piece?"

"Traffic in Rio." Stuart looked calm, but I don't think he liked the chaos any more than I did. Sitting back, I tried to relax. I had already decided I was not going to drive in Rio.

With my eyes glued to the road, I hadn't paid attention to our surroundings. Now, as we approached the city, I gasped at what I saw. On my left, the intense blue of Guanabara Bay. Straight ahead, Sugarloaf. Steep forest-covered mountains in the distance.

Corcovado with the statue of Christ on top. Tall white buildings on the right—Copacabana. On that clear sunny day, it was all more spectacular than I had imagined.

We continued on to Avenida Atlantica, along Copacabana's curved coastline, bordered by hotels and apartment complexes. The wide beach, already crowded at that early hour, stretched for miles ahead.

Hotel Luxor in Copacabana would be our home while Stuart and I both took intensive Portuguese language training. A nanny would take care of Jennifer while we were in class. I hated leaving the baby but knew I needed to learn Portuguese if we were going to live in Rio for three years.

Our hotel room faced the Atlantic. We sat on the little terrace every morning with a breakfast tray of sliced papaya and good strong coffee, waiting for the nanny to arrive so we could leave for our lessons at the embassy.

⤚

I soon found out that Stuart would frequently be away. As a Foreign Service regional medical officer, he not only ran the medical unit at the embassy, caring for State Department, CIA, USIS, USAID, and U.S. military personnel and their families, but traveled to our other embassies and consulates in South America. He saw patients and held informal meetings to inform the embassy community about the risks and medical problems of the region. His visits reassured employees and their families. At local hospitals, he evaluated medical equipment and diagnostic capabilities at labs. He got to know the local doctors and dentists and learned about their training and medical qualifications. From Rio, he had a large region to cover— embassies in Uruguay, Paraguay, Argentina, as well as consulates in Brazil.

On his first trip to Brasilia, Stuart asked me to join him. He was going to visit the temporary embassy office in Brasilia, set up in anticipation that the American Embassy would eventually be relocated there.

From the plane, I looked down on the barren red plateau, so different from Rio's luxuriant landscape. Building Brasilia and making it the country's capital was a dream that went back to the nineteenth century. The plan had been to bring people from the thickly populated coastal cities to the isolated area in the country's interior. In just four years, Oscar Niemeyer's futuristic vision had become reality.

The following morning, while Stuart saw patients and met with local doctors, I explored the city. Along the deserted boulevards, stark concrete buildings dominated. An artificial assemblage of Le Corbusier-inspired structures had sprouted on an orderly grid of streets. Devoid of any embellishments, the modernistic buildings had clean sweeping lines but a sterile, antiseptic feel.

The thought came to me that the city had been conceived in the mind of an architect more preoccupied with form and structure than with thoughts about what makes a city livable. But then— and it came as a lovely surprise—I saw the ornamental pools with tropical plantings. I sat at the edge of one and watched the swaying foliage reflected in the water.

Even with that green organic touch, though, Brasilia lacked charm. Maybe it was because it had no hills to provide soft contours for a meandering road. No river to disrupt the grid-like plan. Perhaps, I thought, charm was spawned only accidentally. Perhaps it took time.

᠕

Not long after our trip to Brasilia, Stuart left on a regional trip. I think he was in Montevideo. No, perhaps he was in Asuncion. He traveled so much, sometimes I lost track of where he was. Now that I think back, he might actually have been in Buenos Aires, but I guess it doesn't matter where he was when he received the telegram. In those days, medical problems from other posts were still often communicated by telegram.

That morning, in one of those places, he was seeing patients at the medical unit when they brought him the telegram. It read, "Brasilia employee injured in hunting accident. Please come at once."

With unreliable phone lines, Stuart had trouble reaching the embassy office in Brasilia. He kept trying. When he finally got through, he was told that George Emblen, an American Foreign Service officer, had been injured in a hunting accident. He was now back in Brasilia after a harrowing trip—first carried on a horse, later by car.

"The stab wound appears to be serious," the officer on duty said.

"Stab wound?" Stuart asked. "I thought he'd been shot."

Crackling static on the line prevented further dialogue. Stuart arranged for the next flight to Brasilia. After a brief stop at the embassy office there, he hurried to the hospital where Dr. Ribeira had already performed exploratory surgery. Dr. Ribeira, one of the doctors Stuart had met on our trip to Brasilia, was a good surgeon with residency training in the United States and spoke English fluently. Stuart wouldn't have to struggle with Portuguese. He was already proficient in the basics but not comfortable discussing more complicated matters.

Dr. Ribeira was waiting in his office.

"Dr. Scheer, so glad you came," he said. "Mr. Emblen has lost a lot a blood on the way back from the Pantanal. But in time, he'll be fine."

"Glad to hear that," Stuart said.

"Unfortunately ..." Dr. Ribeira hesitated. "The barrel of the rifle penetrated the lower abdomen."

"What? I thought he'd been stabbed!"

Dr. Ribeira explained that it had, in fact, been a bizarre accident. The hunting guide had spotted a jaguar, and as they stalked it, the animal suddenly sprang at them from dense underbrush.

"Ordinarily, jaguars don't attack," Dr. Ribeira said, "but apparently this one was protecting her cubs."

The jaguar had lunged and swiped at George. Its claw caught on his brass belt buckle, and George was thrown up in the air. When he came down, still gripping his rifle, he landed on the tip of the barrel. It penetrated the lower abdominal wall and went up to the diaphragm, bruising it badly.

"He's very lucky other vital internal organs weren't harmed," Dr. Ribeira said.

"Very lucky, indeed."

"But the curious thing is," Dr. Ribeira shook his head in disbelief. "There's not a single scratch. Not a single bruise from the jaguar's claws—only the rifle barrel wound."

Dr. Ribeira added that he was concerned that the patient seemed to have been traumatized by the experience.

As Stuart got up to visit George, Dr. Ribeira asked him if he had ever been to the Pantanal region. Stuart told him he had not, and Dr. Ribeira urged him to visit the area, about five hundred miles west of Brasilia, where Uruguay, Brazil, and Bolivia meet. A landlocked river delta, teeming with marvelous wildlife.

"Quite amazing, actually," Dr. Ribeira said.

On the surgical floor, Stuart went to the patient's room. Lying on his back, George, very pale, appeared to be dozing. Stuart sat down and waited—grateful for a few minutes to mull the peculiar circumstances of the accident. When George woke up, Stuart pulled his chair near the bed.

"George, how are you doing?" he asked.

George's eyes were open but staring straight ahead.

"You'll be up and about in no time at all," Stuart went on. "Probably be a little tired for a while from the loss of blood. Only to be expected."

George finally focused on Stuart. Minutes passed. He tried to say something but trailed off. Stuart wondered if it was the medication.

"I keep reliving it over and over … it was terrifying."

He struggled to stifle a sob.

"Like lightning … lunging at me. God, I'd no idea how huge … the smell … her hot breath …"

"Take it easy, George. It's over now. Try to get some sleep."

"I thought I was a goner. It was … it was … it was …"

Stuart put his hand on George's shoulder.

"I don't know what happened. I was yanked up, tossed up …"

"George, it was a freak accident," Stuart said.

"Thought I'd died."

"You'll be just fine."

"It's not that, Dr. Scheer. Something else … it bothers me. You know … I'd only thought of a jaguar as a trophy."

"Of course, George, jaguars have that magnificent pelt."

"Not the pelt. Just a trophy. Never imagined it as a powerful … breathing animal."

George was silent for a moment.

"Can't get over it. My rifle. The jaguar got me … with my own rifle."

"What strange irony," Stuart said when he finished telling me the story.

"Maybe poetic justice," I answered.

✌

I often thought about Stuart's mother's disappointment that we left New York. I would remember our last dinner together, how she tried once again to persuade Stuart to open a private practice there. She had often expressed that same wish to me. Whenever she mentioned it, I was never able to think of what to say. I would just nod politely.

After Stuart told me about the hunting accident, an answer coalesced in my mind. I imagined how I would explain it to her. I would tell her that her son, the man I married, was hungry for the world—as I was. That the day-to-day routine in a medical practice in New York would deaden him. He wouldn't have the opportunity to travel all over South America. I would tell her he liked the challenge of caring for patients in difficult circumstances, establishing rapport with local doctors, visiting their hospitals, and learning about tropical diseases. And in New York, would he come across patients who hunted jaguars in a remote wilderness?

I hoped she would understand.

Our daughter, Jen, with kitten in Rio, 1969.

FOUR DAYS

WE MOVED INTO an old stone house in Ipanema. Just a block from the beach, hidden behind high-rise apartment buildings, it was one of the few houses remaining in Ipanema. The spacious living room's four sets of French doors led to a covered stone patio and a garden enclosed by a high wall.

Thick tropical vegetation had taken over the garden and blocked walkways. Even though the garden needed a lot of work, we were fortunate to have this private refuge, away from the busy street. The overgrown vegetation was proof that Silvio, who was taking care of the garden for us, wasn't a real gardener and probably knew very little about gardening. But then, I knew even less.

Sprawling vines camouflaged the wall. I suggested to Silvio that he trim the vines back a bit. Perhaps misunderstanding my instructions, he cut them to the ground. When I came out into the garden, I was dismayed to see the stretch of crumbling, discolored wall that now marred our garden view.

Silvio pointed to the sky. "American man on the moon. How he get up?"

It took me a minute to realize he was referring to the news that Apollo 11 had landed on the moon. Neil Armstrong's first steps had been broadcast around the world. Silvio couldn't imagine how it could be done. I, an American, would be able to tell him. I was taken aback. How could I explain the moon landing? It was too complicated in English. In Portuguese, impossible. To distract Silvio from his question, I pointed to the ugly, bare stretch of wall and asked him why he had cut down all the vines.

In Rio, we felt removed from events in the United States and elsewhere in the world. Rarely listening to radio broadcasts or watching TV, both in Portuguese, we learned of breaking news and significant events through the embassy. The previous year, we had been shocked by the tragic news of Martin Luther King's assassination and, a bare two months later, Robert Kennedy's death. The landing on the moon was, for a change, welcome news.

❧

Some weeks later, on the afternoon of September 4, 1969, I was upstairs getting the room ready for our new baby. I was nine months pregnant with our second child, with the due date predicted for that week. I heard a knock at the front door. It was Silvio carrying Suzie, our kitten. Her head drooped at an odd angle and her rigid legs stuck out. Suzie was dead.

Poor Suzie. How upset two-year-old Jen would be. Suzie had come to us only a few months ago. Taking the kitten's body, I regretted my annoyance at her habit of brushing her furry flanks against my legs, weaving figure eights in and out. Nudged aside, she would immediately return and continue her irritating looping. But she had been a sweet kitten, and now she was dead.

Carrying Suzie, I passed the frangipani tree near the garden wall. The usual sweet scent of its creamy blooms seemed off, as if a feral muskiness had been added. Suzie's body felt heavy as I walked toward the garage. The late afternoon sun scorched. A faint nausea washed over me.

The garage was cooler. I put Suzie down on the concrete floor, trying to guess what happened to her. Probably rat poison at the apartment building. I knew Stuart would want to have her examined to rule out rabies.

As I straightened up, a sharp contraction took my breath away. I leaned against the garage wall. I had been experiencing intermittent pangs and twinges throughout the day, but this was real. I was going into labor.

Through the open veranda doors of the living room, I heard the phone ringing. Stuart was calling from the embassy.

"Look, Dag," he said when I answered, "something's happened."

"What?" I asked, impatient to tell him my news.

"Ambassador Elbrick has been kidnapped. I've got to get to the residence to be with Mrs. Elbrick when she finds out. She'll be in a state of shock. I'll see you later."

"No, wait. I think I'm going into labor."

"Oh, no. Not now." After a brief pause, he added, "Get your things ready for the hospital. I'll come as soon as I can."

It was dark by the time Stuart came home and we set off for Amparo Feminino, the German Hospital for Women. I hadn't visited the hospital but knew that it was far, in Zona Norte, a teeming industrial zone with grim streets, grimy alleys, and the concentrated misery of housing developments for the poor. The traffic there was even more congested than in other parts of the city. Motorcycles wove in between overloaded trucks spewing diesel fumes, and pedestrians crossed at unexpected places. I began to wonder about my German-trained obstetrician's choice of hospital, but he had assured me that Amparo Feminino was a good maternity hospital.

Between ever-increasing contractions, I tried to listen to Stuart.

"Right in the middle of examining a patient, I got this urgent call from the security officer. I rushed through the waiting room, full of patients waiting to see me. He told me about the ambassador and that I must go to the residence right away to be with Mrs. Elbrick."

"How did it happen? I mean, the kidnapping."

Stuart explained that the ambassador's Brazilian driver had arrived back at the embassy, distraught and incoherent, breaking down in a garble of English and Portuguese. The security officer pieced together what happened. After lunch, the driver was taking the ambassador from his residence back to the embassy when a red Volkswagen swerved in front of them. Another vehicle pulled behind, blocking in the ambassador's Cadillac.

I groaned as another strong contraction gripped me. When the pain subsided, I told Stuart to go on.

"Three armed men got into the Cadillac and ordered the driver to drive up to the top of Corcovado. There, they dragged the ambassador out of the car, pushed him down onto the floor of a van, and covered him with a rug."

"How much longer to the hospital?" I asked.

"Not long. We're almost there."

"Was the ambassador hurt?"

"I don't think so. They set the driver free and gave him some sort of note."

"You hurried to be with Mrs. Elbrick?" I asked. "She must have been terrified."

"When I arrived at the ambassador's residence, she already knew about it. But there she was, wearing her paisley turban, sitting calm and composed. I couldn't believe it. I told her how calm she appeared. She said, 'Dr. Scheer, I am the daughter of an admiral, after all.'"

Prior to his posting in Brazil, career diplomat Charles Burke Elbrick had been the ambassador to Portugal as well as Yugoslavia. As an ambassador's wife, Mrs. Elbrick had learned the fine art of official decorum and formal restraint.

Seeing that Mrs. Elbrick didn't need him, Stuart had excused himself.

"I'm sorry, Mrs. Elbrick, I'll have to leave because we're going to have a baby tonight."

It was midnight when we arrived at the drab concrete hospital buildings. I lay down on the narrow iron bed. Stuart sat near the window on the one chair in the stifling room.

"God, it's muggy," I said. "Could you open the window?"

I tried to distract myself from the now excruciating pain by concentrating on the traffic noises in the street below.

After a long five hours, Nicholas Stuart was born. At the sink in the corner of the delivery room, a nurse held him upside down under the splashing tap water. A healthy, shrill cry filled the room. I wasn't sure whether he was protesting the bracing cold water or whether, perhaps, he was objecting to being brought into the world at such unsettling times, under such chaotic circumstances.

Friday went by in a haze. The nurse wheeled in the bassinette for a few minutes, and then I was alone again. As I dozed during the sticky heat of the afternoon, a floral scent filled the air. I dreamed I was walking in a garden. Waking, I saw the source of the sweet fragrance. On the windowsill stood a large vase filled with red roses.

"Thanks for the roses," I told Stuart when he appeared in the doorway that evening. "They're gorgeous."

A puzzled look crossed his face, and he went to the window to read the card tucked in among the stems.

"Dear Mrs. Scheer," he read. "To celebrate the birth of your son. Elvira Elbrick."

We looked at each other. She had thought about us at such a difficult moment?

Not having slept the night before, Stuart was exhausted. He had shuttled in horrible traffic between the hospital, our home in Ipanema to check on Jen—who was being looked after by our nanny—the embassy medical unit, the ambassador's residence to be with Mrs. Elbrick again, and now to visit me in the hospital. I was happy to see him and anxious to hear news of the ambassador.

"Not good news," he said. "The ransom note said that an ambassador is worth a great deal."

"How much do they want?"

"They don't want money."

"What then?"

"They want fifteen political prisoners to be released. Oh, and an anti-government manifesto to be broadcast nationwide."

Two terrorist groups, the National Liberation Action Group and the October 8 Revolutionary Movement—or MR-8—had set the deadline for their demands to be met by Saturday afternoon, less than twenty-four hours away.

"I think they'll release the prisoners," Stuart said. "But in twenty-four hours? They're in jails all over Brazil and need to be flown out of the country by the following day."

Ambassador Elbrick's predecessor, Ambassador Tuthill, had kept a bodyguard, always changing his route between the embassy and the residence. But Elbrick, arriving in Brazil only a month and a half ago, had ignored the security officer's advice and refused, in writing, protection from Brazilian security guards.

"Go home and get some rest," I said to Stuart. "Check on Jen. I miss her."

"Don't worry, she's fine. Helena is taking good care of her."

Alone again, the hours dragged. In this out-of-the-way hospital,

I didn't expect any visitors. My son was occasionally brought to me, but those happy moments were quickly replaced by my fear about the kidnapping. In oppressive heat, I sat staring at the bare walls, listening to the traffic noises, too distracted to write letters or to read. By late Saturday afternoon, after having made his usual rounds of home, the embassy, and the ambassador's residence, Stuart came by. I knew he would only be able to stay for a moment. As they brought the baby in for him, he told me the good news.

"They've released the prisoners. They've been rounded up, and the manifesto has been broadcast."

"That's really good news. Mrs. Elbrick will be relieved."

"Not yet. The ambassador hasn't been freed. If all goes well, he will be. I wish I could stay longer with you and the baby, but I've got to rush off."

I was still in the hospital on Sunday, and the many hours of the morning were followed by interminable hours of the afternoon that dragged on into a bleak evening. I sat in the sweltering heat, waiting for Stuart, waiting to hear if the ambassador had been released, waiting for the baby to be brought to me.

I was thankful the delivery had gone well and our son was healthy and beautiful. But at the same time, I was desperate to know what was happening with the ambassador. I felt helpless and confined. Like a captive. As the evening wore on, I knew Stuart wouldn't be coming.

What if the ambassador wasn't released? What would happen? I realized I didn't understand anything about the political turmoil in Brazil. Why had the United States supported the military takeover in 1964 that ousted João Goulart? Had that been the right thing to do? What had started as a temporary military regime had become a rigid dictatorship lasting for years. How oblivious I had been about the political situation—feeling safe, as an American, protected by diplomatic immunity. How quickly illusions can erode.

୬

On Monday, Stuart came to the hospital to drive our son and me home. Cradling the baby in my arms, I listened to the events of the previous day.

When Stuart arrived at the ambassador's residence, it was crawling with staff from the embassy, the CIA, and senior State Department officers flown in from Washington to debrief the ambassador upon his return. If he returned.

A room had been set up for the debriefing. In the marble foyer leading to the huge living room used for formal receptions, small groups waited anxiously, recounting and reconstructing details of the events. The demands in the ransom note had been met, but still no news of the ambassador's release. As the day wore on, an uneasy foreboding settled on the gathering. Tension escalated. Would the guerrillas release the ambassador? Would they make additional demands? The room was thick with suspense, the growing anxiety palpable.

Stuart was making his way through the milling entourage when he heard loud knocking at the front entrance. With the butler nowhere in sight, he rushed to open the locked door. Haggard, his tall frame stooped, a bandage on his forehead, his rumpled white shirt and finely tailored gray suit no longer impeccable, stood the ambassador.

"Welcome back, Mr. Ambassador," Stuart said.

"Good to be back. Where's Elfie?"

Rushing through the crowd, the ambassador ran up the grand staircase just as Mrs. Elbrick was descending. An embarrassed and uncomfortable silence fell on the gathering as, overcome by their emotions and oblivious of the crowd, the Elbricks embraced—a touching but rare lapse of decorum for these scrupulously formal and seasoned diplomats.

In an upstairs bedroom, set up as an examining room, Stuart tended to the ambassador's head wound.

"I was under a rug in the back of a van. No idea where they were taking me," the ambassador said.

"What happened to your head, Mr. Ambassador?"

"The van stopped. I was dragged out ... someone put a gun to my head." The ambassador pointed to his right temple. "I thought it was the end. They were going to kill me."

The ambassador's voice broke as he relived the terror of the moment, pent-up emotion overwhelming him. He breathed deeply, struggling to regain his customary composure.

"I pushed the gun away," he continued. "That angered him, and he struck me on the head with it."

"It's not a bad wound, Mr. Ambassador," Stuart told him.

Downstairs, the crowd's worry had been replaced by relief, and a celebratory atmosphere could be felt when the ambassador walked into the room. With clipboards and notebooks, the senior officials waited to record the details. In control of his emotions now, in a professional, businesslike manner, the ambassador told his story.

"My captors are young, intelligent, and dedicated political activists. They were driven to terrorist acts against the harsh military government in desperation about the political situation. After the blow to my head, I was actually treated well. At first, the guerillas were confident their demands would quickly be met. After all, the U.S. had supported the military takeover and they could not, in theory, allow the American ambassador to be harmed."

In the hideout, the captors and Elbrick began a dialogue. The guerillas were surprised by the ambassador's respectful dignity. They realized that Elbrick understood their revolutionary commitment and the reasons for the kidnapping. Mutual respect developed between the captors and the captive. But as time passed, first hours and then days, and no news of the release of prisoners was announced, tension in the hideout mounted. The ambassador feared that, being new to terrorist tactics, the guerillas hadn't imagined the possibility that their demands might not be met.

"I began to suspect that things might not evolve as the guerrillas had intended," Elbrick continued. "The wait was excruciating. I was afraid they might be forced to kill me."

The ambassador struggled to continue. "I began to have serious doubts that the demands would be met. Not in time anyway. By Saturday, I felt anything could happen."

Still in captivity on Sunday, Elbrick was unaware that the political prisoners had been flown out of the country and didn't know the manifesto had been broadcast. He hadn't been told the demands had been met.

"They came in and led me to the van waiting outside. I thought it an ominous sign. I was sure they were going to take me somewhere, kill me. The van took me to a neighborhood I didn't recognize. At a busy intersection, they told me to get out. I stood in the unfamiliar street not knowing what to do. A taxi pulled up. The driver said he recognized me from the news reports. He was kind and drove me back."

As he finished the debriefing, the ambassador looked drained. The senior officials sat in silence, some still scribbling notes.

"Now, if you will excuse me, I must go to Elfie."

❧

As Stuart finished his account of the ambassador's safe return, I held the baby close and pondered the significance of what I had just heard. Would the kidnapping change our lives in Brazil? Was this an isolated incident or a turning point, a precursor of a pattern of terrorist tactics to come? Would its ripple effect change the way America was perceived worldwide?

I thought about the remarkably dignified role the ambassador had played, admired his instinctive code of correct and appropriate conduct. This stately old-school diplomat had undoubtedly played difficult roles many times before in his life, so that noble and respectful conduct had become ingrained, embedded in his very core. And Mrs. Elbrick, on the most traumatic and distressing day of her life, had thought to send me roses.

I thought about Stuart too. In the last few days, he had played various roles, and I knew he had played them well.

Ambassador Elbrick later supported amnesty for the kidnappers but was criticized for doing so. He was condemned for saying positive things about the urban guerillas and for demonstrating a willingness to understand what they had tried to accomplish.

Fernando Gabeira, mastermind of the kidnapping, wrote the following in his memoir.

"One of the things I learned from Ambassador Elbrick was how to behave with dignity when being held captive by armed men."

CARNIVAL

YEARS LATER, AFTER one of our frequent moves from country to country, I unpacked a box of LP records and arranged them on the shelf in alphabetical order—the Third and Eighth String Quartets by Shostakovich, Mozart's *Requiem*, Brahms' *Double Concerto*, *Vier Letzte Lieder* and *Metamorphosen* by Richard Strauss. Then I came upon an LP that puzzled me. Where should I put *I've Got Dem Ol' Kozmic Blues Again, Mama*? The garish cover depicted the singer in concert, face almost obscured by a huge tumble of frizzy hair. Undecided, I started to put it aside when I noticed, scrawled diagonally across the front of the album in blue ballpoint pen: "To Dr. Scheer, with Love, Janis."

"Where did you get this?" I asked Stuart when he came home that evening.

"Oh, I'd forgotten all about that."

One morning in the medical unit, while we were still living in Rio, Stuart had received a call from the Marine guard on duty at the front entrance of the embassy.

"There's a couple here. They want to see the doctor," the guard said.

"Do they have an appointment?" Stuart asked.

"No, they don't."

"Well, okay, I can squeeze them in. I'll see them as a courtesy. Please escort them to the medical unit."

As the couple entered, Stuart was startled by the young woman's appearance. Even for a flower child, her outfit was boldly glitzy— purple silk bell-bottom pants, lace blouse that looked as if it had been made from an old curtain from her grandmother's kitchen, strand upon strand of beads, jangling bangles on her wrists, a disheveled mane of long curly hair, huge round glasses that couldn't hide her bad complexion.

Stuart recognized her. It was Janis Joplin. She was with a tall young man with dark shoulder-length hair who was holding his right elbow. Stuart asked them to sit down. Janis slumped in her chair. Despite the theatrical clothing, she looked waiflike and plain. It was as if without the electrifying propulsion of her raucous voice, the energy had been sucked out of her. She looked wilted.

"I'm still kinda shaken," she said. "We've been in an accident. The car in front of us swerved and made us crash into a wall. We were both thrown off."

"Off?" Stuart asked.

"Yeah, a motorcycle."

"In this traffic?" He couldn't believe it.

Janis had hit her head, and David, her young man, had a gash on his arm. As they picked themselves up on the side of the road, Janis tended to David's bleeding wound.

"Janis took off her green stocking and wrapped my elbow," David said.

Stuart was appalled by their recklessness, but refrained from showing it. Traffic in densely populated Rio was utterly insane, chaotic, and dangerous. When we first arrived, we had been warned that Brazilians drive like madmen and ignore basic traffic rules.

Even crossing a busy street could be a nightmare. Riding a motor-cycle in Rio was a crazy, suicidal thing to do.

It was not all that uncommon, especially in Zona Norte, the northern part of the city, to see a dead body lying in the street, probably a pedestrian who had been run over while trying to cross a congested avenue. We had seen such bodies surrounded by burning candles and flowers or fruit. We thought it was macumba, spirit worship, or some other ritual. The body might remain in the street for many hours before the police arrived to take it away.

In the treatment room, David winced as Stuart unwrapped the stocking. The wound, now caked with blood, was stuck to it. Finally succeeding in pulling it off, Stuart swiveled around to discard the soiled stocking.

"No! That's Janis's," David protested.

Setting the stocking aside, Stuart washed and disinfected the abrasion, applied a gauze dressing, and bandaged the elbow. When finished, he somewhat reluctantly took the green stocking and wrapped it once again around David's elbow, on top of the clean dressing and bandage. He suspected that David believed an article of Janis's clothing would help the healing process. It was the first time he had incorporated macumba in his medical practice.

Janis's neurological examination revealed no abnormalities. Parting her tangled hair section by section, Stuart found a few scratches and some clotted blood on her head but nothing serious. As a precaution, he sent her to a radiologist to make sure there were no skull injuries.

During her subsequent visits to the medical unit, Janis talked about herself and why she had come to South America.

"I'm having a bad time," she said. "No one liked my last record-ing. It's different."

In her latest recording, she had changed her wildly popular

psychedelic rock style for a more mellow blues sound. She wanted to go in another direction with her music and had dissolved the Kozmic Blues Band. She thought she might start a new band when she went back to the States.

"I need some time off. I'm stressed out. I mean, ten concerts a month is crazy. Traveling all over the country."

"Time off sounds like a good idea," Stuart said.

"I've got to get off the drugs and alcohol. Look what it's done to me!" She pointed to her heroin-ravaged complexion.

But while in Brazil, Janis wanted to experience Carnival. Stuart understood and agreed that Carnival in Rio was something Janis would appreciate.

During Carnival, Rio comes alive. For the dizzying revelry that dates back to ancient rites celebrating life, the city is a magical setting. To the cariocas, these four intoxicating days make the rest of the year, and probably life itself, worth living. Schedules, routines, even reality are suspended. Restraints and constraints are lifted, frustrations evaporate, inhibitions forgotten. A mass phenomenon of contagious festivity with no expense spared.

In Ipanema, the rich emerge from their luxury beachfront apartments and the poor stream down from their flimsy shacks perched on steep hillsides. They spill into the streets in the oppressive tropical heat and mingle in a teeming mass of sweating humanity. Frenzied, maddeningly repetitive drumbeats transform the clogged streets into a kaleidoscopic, pulsating revel. Exhilaration boils over into a feverish *allegria*. Samba dancers, with their dazzling masks and glittering costumes in bold clashing colors, parade in the street. Extravagant fantasies and passions are lived out. For the irrepressible cariocas, it is a feast for all the senses. But above all, it is a celebration of the body.

Propelled by the samba, a musical drug, young women, whose taut bodies in their bikini-clad lives have not yet been touched by gravity, gyrate sensually through the choked *avenidas*. Men, with swirling emotions and desires unleashed by excesses, follow them on the prowl. The desperate merriment, as if animated by an electrical current or some primal force, induces a collective delirium.

For Stuart and me, during Carnival there were parties and lots of *cachaça*. Out on the street, impulsive, pervasive music persisted and reverberated, and we tried our samba dance steps. But the throbbing rhythm overwhelmed, became obsessive, almost unbearable. Just when it seemed the peak had been reached, couldn't be sustained, the music would accelerate.

Through sweltering days and whirling humid nights, the spectacle continued. In some parts of the city, it spiraled out of control, and there was, as always, violence. Eventually though, as fatigue set in, the tempo diminished. Euphoria gave way to exhaustion. The delusional spree of the cariocas had been played out. It was a catharsis that made difficult lives more livable, at least until the following year.

A few days after Carnival, Janis came to the medical unit and brought the autographed LP for Stuart.

"I need some methadone," she begged.

"I have none," Stuart said.

"Please, any narcotic, anything. What about cough syrup with codeine?"

Janis was desperate.

"No." Stuart insisted. "Janis, you've got to get off drugs. And you have to stay off drugs. Otherwise, you're going to die."

And she did, eight months later, in California, of a heroin overdose. She was twenty-seven. Her life had been no less chaotic than Rio's frenzied Carnival.

❦

"Heard about my next assignment," Stuart said one evening as he hugged our kids, who had run up to greet him. A telegram from Dr. Mishtowt, the director of the Foreign Service medical program, had arrived that morning.

"Mishtowt wants me to go to Vientiane."

"Vientiane?" I echoed, putting down the dishes I was carrying to set the table for dinner.

"Laos."

"But Laos is next to Vietnam," I said.

"Vientiane is far from the border." Stuart attempted to reassure me.

For the next week or so, we struggled with misgivings about going to Laos. I started to pay more attention to news about the war in Vietnam. I would sit outside and watch Nick and Jen playing on the lawn and read whatever I could find about Laos.

Although theoretically neutral, Laos had been drawn into the war in Vietnam. In secret missions, the United States was providing aerial and logistical support to the South Vietnamese Army's effort to disrupt the traffic on the Ho Chi Minh Trail, the supply corridor that ran along the eastern border of Laos. The attacks targeted North Vietnamese trucks carrying troops and supplies south along the trail to infiltrate South Vietnam from the west. At the same time, Pathet Lao, the Laotian communist insurgency movement, was advancing and taking regions in southern Laos and Hmong areas north of Vientiane. In short, Laos was a war zone.

I was worried. How could we go to a region of unrest? We had to keep the children safe.

About a week later, news came that the Foreign Service doctor in Addis Ababa had resigned. Dr. Mishtowt offered Stuart the option of going to Ethiopia rather than Laos. We were more than relieved. Not that we knew anything about Ethiopia other than that it was in the Horn of Africa—safer than Southeast Asia. Haile Selassie, as emperor, had ruled for four decades. The country, never colonized, had retained its own unique language and culture.

The three years in Brazil had sped by. In a few months, we would be leaving. First there would be home leave in the States to visit our families in Cleveland and New York, and then organizing our move to Ethiopia.

As our departure approached, I regretted that we would be leaving our good friends, but, of course, they too would be leaving to work at other embassies on other continents. I began to realize that Foreign Service people's lives are a succession of overseas posts. Fine friendships readily formed are suddenly disrupted by new assignments. Occasionally, paths might cross again at another embassy in a different part of the world. More often, though, over the years, we would lose contact, never to meet again. Our lives would be fragmented, shaped by experiences in each new country.

Our nanny, Askale with Nick and Jen.

ILLUSORY PROTECTIVE BUBBLE

AS THE PLANE began its descent toward the Addis Ababa airport, I pressed my face to the window. Abruptly, the brown desiccated terrain we had been flying over gave way to steep escarpments and the green forests of Ethiopia's highlands. A vague blue haze hovered over the sprawling city. I would soon know the smell of that haze—evening cooking fires burning eucalyptus branches. Sharp and medicinal, like Vick's cough drops.

Clutching her latest Dr. Seuss book, four-year-old Jen slept beside me. Nick, still a toddler, squirmed on my lap. A twinge of apprehension marred my excitement. I tried to imagine our life in Ethiopia.

We moved into our embassy-rented house on Mesfin Harar, the main road leading out of Addis Ababa. A high wall shielded our garden from the street where drivers honked horns to clear the way through masses of people on foot, on bicycles, herds of goats, sheep, stray chickens, and plodding zebu. Leaving trails of exhaust fumes and dust, overcrowded buses passed back and forth.

Through the grillwork of the front gate, I watched the unending procession of donkeys weighed down by huge loads, women in white *shammas* with embroidered hems holding bright umbrellas as protection from the searing high-altitude sun. Barefoot women carrying cumbersome bundles of sticks.

Our high wall secluded us. It also separated us from Ethiopia itself.

Inside our walls, walkways crisscrossed lawns. Passion flower vines twisted around the entrance gate. Tall cannas, in discordant reds and yellows, camouflaged the stone wall. By the front steps, milk-white calla lilies bloomed on tall stems.

At times, from a large drain pipe at the base of the garden wall, a one-eyed feral cat emerged. A pathetic stray, its grungy fur spiked in messy tufts. Its limping, skulking gait reminded me of the hyenas whose howls we heard at night as they scavenged for carrion on the outskirts of the city.

Cutting lilies to put in a vase one day, I saw the furtive cat crawling out of the drain pipe. Nick and Jen, playing nearby, spotted it too. They dashed to play with it. The cat hissed, bared its claws, ready to pounce. The kids tried to catch it.

"Here, kitty, kitty!"

"Leave it!" Stuart shouted from the top of the steps. "Stay away from that cat. You are not to go near it."

"But we love that cat." Disappointed, Jen faced her father, hand on hip.

"Take the kids into the house, Dag. Keep them there. There's a lot of rabies in Ethiopia. I'm going to get a box and take that thing away."

I dropped the flowers and hurried the children into the house. When I came out again, Stuart had gotten the cat into a big cardboard box. The trapped cat lurched from side to side. Carrying the ungainly box, Stuart made his way to the garden toolshed at the back of the house. I guessed he was going to put the box there so he could get his car keys and drive to release the cat somewhere far from the house.

I sat down on the low stone wall next to the laundry room near the shed. Damp sheets flapped about on the clothesline, shielding me from the blazing sun. In the laundry room, Askale, our nanny and maid, fed a load of wash through the wringer of the old-fashioned washing machine. The ancient appliance, its tub set on legs, had to be filled from the garden faucet and emptied through a hose to a drain outside. A tedious chore.

The box for the cat was left over from the movers who had delivered our household shipment. My cheeks burned as I recalled moving day.

The grand piano sat on the lawn without its legs. Twelve, maybe fifteen Ethiopian moving men, rounded up from the street, milled about. The piano had been shipped from Brazil, our last post. The thin, undernourished men looked at the piano's shiny black surface, the smooth curve of its side. They had never seen anything like it and had no idea what it was or what purpose it served. They didn't know how to get the immense, awkward thing up the front steps and into the house. The Mason & Hamlin had been a wedding present from Stuart's parents. Three hefty men, with thick straps wrapped around the piano, had carried it up the stairs to our third-floor apartment in New York. Now this extravagant gift was out on the grass. Stuart's instructions for everyone to lift at the same time were not working.

The movers inside the house were unpacking our household items. In the living room, men crouching beside boxes unwrapped kitchenware. One of them held up a rolling pin and examined it, trying to figure out what it was. Perplexed, he shrugged and used it to tap another man's head. Next, a muffin tin was pulled out. Another strange thing they had never seen. More boxes were opened in the dining room. When a hand mirror was unpacked, the men chuckled at their reflections. My hairdryer was next. In that era of big hair, it was one of those dryers with an orange plastic hood. The men gazed at it uncomprehendingly. They didn't know what it was—couldn't even begin to guess its use. They passed it around, convulsed with laughter.

Why was my life filled with these ridiculous items? I asked myself as I watched. The movers probably lived in a thatch-roofed *tukul* with one cooking pot and a gourd for carrying water. And we had all this stuff. I never even baked muffins!

Unable to bear the humiliating charade any longer, I asked the men to leave and unpacked the rest of the boxes myself.

Commotion from inside the shed startled me. The cat had gotten out of the box. It screeched and yowled maniacally as it tried to escape the shed. Scampering around, it knocked over garden tools with loud thuds. I heard Stuart's frantic steps. More loud thuds—then silence.

Stuart emerged from the toolshed.

"The cat's dead—clawed itself out of the box. Had to clobber it. It was attacking me."

"There's blood spattered all over your face ..." I began. He cut me off.

"We're getting a dog. The kids need a dog." Without looking back, he entered the house.

It occurred to me he may have been thinking about that part of the physicians' creed: First, do no harm ...

Stuart was right about rabies. It was a big problem in Ethiopia. As part of a preventive program, we got pre-exposure rabies vaccine. A series of injections—the first followed by the second a week later, another one a month later, and a booster every two years, each shot carefully noted in our immunization record.

I quickly learned about the many tropical diseases in Ethiopia, even some long-forgotten ones—medieval afflictions we thought had disappeared ages ago. Leprosy and plague still occurred in rural areas. A plague vaccine was also on our list.

"And what's the gamma globulin shot for?" I had asked Stuart.

"Hepatitis from unsanitary food handling. We need a GG injection every six months."

"Our little yellow immunization record is going to get filled up quickly."

We worried about diseases for which there were no vaccines—gastrointestinal bacterial and parasitic diseases like salmonella, shigella, giardia, and amoeba, all common here. I filtered and boiled our water, but suffering from one of these ailments was part of living in Ethiopia.

Our family's Sunday dinner routine was taking chloroquine tablets, the antimalarial medicine. Because of its altitude, there was no malaria in Addis Ababa, but we were planning to travel to other regions.

"No, I'm not taking it, Daddy," Jen said one Sunday.

"You have to take it, Jen."

"No, it's yucky."

"I know it's bitter and hard to swallow, but if you don't take it, we can't go camping."

"Well, okay, just this once."

I came to realize that in this country, ravaged by poverty and disease, we Americans lived inside an invisible—and illusory—protective bubble of careful precautions, injections, and medicines. It reassured me that we would stay healthy.

After we got settled in the house, our new embassy friends, Frank and Beth, invited us to join them and their three small children on a trip to another part of the country. We packed all the food and water for the nine of us for the four-day trip. That morning, while the Land Rover was being loaded with military precision, the kids ran around excitedly, watching the tents being secured on top and gasoline-filled jerry cans strapped to the front. Every available space inside was crammed with containers of water, boxes filled with food, and anything else we might need.

Frank drove, and Beth sat in the front with their baby Nathaniel on her lap, an East African bird guide in her hand. The variety of birds in Ethiopia was incredible. A dozen miles out of Addis, the paved road ended. We bumped along dusty roads full of potholes. Beth pointed out the feathered jewels that were sunbirds—an iridescent flash of amethyst plumage. We watched the undulating flight of crested hoopoes and identified the cobalt-colored rollers.

On a barren plateau, Frank, thinking he might have missed the turn, stopped to spread out his map on the steering wheel. Out of nowhere, a crowd appeared—tall men, walking sticks slung across their shoulders, their *shammas* draped around lean bodies, women bent over from heavy loads. They surrounded the vehicle and stared at us. One woman, even thinner than the rest, with dark circles under her eyes, carried a tiny baby on her arm. She pushed herself through and stretched out her emaciated arm. Beth reached into the basket at her feet to get some bread. Stuart put a hand on Beth's shoulder.

"Don't open the window, Beth. The baby has smallpox."

We drove away.

"How can you tell?" Beth and I asked in unison.

"On the baby's face, pustules. Unmistakable. You know," he continued, "modern medicine has almost eradicated smallpox. But not here. Over twenty-thousand cases just last year."

We drove on in silence, thinking of our five healthy children.

After the exhausting drive over dusty, corrugated roads, a shady spot under tall trees on the banks of the mud-colored Awash River looked inviting, a good place to set up camp. We climbed out of the cramped Land Rover. The kids ran down to the water's edge. Stuart and Frank pitched tents while Beth and I gathered firewood. A cool breeze dissipated the suffocating heat. After a quickly improvised meal, we relaxed around the fire and watched its gold reflections on the water, the showers of sparks when burning logs collapsed. Never had the sky appeared so immense, the stars so visible. We washed the pots and dishes in the river but didn't linger near the water's edge. Earlier, on the opposite bank, we had seen a crocodile. We doused the smoldering ashes and crept into our tents.

The night was alive with sounds. Strange croakings and yelp-ings. A grunt followed by a snort. Unidentifiable noises. Nearby something crawled through the dry scrub brush. Dead tired, we huddled in our sleeping bags and slept deeply.

In the morning, just outside our tent, we saw a curious mark—a winding pattern across the sand, as if something had been dragged to the river.

"Maybe it was a crocodile," Jen said, poking the four-toed imprints with a stick.

I shuddered and tried not to think about it.

Loading the Land Rover in the midmorning heat seemed more arduous than it had the day before. Finally ready, we headed south toward the Rift Valley lakes, through a scrubland of tall grasses. The Land Rover churned up thick clouds of dust. Overhead, the blinding equatorial sun burned. An occasional acacia tree shimmered in the vibrating air.

By late afternoon, we reached Lake Zwai. Along its shores, thick with reeds, we searched for signs of hippo, for we had heard they could be spotted here. White pelicans circled against a cloudless sky. Yellow-billed storks waded in the reeds near the shore. In a boat made of bundles of reeds tied together, standing tall like a Giacometti sculpture, a thin man with a long oar rowed by soundlessly.

We continued on to Lake Langano, where the coarse white sand on the shore seemed an ideal place to unload our gear and set up tents. The lapping sound of the waves soothed. The kids, tired and dusty, scrambled down to the water, the color of milky tea. I watched Stuart put his arms around their shoulders and explain that they couldn't wade in the water.

"Why not?" Nick and Jen demanded.

"Well, because of the snails."

"I don't see any," Jen said. "Where are they?"

"On the reeds underwater."

I watched as farther along the shore, Ethiopian children splashed and waded in the water. A fisherman dragged a boat filled with the day's catch onto the beach. A calm everyday scene. They had probably noticed brown snails on the reeds. But did they know about the connection between them and a disease? I was sure these lake people had never heard of schistosomiasis.

"It took clever scientific minds a long time to figure out the organism's complicated life cycle," Stuart explained to Frank and me. The tiny snails don't cause the disease but harbor the organism that does. That organism morphs through a logic-defying cycle of stages. During its free-swimming stage, the larvae attach to and penetrate the skin of a swimmer or someone wading in the water.

"It's hard to diagnose," Stuart added. "Once diagnosed, though, schistosomiasis can be treated by a single dose of medicine. But the thing is, you can't get the medicine in these parts."

"Damn it, Stu," Frank said. "I really wanted to go in and wash this layer of dust off. But, hey, I'm sure glad we've got you along."

It seemed that no matter where we went in this country, we bumped up against some depressing reality. Each time, with a sickening jolt, I realized how big the difference was between our privileged lives and the lives of Ethiopians.

MANY WAYS OF DYING

AT THE DIPLOMATIC reception, Marian Adair, wife of the American ambassador to Ethiopia, made her way toward me through the crowd.

"Mrs. Scheer, or may I call you Dag?"

"Of course, Mrs. Adair, please do."

"I've heard so many good things about Dr. Scheer. You're both such a great addition to our little community here. But I wanted to tell you about my wonderful idea. Wives need to be busy here too, you know. I'm starting an egg-decorating workshop on Mondays. Please, won't you join us?"

I was taken aback. Egg decorating? I took a sip of my wine. A matronly but still pretty woman, with white hair in tight curls and bright lipstick that had left a red smudge on her glass, Mrs. Adair was smiling and waiting for my answer.

"Of course, Mrs. Adair. How can I refuse your lovely invitation?"

∽

On my way to Mrs. Adair's workshop the following Monday, I stopped at the medical unit on the embassy compound, not far from the ambassador's residence. In the examining room, a little drama was taking place.

"I am afraid, Dr. Scheer, that her leg is badly fractured." Ato Chane, the lab technician, stood in the doorway with the still-wet X-ray in his hand. Stuart glanced to where she was lying. Soft brown eyes gazed back. As he gently stroked her head, she quivered and pulled away, evading his touch.

Stuart was used to puzzling diagnostic problems and difficult emergency situations, but he was not prepared to tend to the broken leg of a gazelle. The delicate creature, her graceful curved-back horns and tawny legs ending in little black hooves, was not much larger than a medium-sized dog. Accustomed to the freedom of the flat plains of Ethiopia, the gazelle, confined in the uneven terrain behind the ambassador's residence, had slipped on a large rock.

In his starched white coat, Stuart usually exuded clinical competence. He hesitated now, though, not sure what to do. Since I was already late for the workshop, I waved from the doorway and hurried out.

Crossing the walled embassy compound shaded by eucalyptus trees, I wondered about the egg-decorating workshop. What came to my mind were those opulent and intricate Fabergé Easter eggs I had seen in a museum, carefully crafted for Russian czars— fabulous treasures of opalescent enamels, lapis lazuli, and precious stones. Trellised with bands of gold and cleverly constructed so that when opened, they revealed a little surprise for Russian czarinas. I doubted that Mrs. Adair created such elaborate concoctions.

More humble had been my mother's Easter egg decorating. Not during the war years, for then, our eggs had no shells. The powdered eggs mixed with water resembled real eggs only in name. But by that time, we had forgotten the taste of a fresh egg. After the war, when we did have eggs with shells again, for weeks before Easter, Mother collected onion skins. There were plenty of them, for her beef stews and thick barley soups were rich with the flavor of onions, although she prided herself for never allowing garlic to cross the threshold of her home. To her, garlic was for people in southern European countries with a less refined cuisine.

The golden crinkly onion skins, saved in a brown paper bag, were boiled in a pot of water with the eggs. The shells turned a lovely caramel color. With the point of sharp scissors, my sisters and I etched Latvian folk designs on our eggs. Easter morning, we ate the decorated eggs, which, to attain that lovely hue, had boiled for such a long time that the pale yolks were rimmed with blue.

At the entrance to the ambassador's residence, I was greeted by the Ethiopian butler. He led me through the vast rooms used for diplomatic receptions and down a corridor to an airy back veranda where Mrs. Adair had already begun her demonstration. In her public role as wife of a congressman from Indiana, she had acquired poise and confidence in front of a group.

Before her, on a long table, she had displayed her work. It was ostrich eggs she decorated. They were readily available in Ethiopia. We had two of them, perched on little wooden stands on our library shelves, which we had bought on our first trip to the Mercato—the huge market that sprawled over a hundred acres near Addis. That morning at the crowded market, we navigated through the narrow passages along with donkeys and chickens. The scented blue haze from the eucalyptus-wood fires barely masked the rank smell of badly tanned leather shields. Chunks of frankincense smoldered on charcoal braziers. Rows of half-foot-high ostrich eggs, from which the contents had been emptied through a tiny perforation at the bottom, were laid out in a ramshackle stall among kitchen utensils and plastic buckets. We bought the eggs and then searched out the more intriguing Ethiopian crafts—biblical stories painted on parchment, old amber and silver jewelry, mysterious musical instruments, brass processional crosses.

"First," Mrs. Adair was saying, "you have to carve away the side of the shell. They're thick, and it's a little tricky." She waved the little tool she used to accomplish this. "Then we're ready to create a tiny, tiny tableau inside the egg."

She picked up one of her decorated eggs. Inside was a miniature living room with furniture, a rug, even curtains at chiseled-out windows, and an exquisite minuscule chandelier suspended above.

"How marvelous. What a delight," the ladies exclaimed.

One egg depicted a nativity scene, another one a minute Ethiopian landscape—a tiny round thatched *tukul* surrounded by scrub brush and a few brown goats. I had to admit the perfection of the diminutive scenes was strangely charming.

"Here is a list of things you need to bring," Mrs. Adair went on. "You might want to start collecting bits and pieces right away. Next Monday we will all, together, begin creating our own tiny tableaux. Won't we? And now, ladies, tea will be served in the dining room."

While admiring the painstaking detail of Mrs. Adair's ostrich-egg tableaux, I realized this endeavor would be time-consuming and was slightly ludicrous. This was not what I wanted to do with my time in Ethiopia. But Marian Adair was the ambassador's wife, and I wasn't sure I could decline her invitation to join the group. By then, I had become aware that as a Foreign Service wife, my participation in the community was part of my husband's performance evaluation. In Rio, my activities had been mentioned on his annual reports. Nothing bad, but I was surprised when Stuart told me.

Foreign Service wives were expected to assume formal representational responsibilities and to participate in community activities and charitable organizations. How a wife spent her time could affect her husband's career. By 1971, this assumption about wives' activities had become an issue.

"Just got this memo, Dag. Take a look." Stuart handed me a memorandum from the State Department.

It has become increasingly clear in the past few years that a reform is urgently needed in the treatment of Foreign Service wives. Few problems have had a more negative effect on morale. The treatment of wives is repeatedly mentioned by resigned Officers as one cause for leaving the Foreign Service.

"I've never been treated badly," I told him. "But I've heard complaints from other wives. Just as it says here."

The memo went on:

> *... a Foreign Service wife was often subjected to excessive demands on her time; to pressure, bordering on harassment, to involvement in projects not of her own choosing; to unwarranted intrusions in her private life; and perhaps worst of all, a caste system which granted wives of senior officers the right to dictate to wives of employees of lesser rank.*

Leaving the ambassador's residence that day to pick up Jen at the nursery school, I knew it probably wasn't wise for me to decline to participate in Marian Adair's workshop. I could decorate a few eggs, get to know Mrs. Adair better.

I walked to the car, and even though the midday sun scorched, I shivered as I recalled the previous week's incident at the school. I had parked and gone into the school to get Jen. When I returned to the car, I didn't notice that during my brief absence, the passenger side window had been opened. As I started the car, to my horror, an arm suddenly reached through the open window, pushed Jen back against the seat, and snatched my handbag. Following a crazy and stupid impulse, I ran after the thief and grabbed my bag back. Jen and I had both been shaken.

That day, there were no frightening incidents at the school, and we arrived home just in time for lunch—our family meal, when Stuart usually joined us. We had already found out that embassy life at a small post like Addis Ababa meant that nearly every evening there was a reception or dinner we had to attend. It was a busy time for us in other ways. Stuart had volunteered to teach clinical diagnosis to second-year medical students at the Haile Selassie Medical School, in addition to his work at the medical unit. I was studying Amharic, struggling with the ancient Semitic language's two hundred Amharic characters—some of them unpronounceable.

Lemma, our cook, had set out bowls of cold cucumber soup, and I caught the aroma of chicken cacciatore simmering on the stove. From an Ethiopian boy by the side of the road, I had bought some tiny wild asparagus spears to go with the chicken.

Lemma had learned to prepare dishes my family enjoyed. An intuitive cook, he would be in demand by other diplomatic households when we left Addis. Yet he didn't eat our food, not even taste to adjust the seasonings. In a daily early-morning ritual, I described how to make the dishes for our meals while he wrote down my instructions in Amharic. In the strange script, his little notebook was filled with my recipes.

"How's the gazelle?" I asked Stuart when we were seated at the table.

"She'll be fine. I called the vet at the U.S. Military Mission. He splinted her leg."

"The military has vets here?"

"Yes, he inspects local meat for their commissary."

"Why?"

"I'll tell you later. Not good lunchtime conversation."

"Madam." Lemma appeared in the doorway and motioned for me to follow him.

It was Martha Schwab, the Peace Corps doctor's wife, on the phone.

"Dag, I'm wondering if you'd like to help me. Dr. Fritschi at the leprosy hospital has asked me to start an informal rehabilitation program for some of the patients. I'm looking for volunteers."

"Sounds like a useful undertaking. But, Martha, you know I'm not a nurse."

"It doesn't matter. It's mostly about getting the patients to do handcrafts. I plan to get started on Monday. Please say you'll join me, Dag."

As I started to tell Martha that my Monday mornings were taken up with Mrs. Adair's egg-decorating workshop, I realized this was my opportunity to do something worthwhile. I agreed to meet her at the hospital.

The Hansen Research Institute on the outskirts of Addis was founded by Norwegian doctors. Dr. Fritschi, the orthopedic surgeon there, had on several occasions asked Stuart to do bone marrow aspirations and smears for leprosy patients with anemia.

Whatever I did at the hospital would be more useful and meaningful than decorating ostrich eggs.

The phone in our hallway often rang in the middle of the night. Stuart, aware that it could ring at any time, was always listening for it. One night when it rang, he hurried to answer as usual. Awake then, I tried to listen but couldn't make out the urgent one-sided conversation. Returning to the bedroom, he got dressed and grabbed his medical bag.

"It's Cynthia," he said, and rushed out.

Oh, no! I thought.

Just a few days earlier at a reception at the ambassador's residence, I had met Cynthia, the bubbly young wife of Jeff Logan, one of the political officers. Pregnant with their first child, she was being seen by a local obstetrician but was planning to fly to Germany for the birth of the baby. Cynthia wasn't due for a couple of months, so it was probably a tummy upset, I thought, nothing serious. I went back to sleep.

The cold breeze from the window woke me. Stuart wasn't back, and I had no idea how long he had been gone. Why hadn't he returned? Where was he? Anxiety gripped me. Addis wasn't safe at night. There had been robberies recently.

It was easy to get lost, especially in the dark. The central part of the city was laid out in disciplined grids of wide boulevards, but in the out-of-the-way areas where most of the American community lived, a confounding maze of unlit, badly paved labyrinthine roads followed ancient caravan tracks. Without signs, the roads often led to dead ends. Stuart was good at navigating by instinct and knew the landmarks. But still …

I slid out of bed and closed the window. Hoping to spot Stuart's car coming down the road, I went outside. Gabre, our old night guard, sat by the front steps wrapped in a thick blanket, for the nights were cold. A regal figure even swathed in a blanket, Gabre had once served in Haile Selassie's Imperial Bodyguards. At night, he guarded our house with a gun in his lap and a large stick at his side. I was happy to have him, as Stuart had to travel and I was often alone with the children.

I shivered and inhaled the wafting eucalyptus smell. Dawn's faint greenish streaks lit up the sky when I spotted headlights. Stuart drove through the gate, and I ran to meet him.

"Cynthia had twins," he said. "Just stopped to let you know. Got to get to the embassy."

From Stuart's unsmiling face, I realized something was wrong. "Premature—they're tiny. There's only one incubator at the local hospital. They're both squeezed in together. I've got to get them to Germany."

He drove off, and I stood there helpless, knowing there was nothing I could do. He would get on the phone and try to arrange a medical evacuation. I could only hope it would be in time.

Americans didn't use local hospitals in Addis because of the outdated medical equipment, shortage of medicines, and lack of well-qualified doctors and nurses. They relied on the embassy's medical unit for health care. The one-story stone building on the embassy compound was reasonably well-equipped with an X-ray machine and a lab for simple diagnostic tests and blood counts. A nurse, an Ethiopian lab technician, and a receptionist assisted Stuart. Seriously ill patients could be evacuated to one of the U.S. military hospitals in Germany.

Stuart called to tell me that the Air Force Base in Ramstein, Germany, was sending a medevac plane for the twins.

"Thank God for the military's quick response," he said. "We're leaving for the airport shortly."

"Will the babies be all right?" I asked.

His "too soon to tell" wasn't encouraging.

Knowing Stuart hadn't taken time to eat, I packed a sandwich and a thermos of coffee and drove to the airport. As I arrived, Stuart and the nurse, each hugging a baby and a hot water bottle wrapped in a blanket, were already heading for the tarmac. Each bundle was, I suspected, an alarming featherweight lightness—the infants' tiny crimped, crimson faces hidden under blankets. Cynthia followed with an unsteady gait.

As part of a plan to evaluate aid programs in Ethiopia's rural communities, Walter Southwick, the embassy's economic counselor, asked Stuart to visit a small up-country clinic.

"Not to see patients," Walter said, "just a simple courtesy visit."

Stuart invited me along. The clinic, not far from Dessie, was a long drive north of Addis. Deciding to leave the children home with Askale, we set out along the road through the eucalyptus forests of Mount Entoto and continued through fields of teff, barley, and wheat. Shaped by the contours of the land, small farm plots surrounded modest compounds of usually a dozen or so round thatch-roofed *tukuls*. Sheep and goats grazed on sparse tufts of grass outside fencing of intertwined thorn tree branches. I saw a field being furrowed with a wooden plow pulled by a pair of emaciated zebu. The scene emerged like a tableau out of the parchment pages of the Old Testament, a life of utter simplicity reminiscent of an era before even the wheel was invented. With no running water or electricity, it was a life of complete self-sufficiency and isolation. A precarious existence, for in times of drought, famine could not be far off. The typical lifespan here was about forty.

I was reminded that there were many ways of dying in Ethiopia.

Eventually the plateau sloped down to terrain broken up by ravines and dry, rocky areas. The road wound along deep gorges. A dusty bleakness, too wind scoured, too sun scorched to cultivate. The small enclaves of *tukuls* were now scattered farther and farther apart. In this crusted wasteland, the gullies twisted and turned in irregular patterns of erosion. Running along the ridge, dozens of baboons bobbed up and down. Scrubby vegetation with the occasional acacia tree or euphorbia—a parched landscape. A dead donkey by the side of the road had attracted a stray dog that, digging in the entrails, tore up bloody mouthfuls. In a circle a few feet away, patiently waiting their turn, black vultures had gathered.

We passed people walking along the road, so Dessie must be near. Perhaps it was market day. According to Walter's directions, we should be approaching the clinic.

"There's Walter in front of that building," I said. "My God, Stuart, I can't believe he's wearing a tweed jacket and a tie." On either side of the drab building, long lines had formed.

"The word's spread that an American doctor's coming," Walter said when we got out of the car. He strode back and forth, pointing to the crowd. "These people have walked for miles, Stu. I need to find someone who speaks English."

We entered the one-room clinic, bare except for a table and chair in the corner and a shelf of medicines. Stuart was not prepared for this. He sat down at the table unsure how to begin. I leaned against the wall.

Walter was back, without his jacket now, tie loosened. Dark sweat stains marked his light-blue shirt. Tesfaye, a young teacher, would translate.

Outside, the crowd waited. These thin people, their *shammas* draped around bony shoulders, suffered not from trivial aches and pains but from bad diseases. A man with an agonizing cough, a woman flushed with fever from some untreated infection or undiagnosed parasite. A small boy with a badly swollen foot hobbled with a makeshift crutch. Mothers carried small children with sunken eyes. Flies clustered around their nostrils and the corners of the mouths. Dreadful eye diseases. I turned away from the vacant gaze of a bluish opalescent eye.

The stifling room swarmed with flies. As the day passed, the lines outside did not get any shorter. Tesfaye searched for words, his scant collection of English nouns and verbs inadequate to describe the variety and acuteness of the diseases here. Stuart listened patiently, nodding from time to time, offering a few words of advice, treating them as best as he could from the dwindling supply of medicines. The afternoon wore on, and I could see his fatigue and stress beginning to show. His shoulders slumped. The khaki shirt, drenched with perspiration, clung to his back.

The people stood in line in heart-rending silence. Despite their misery and suffering, they waited with resignation and dignity. Their harsh lives had taught them the pointlessness of impatience, the futility of anger. After each brief consultation, the deep, respectful bow with which they thanked Stuart made me believe that somehow he had managed to communicate his concern and caring, that he had perhaps even produced a glimmer of hope.

It was night when we left the clinic to drive back to Addis. Stuart hunched over the steering wheel to better see the unfamiliar, unlit road. We were both tired. More than tired. I felt numb. It had been a sobering day.

"What are you thinking?" I asked.

"About all the medicines stocked in our medical unit."

I couldn't see Stuart's face in the dark, but the curt answer betrayed his frustration. Without medicines, without labs, even a well-trained doctor could do very little. The raw sores would continue to fester, nothing would soothe the coughs, frail babies wouldn't survive. The grim reality, the heartbreak of it all.

We drove back to Addis in silence.

⤚

One day Stuart came home from the embassy and handed me a white envelope. Inside was an invitation from Cynthia Logan. For a christening.

Her babies, Ginger and Craig, did just fine.

TRAVELS WITH THE SECRETARY

AFTER OUR TWO years in Ethiopia, Stuart was assigned back in Washington DC to work at the State Department coordinating its overseas medical program. In February of 1974, he was asked to accompany Secretary of State Henry Kissinger on an official trip to Mexico City to attend the Tlatelolco Conference. Twenty-four Latin American and Caribbean foreign ministers were gathering to discuss opportunities for cooperation among their countries and the United States.

"Easy trip, no problems," Stuart said when he got home. "Four days, one city."

A doctor from the State Department went along on these official trips in case a medical problem arose. He provided care for the secretary and his staff as well as the security detail, the press, and the air force crew of the secretary's plane.

"Hope everyone stays healthy on these trips," I said. "No medical emergency."

"Yep, medically I'm *it*."

"What happens if you get sick?"

"I can't get sick."

That fall, he was asked to accompany Kissinger on another

official trip. This time seventeen countries in eighteen days. An ambitious trip.

I recently spread out a world map to trace the itinerary. After marking the capitals of the seventeen countries, I drew a line connecting them. It formed a crazy zigzag across a huge part of the globe. I thought of the mindboggling amount of planning for such an elaborate undertaking.

Why these particular countries?

I probed the State Department's archived transcripts and *New York Times* articles on the official meetings in these countries. I wanted to learn what topics might have been discussed. My research turned into quite a history lesson on the problems of the world. A snapshot of trouble brewing in far-flung places. The year 1974 was a pivotal time.

Stuart told me that for these trips, the State Department had equipped an Air Force Boeing 707 with a bedroom for Kissinger, a staff office, and a conference room fitted out in the front of the plane. The doctor sat in the back along with the press and security officers. Luggage racks had been configured into beds, but only for the more senior staff.

In Moscow, the first stop of the trip, Kissinger was meeting with General Secretary Brezhnev, Foreign Minister Gromyko, and other Soviet officials.

After a stop in Copenhagen, the plane landed in Moscow late at night. It was past midnight when Stuart got to his hotel room. Getting ready for bed, he reached for his toothbrush and knocked over the water glass beside the sink. It broke and started to roll off the tile counter. As he tried to grab it before it crashed on the floor, the jagged edge of the glass dug into his hand. Blood spurted on white tiles and bathmat. Stuart reached for his medical kit. A thick rubber band twisted over the base of the badly cut finger worked as a tourniquet. After a few moments, the finger turned numb, then white. When the bleeding stopped, he cleaned the deep laceration under running water and dried the skin. With his left hand he managed to pull the edges of the wound together and secured them with butterfly bandages. No one needed to know about this.

"As the doctor accompanying the secretary of state," he told me later, "how could I have a medical emergency myself? Not on the first day."

The next morning, along with the press, the security contingent, and numerous aides, Stuart accompanied Kissinger to the Kremlin. In the era of "mutually assured destruction," the crucial topic was the Anti-Ballistic Missile Treaty. Emerging from such intense, complex, strategically sensitive sessions, Kissinger engaged in friendly chatter with his entourage.

In passing, he remarked to Stuart, "Doctor, I am foaming at the mouth!"

Kissinger's humorous remarks and relaxed banter masked the tense seriousness of the ongoing talks. Kissinger's hands, however, gave away the unrelenting stress the secretary of state must have suffered. His fingernails were thoroughly bitten down.

"What's Kissinger like?" I asked. "In person."

"He's not a tall guy. Shorter than I, maybe five foot nine," Stuart said. "In photos you don't see it, but there's an aura about him, a presence."

The visits didn't always go smoothly. In New Delhi, Kissinger was given a cool reception. The two countries' relationship had been marred by U.S. support of Pakistan during the 1971 India-Pakistan war. Unexpectedly, the day after Kissinger's arrival, Prime Minister Indira Gandhi left for Kashmir. The sudden departure was interpreted as a snub to Kissinger.

In Dhaka, the topic was famine. Just three years after independence, Bangladesh was ravaged by monsoon floods along the Brahmaputra River. Mass starvation spread across the country. It was the worst *famine* in decades, and Kissinger promised that the United States would do all it could to help.

"As expected," Stuart said, "the state dinner in Dhaka was less elaborate than in other capitals. Still, long banquet tables were lined with brimming bowls of prawn curries, masala goshts, dals—all pungent, served with rice biryani, mango chutneys, baskets stacked with naan and puri."

"Sounds pretty elaborate to me," I said.

"Oh, and no alcohol. Muslim country. Lassa, the yogurt drink, and chai, a sweet tea, and pitchers of water. I cautioned everyone against the yogurt drinks, even the water."

As the entourage approached the banquet table, they asked Stuart what they could eat, what they should avoid. He told them he didn't know, just to watch what he ate. Nancy Kissinger smoked her way through the whole dinner.

Stuart himself was not lucky. He became acutely ill. Ingesting maximum doses of Lomotil that night, he pulled himself together before the early departure for Pakistan.

In Rawalpindi, Pakistan, Kissinger's meeting with Prime Minister Bhutto lasted three hours. To find out what they talked about, I printed out the fifteen-page memorandum of their conversation, stamped SECRET across the top. A thick black line through it meant the memo had been declassified, each page marked with an executive Order 12958 declassification authorization.

Trying to make sense of the topics discussed took considerable effort on my part. Among other issues, Bhutto asked Kissinger to provide U.S. military equipment so Pakistan could defend itself against India's territorial ambitions. Reading their convoluted dialogue was a primer on tricky diplomatic discourse. I noticed how Kissinger and Bhutto respectfully tiptoed around the issues. A verbal sparring, if you will. Each alluding obliquely to terms of negotiation and what they were trying to accomplish.

"Did you attend these meetings?" I asked Stuart.

"No. Usually I just hung out with other staff somewhere outside the conference venues. I did attend the state dinners, though. In Rawalpindi, the dinner was in a tent at Bhutto's residence. Huge tent as big as a football field."

The trip continued. After a five-hour stop in Afghanistan, they landed in Tehran for a meeting with Shah Reza Pahlavi about oil prices. OPEC had imposed an oil embargo against the United States in retaliation for its support of Israel.

"Oil prices," Stuart said. "Big issue for Kissinger, what with gas prices skyrocketing all across the U.S. People hate the fifty-five mile-per-hour speed limit."

"I hate the long lines at filling stations," I said. "Maybe it's time to get one of those Japanese fuel-efficient cars."

After the official talks, there was a rare sightseeing excursion—a helicopter tour of Isfahan, once one of the most celebrated cities in the world. From the helicopter, Stuart searched the dun-colored landscape for the Persian-Islamic architectural gems. The bulbous, mosaic-tiled dome of the Shah Mosque appeared. The aircraft tilted to provide a close look of the huge bluish dome glistening in the sun, then circled. Minarets and more mosques sped by in a merry-go-round fashion. Again, the blue dome and the great Naqsh-e Jahan Square, laid out in plantings of formal patterns like an enormous green Persian carpet.

෯

214 | DAG SCHEER

214 | DAG SCHEERe214 | DAG SCHEER

Romania and Yugoslavia were quick stops. Ceauşescu requested Kissinger to include Romania in the Most Favored Nation status to facilitate trade and economic growth. I found just reading the archived transcripts of these complex meetings exhausting and began to admire Kissinger's stamina. But here and there in the dry documents, a bit of humor caught my eye. In discussing the cumbersome Arab-Israeli peace process with Tito, Kissinger quipped: "The trouble seems to me to be that Arabs can never make up their minds whether they want to make policy or epic poetry."

Covering that many countries in such a short time required precise scheduling. For the early departure each morning, luggage had to be packed and placed outside the door the evening before. Nancy Kissinger, tall and slim, frequently photographed for *Vogue*, meticulous about her appearance, came down one morning dressed as usual in a stunning Chanel suit, fur coat, matching hat, long gloves but with a pair of much-too-large men's loafers.

"These are Jerry Bremer's loafers," she said, pointing at her feet. "I need to get my boots from my suitcase. Now!"

Nancy was upset. Stuart understood perfectly. In Moscow, he had set out his suit, shirt, tie, belt, shoes, socks. Later that evening, suitcase already gone, he realized—no underwear. He put on his suit, ran downstairs just as the luggage truck was about to depart. The confused KGB looked on as Stuart clambered onto the truck, identified his suitcase, and retrieved the missing item.

The stop after Yugoslavia was Rome for the UN's first World Food Conference. The attending world leaders examined global food shortages and, in particular, the famine in Bangladesh. At the Assembly, Kissinger surprised everyone with the improbable statement that with agricultural and technological advances, "in ten years no child will go to bed hungry."

Kissinger's plane continued its zigzag across continents for another five or six days, eight more countries. Egypt, Saudi Arabia, Jordan, Syria, Israel, Tunisia, and Morocco.

"I started to lose track of where we'd been," Stuart said. "Or where we were headed next."

In Jerusalem, he did remember going along with Kissinger to Prime Minister Rabin's home for dinner.

"A rather modest house for a world leader," Stuart said. "I sat in the kitchen and watched Mrs. Rabin prepare dinner."

In those eight countries, Kissinger's agenda was the peace process in the Middle East, an attempt to strategize order from a chaotic situation that threatened to implode. What emerged after the slithery process of negotiating with Arab and Israeli leaders was the recognition that further American-sponsored diplomatic progress in the Middle East was at least possible. Kissinger's incremental and persistent efforts to convince the Arab states and Israel to negotiate established the groundwork for the 1978 Camp David Accords. Although his legacy is still controversial, Kissinger had the rare ability to view the world in conceptual terms and to imagine what America's place in the world might be.

As I was writing this, I asked Stuart his impressions about traveling with Kissinger. I expected to hear about the jet lag, the stress of the frenzied scurry from country to country, the excitement of seeing world leaders up close, the drama of history being made. I imagined he would have grandiose comments about the great privilege, the responsibility. That he would describe the trip as unforgettable, a once-in-a-lifetime opportunity. Instead, he simply said, "It was part of my job."

∽

Ten years later, in June of 1984 while we were living in Bonn, Germany, Stuart was asked to go on a trip with Secretary of State George

Shultz. President Reagan, at the invitation of Margaret Thatcher, was attending the G7 Economic Summit meeting in London and had requested Shultz to accompany him. In the motorcade driving to and from official functions, the Secret Service assigned Stuart to an ostentatious dark-blue Mercedes stretch limo. He was the only passenger with the driver. In front of his vehicle in the motorcade were the usual two lead cars. Behind his Mercedes was a rather ordinary American car, armored, for Schultz, followed by all the other vehicles. As the motorcade progressed down London streets, people waved at the Mercedes. It was obviously the dignitary's car in the motorcade. Stuart waved back. A rather curious arrangement, he thought.

The following year he went on an eight-day official trip that was termed Secretary Schultz's "B trip." After starting out in London, it went to Brussels and then continued on to Bonn, Berlin, Bucharest, Budapest, and Belgrade.

In Brussels, Stuart was assigned to ride in a huge and imposing silver BMW. Secretary Schultz traveled behind him in a modest vehicle. As they drove through the city, people waved at Stuart in the luxurious BMW. Schultz rode by unnoticed. Stuart figured out the scheme—the doctor was being used as a decoy.

THE DINNER PARTY

WE BOUGHT A contemporary brick and frame house with soaring interiors and floor-to-ceiling windows in Oakton, Virginia. It was a long commute to Washington for Stuart but the woodland setting ideal for our children.

We often entertained friends we had met in Brazil and Ethiopia, also on assignments in Washington. On one such evening, our guests departed at midnight. I closed the front door against blasts of icy winter wind. It had been a lively gathering, filled with reminiscences about Ethiopia where we had met the Thornes and the Milbrooks, who along with another couple had come for dinner.

The Thornes were leaving for Egypt—he would be director of the Sinai Field Mission. The Milbrooks' next assignment was Ghana. Carol and Bill, our neighbors, had fit right in with the Foreign Service couples. Bill worked for the Secret Service and Carol was a Pan Am flight attendant, a glamorous job then, when flying was still an agreeable adventure.

This well-traveled group had appreciated my rather exotic Brazilian menu. On a cold winter day, nothing is more comforting than a pot of black beans simmering on the stove, filling the kitchen with whiffs of smoked bacon, chorizo, and pork ribs with garlic and herbs. In poor Brazilian households, such a *feijoada completa* would also include pig snouts, tails, and assorted salted meats. My version omitted those cuts. This typical tropical feast, with the meats arranged on a platter surrounded by a pot of black beans, bowls of rice, and green kale, made an attractive buffet spread. *Farofa,* seasoned manioc meal, added a crunchy texture—sliced oranges, acidity and color. Caramelized custards, somewhat too rich but a tradition, ended the meal.

After the party, Stuart and I collected the glasses scattered about the living room, loaded the dishwasher, and washed the silver and china by hand. With stove and countertops spotless, we sprawled in the living room. Stuart threw a log on the still-smoldering embers in the fireplace and poured some brandy. The logs flamed up, and the brandy, fiery in the throat, radiated a glow in our cheeks. We lingered, trying to prolong the expansive mood of an enjoyable evening spent with friends.

Later upstairs, we couldn't have been sleeping long when we were awakened by loud knocking at the front door.

"Probably one of our guests." Stuart groaned as he rolled out of bed. "Somebody's left a scarf or something." Putting on a robe, he dashed downstairs.

Still groggy from the brandy, I fell asleep again.

I woke up shivering in the freezing room. Running downstairs, I was hit by an icy gust of wind. The front door was wide open.

Outside, thick snowflakes swirled. Except for a barely perceptible hiss of snow, there was silence, an ominous silence. No sign of anyone. No cars. No footprints. If there had been any, they had been obliterated by the fresh snow. I checked the garage. Our two cars were where they should be. Back inside, I closed the door. At the foot of the staircase, the dog slept.

My heart raced from a horrible premonition. Surely, Stuart would have shouted up that he was going, would have closed the door. Where could he go in his robe and slippers? In the middle of the night? He had vanished. I was certain he hadn't left of his own free will.

Still, I told myself there must be a simple explanation, except I couldn't think of what it might be. Disturbing possibilities flashed before me. Absurd thoughts orbited around the unthinkable.

Who had pounded on the door? At night? In the middle of a snowstorm?

I shuddered, not only from the cold but from a sense of dread. In a sudden panic, I ran upstairs to check on Jen and Nick. They were both asleep. Back downstairs, I paced from room to room in the dark house, afraid to turn on the lights. Someone might be prowling outside. Through the window, barely discernible contours of trees appeared distorted, branches weighed down by snow.

Whorls of anxiety knotted my stomach. I needed to do something. But what? I should call the police. But how could they get here in this storm? And what would I tell them? What could they do?

It started with a throbbing carotid artery in my neck, then the painful pressure behind my left eye—a migraine. I pressed my hands against my temples, trying to ease the sudden pain. I had trouble breathing, as if something were pressing down on me.

I should go upstairs and get my migraine medicine, get a sweater. The house was freezing. But I couldn't summon enough energy to go up. I should be doing something. But what?

Unnerved by the deep stillness in the house, I wandered back and forth. Awful scenarios flashed through my mind. I tried to push them aside, but the alarming thoughts crowded out sane and logical explanations. Had Stuart been kidnapped? But why? We were in the States now, not Brazil.

I thought of other nightmarish incidents, other nights I had been awakened feeling helpless with terror. It was that same dread

I had faced as a child sitting in a dark cellar, waiting for a bomb to explode through the roof and the walls to come down, crushing me.

I must get dressed, get in the car, and search the neighborhood. But the streets hadn't been plowed. I could get stuck somewhere. I couldn't leave the children alone in the house. I had to stay here.

A terrible thought stunned me, as if I had been struck. Was something going on that I didn't know about? Was Stuart involved in some secret activity? Why didn't he tell me?

He could be in danger. I was wasting precious time roaming around the house, grappling with unfounded suspicions. I had to get help.

I thought of Bill, our neighbor. He worked for the Secret Service and would know what to do. In the dark kitchen, I groped for the phone book in the drawer. I turned on the lights to find his number. I dialed. Drifts of snow were piling up against the sliding door.

The phone rang fifteen, twenty times. No answer.

He must be there. "Pick up the phone," I repeated over and over.

Bill and Carol had left our house to go home after the dinner party. They had to be there. There was no one else I could call. Just as I was about to hang up, Bill's half-asleep, surprised voice answered.

"Please, Bill, something's happened."

He recognized my frantic voice. "What's going on, Dag?"

I quickly told him.

"I'll be right there. Give me a minute to get my gun."

Gun? I remembered the old night guard sitting on our porch in Addis with a gun on his lap. I recalled the gut-wrenching feeling I had when Stuart hadn't returned from an emergency call in the middle of the night.

I hung up and thought I better call the police. They would ask me what was going on. What exactly could I tell them?

Through the window, I saw the beam of a flashlight swinging back and forth among the trees. It must be Bill searching the woods. As I went back into the kitchen to call the police, I heard the front door open.

It was Stuart, wet hair plastered down on his forehead. We stared at each other. He brushed snow off his shoulders, and I suddenly realized how distraught and disheveled I must look.

"Where've you been?" I asked. "You look awful."

"Our neighbor. From the old farmhouse down the road."

Overwhelmed by my relief that Stuart was safe, it took me a moment to react to what he was saying. "Knocking on our door? Why?"

"He was frantic. His kid was having convulsions."

Desperate, the neighbor had run to our house for help. Stuart raced down the road with him to reach the ailing child as quickly as possible.

"How's the boy?" I asked.

"He's fine now."

"You didn't close the door."

"I didn't? Oh, God, sorry about that."

"So, what happened? You took him to the hospital?"

"No, the convulsions had stopped by the time I got there."

Stuart had told the frantic parents to take the child to the emergency room right away and promised to check in with them in the morning. They had bundled up the child and left for the hospital a few minutes later.

"So, where've you been all this time?"

"What're you talking about?"

"You've been gone for hours. Where have you been?"

"I ran back. Rushed back—thought you might wake up and get worried. It's only been, what? Fifteen … maybe twenty minutes?"

"I thought you were gone for hours."

His minutes had been hours to me.

I thought afterwards about how the pleasant evening had skidded into something awful. How fragile the scaffolding that supported our daily lives. One piece dislodged, and everything crumbled. How for a moment, in my anxiety, I had even doubted Stuart. I had imagined he might be involved in something I didn't know about. How absurd.

My panic had warped time. I had relived exaggerated fears I had long forgotten. Irrational but undeniable. An indelible residue of old, frightening events, lodged in the subconscious, had surged up.

⌘

After eighteen months of administrative work in Washington, Stuart was waiting to hear about his next assignment. We had started to think about the impact of Foreign Service life on Jen and Nick—fragmented childhoods spent in countries abroad, separate life segments distanced from grandparents, aunts, uncles, cousins. Our small family unit was sufficient in itself, but was that enough? What did our frequent moves do to all of us? Every few years, a new home, new school for the children, new friends, new country, new language.

Yet I had become increasingly aware that Stuart loved his work overseas—running a medical unit, being responsible for the health of a close community, interacting with local doctors. He thrived on being challenged by the unexpected and the refreshing absence of a dull routine. Above all, he found it professionally rewarding to practice medicine in diverse and often difficult environments.

Stuart was lucky in that he could choose where to go on his next assignment. The medical program needed doctors in Tunisia, India, and Laos.

"What do you think?" he asked.

"Not Laos!" I said.

"How about India?"

"No, Tunisia," I said. "I want to live in Carthage."

My quick and rather frivolous answer was due to the fact that I was taking a French literature course at a local university and reading Flaubert's *Salammbô*, set in Carthage, the legendary site where Phoenician, Roman, and Byzantine civilizations once flourished. Flaubert had made Carthage come alive for me with his stunning atmospheric descriptions. It's a brilliant and exotic work that was called erotic, sadistic, and decadent when first published and was said to have been written by someone with an obsessive and neurotic mind. Nothing I had ever read had invoked such a powerful vision of an imagined place.

Of course, the final decision of going to Tunisia couldn't be based on my enthusiasm about Flaubert's book. We had to consider more practical aspects, such as a good school for our children and learning about the region Stuart would have to travel to for his work. An especially important factor in our choice of assignments was the political stability of an area.

But what would I find in Tunisia? Painters like Paul Klee and Wassily Kandinsky sought its sun-drenched landscape steeped in light. When Klee visited Tunisia, he described how "the limpid light of North Africa awakened my sense of color," and he made the sojourn the turning point in his life and art. Tunisia, a land bathed in transfiguring light. Would my eye be keen enough to perceive it?

PART FOUR

CARTHAGE

IT DIDN'T TAKE me long to discover the outdoor market in Tunis that stretched on and on for many city blocks. Early in the morning, I would wander down the narrow aisles, jostled by crowds toting vegetable-laden baskets. Among the women, many were covered head to toe by the traditional white *sefsari*. Despite the bustling activity at that early hour, I braved the crowds, as morning was the best time to find the freshest produce from local farms.

Picked at dawn in nearby orchards, oranges and lemons still held the dampness of dew. I caught a whiff of a rich earthy smell from the heaped-up carrots, potatoes, heads of cabbage no bigger than grapefruits, and purple-tinged turnips just dug from fertile plots surrounding Tunis. Strident vendors hawking eggplants, onions, and plump fennel bulbs beckoned from all sides. At a stand, leathery soil-worked hands with cracked fingertips arranged whorls of zucchini flowers on trays. A man with a wilting carnation tucked behind his ear sat cross-legged next to a brazier of hot coals. From a black teapot, he poured tea into tiny glasses lined up in a row.

Women, crouched on straw mats, plucked just-killed chickens. Stray feathers drifted about. On a table, rows of scrawny birds swarmed with flies. Usually, I bought a chicken, but that day I needed lamb. On my way home, I was going to stop at the roadside shack where marbled slabs of tender meat hung from hooks.

I searched for the stand where shriveled red peppers, strung up with twine, looped against a blue-and-white striped awning. The old woman, filigree tattoo on her chin, was setting out a basket of hot peppers. From a black clay bowl, she spooned out a large dollop of harissa for me. The spicy paste of mashed peppers, garlic, and chilies would add the obligatory kick to the couscous I was planning to prepare for friends that evening.

A Bedouin girl in a lime-green and pink blouse sold dates. Silver bracelets clinked on her thin wrist as she whisked away wasps from the oozing clusters. She offered me a date, and I bit into its sticky sweetness as I waited my turn at a table sagging from pumpkin-size squashes. With a rusty cleaver, the vendor lopped off a generous wedge of the orange squash and dropped it in my *panier*.

Farther down, a woman sat surrounded by burlap sacks of grains. With a practiced gesture of her henna-painted hands, she twisted a cone from a bit of newspaper and scooped in the hand-rolled couscous.

Here and there in the dense crowd, I spotted thin-waisted French ladies. A couple of them knelt by a crate, searching for a melon of that perfect aromatic ripeness. It amused me that they wore linen dresses and heels to the market. My attire was more casual—wraparound denim skirt over a white tennis outfit. After-wards, I was going to join friends at the Tunis Tennis Club.

Next to the melons, olives glistened in blue Nabeul pottery— black, green, some in brine, some in oil. In the morning heat, cloying smells of overly ripe melons, eviscerated chickens, and briny olives made for a queasiness-inducing mix.

Displayed on large fig leaves, prickly pears and ripe figs looked tempting. Mounds of strange, plum-sized yellow fruit were piled up next to a wicker tray with pomegranates, spilling out tiny ruby seeds. Seeing the luscious fruit felt like a vitamin surge. I strolled along the congested aisles trying to prolong this, the least complicated part of my day. Despite the din and chaos of the market, I sensed its order, its rhythm. The clamor blended into white noise. Morning light bathed and transformed colors with surreal clarity.

Mingling with the crowd, I felt that a market such as this could have been from another time, could have existed hundreds of years ago, maybe even thousands. In ancient Carthage, women could have come here to buy olives, a cook from a Roman household may have scanned the stalls for the juiciest apricots and sweetest lemons, or a young child might have been sent to buy almonds. I was overcome by an eerie sensation of time dissolving, of a connection to the ancient people who may have once walked along these aisles.

The rope handles of my loaded *paniers,* digging into the palms of my hands, jolted me back to the present. As I left the market, plucky barefoot boys followed. One, not more than four years old, tugged at my skirt impishly and offered to carry my baskets for baksheesh. The street-smart urchins, old beyond their age, grabbed the coins from my extended hand and scampered away.

Outside the tennis club, I opened the trunk of the car and reached for my tennis racquet when a man's voice startled me.

"*Mademoiselle!*"

Was he talking to me? I looked around. No one else here. Must have been calling me.

"*Mademoiselle!*" The tough-looking dark-haired man with an

unlit cigarette in the corner of his mouth approached. What did he want? I should dash into the club, I thought.

Too late. He strode toward me. *"Mademoiselle, s'il vous plait, avez-vous du feu?"*

Of course. He was only asking for a light for his cigarette. But what a deep resonating voice he had. As I fumbled in my tennis bag for matches, I realized who it was. Zorba the Greek.

He towered over me. Craggy face, thick, unkempt brows, deep lines around the mouth. I handed him matches, and he lit the cigarette, cupping the flame with a large, veined hand. Intimidated by his presence, his nearness, I lowered my gaze. Inhaling deeply, he handed back the matches and, with a *"Merci bien, mademoiselle,"* disappeared into the club.

I leaned against the car to compose myself. Anthony Quinn, as compelling in the flesh as on the screen. Maybe more so. Stuart and I had seen the movie *Zorba the Greek* at the Wheelus Theater in Tripoli, Libya, a dozen years earlier. But it was as if I hadn't just seen Quinn, but Alexis Zorba himself. The irrepressible man of the sixties film. Uninhibited and passionate, savoring each moment to the fullest.

I thought of that unforgettable scene in the film when Zorba said, "I have hundreds of things to say, but my tongue just can't manage them. So, I will dance."

He threw off his jacket and slowly rolled up his shirtsleeves. Snapping fingers, arms out, he began to dance. Slow, seductive steps. I could still hear the haunting bouzouki music. Silhouetted against the bare rocks of sun-drenched Crete, Zorba twisted and glided. Mesmerized, Stuart and I had watched Zorba dance—aware perhaps for the first time of the power of dance, the way it conveyed what words could not express. Then the rhythm accelerated, grew wilder, and

Zorba threw back his head in laughter—or more like a howl. Expressing what exactly? Rapture, the joy of living? The anguish? After the movie, Stuart and I drove back to my villa in Giorgimpopoli. Still under Zorba's spell, we put on our own bouzouki music. As if animated by Zorba's spirit, or as if we had drunk too much ouzo, we danced. Stuart rolled up his sleeves. We snapped our fingers. Arms extended at shoulder height, we danced. We had absorbed Zorba's vitality, his passion. Uninhibited, we glided and twisted in our own joyful version of his dance. Finally, exhausted, we collapsed on the floor, breathless with laughter. How alive we had felt.

Seeing Quinn in this chance meeting had, by some weird mechanism or mysterious power, unlocked the nostalgic memory of that evening. Briefly, a long-forgotten moment had surfaced. An echo of an old and intense emotion. From where had it come? A moment of encapsulated radiance had suddenly blazed up.

⁓

When in Tunis, Quinn often came to the club to work on his tennis game with the Romanian pro there.

Franco Zeffirelli was filming *Jesus of Nazareth* in Tunisia, with Quinn as Caiaphas. The eroded ravines and crackled moon-like topography of the southern part of the country were perfect settings for filming the Holy Land. Tunisia had also been an ideal set for the distant galaxies of *Star Wars*. Luke Skywalker's home on the mythical planet of Tatooine was, in fact, a dwelling in the small Berber town of Matmata, constructed underground as protection from the unforgiving desert heat. In that ochre land of bare hills and dry riverbeds, the corrugated terrain scattered with the occasional scrubby tree or lone date palm, the annual rainfall was measured in millimeters.

While Tunisia's landscape was ideal for the film industry, day-to-day living there could be stressful. Every Monday morning, four of us met at the Tennis Club, a complex of about a dozen unkempt clay courts enclosed by a chain-link fence covered by tattered green canvas sheeting. After a few sets we would chat, sipping lemonade at the little tables outside the clubhouse.

Getting together on those mornings, we shared our daily frustrations. All four of us, Kathy, Noelle, Fiona, and I, had young children in school. Our Jen was in third grade and Nick in first. We worried that the American Cooperative School had no art, music, or physical education for our kids. The school bus service was so unreliable, we often drove our children to school. Stuart was frequently away to see patients at medical units in embassies in Libya, Algeria, Morocco, and Egypt. Left alone so often with the children, I found it hard to make decisions on my own.

Kathy's family, along with many Foreign Service personnel, had just been evacuated from Beirut because of the civil war there—a traumatizing experience for her and her boys. To make matters worse, she had no idea where her household goods were and had to stay at the Amilcar Hotel until they arrived. My French friend Noelle, whose husband also frequently traveled, had begun an extramarital affair and was beginning to realize there would be consequences for her family. Our fourth player, Fiona, the wife of an officer at the British Embassy, had just arrived in Tunis. Not speaking any French at all, she found even simple chores like grocery shopping a frustrating ordeal and wasn't sure she would like living in Tunisia.

That Monday, we had just begun our second set when, in the middle of a really good rally, Fiona suddenly dropped her racquet. We stopped playing and looked to where she was pointing. Through one of the strategically torn holes in the green sheeting that covered the chain-link fence, a man's dark erect penis was thrusting through.

We stood there, shocked.

Red in the face, Fiona was the first to react. "In broad daylight. Disgusting."

Kathy didn't wait. Waving her tennis racquet, she ran toward the fencing to chase the offender away.

"The club manager needs to be told. Noelle, you go tell him," Fiona said.

Noelle laughed and showed no intention of going.

Clearly upset, Fiona wanted to leave at once. But we needed her to finish our set and persuaded her to stay. We continued to play but could no longer concentrate on the game. All of us were wondering if, after this, we would ever come back to the club.

We did go back, and once in a while it happened again. Embarrassing and annoying. But we didn't want to give up our Monday-morning tennis.

How naive we were then. When I think of it now, I truly cringe. In Tunisia, when out on the street, many women still covered themselves. And there we had been, our little group of women, wearing short tennis skirts that exposed our white thighs. Hair loose, we raced to hit balls, laughing and squealing idiotically after an especially good rally. In the sweltering heat of those late mornings, our drenched sleeveless tops clung. When we bent over to retrieve stray balls, our lacy tennis briefs (the fashion then) were revealed. Tossing the ball high into the air, preparing to hit a serve, we exposed our perspiring armpits. To Tunisian men, we were pornography.

After four months of lodgings in El Menzah V, a modern suburb of Tunis, we moved into an embassy-owned house, Villa Laetizia, on Rue Astarte in Carthage. Behind its high wall, the whitewashed Art Deco house with decorative blue grillwork was surrounded by lemon trees, plantings of hibiscus, and white geraniums. Stone paths led past an old fig tree and a mimosa that arched over the kitchen door. Even on the hottest days, the high-ceilinged, thick-walled rooms remained cool. In the garden, several large fragments of fluted Roman columns, retrieved when the foundation was dug, were daily reminders of the complex and layered heritage of Carthage.

Rue Astarte ran along the foot of Byrsa Hill, the heart of ancient Carthage, the fabled empire of Hamilcar and Hannibal. On top of the hill, there was not much left to see of the splendid city of two millennia in the past. The giant aqueduct that had once brought water from the hills of Zaghouan collapsed long ago. The sixty-foot-high wall of fortifications, enclosing Byrsa Hill, had crumbled into oblivion. Remnants of the Temple of Eshmoun lay buried under the domed nineteenth-century Cathedral of St. Louis. Among tall tufts of weeds, chunks of marble from toppled columns lay strewn underfoot.

Deep down underground, pottery chips, coins, and bits of jewelry, covered by layers of ash, were still being unearthed. One day archeologists would examine and piece together the fragments. Historians and linguists would reconstruct and interpret the finds, bringing to light the mysteries surrounding this legendary civilization that sank into obscurity.

Not far from the hill, excavated stelae with barely discernible inscriptions, painstakingly analyzed, provided clues about the deities that were once worshipped, some of them angry gods like Moloch. Unearthed urns contained remains of bones. Tiny, charred bones of infants and children. Were they the remains of child sacrifices? Scholars continue the debate.

If true, this practice is unimaginable to us. What terror and desperation could have driven the Carthaginians to such extreme measures? Could it be that when drought threatened, when nothing remained in cisterns but a stagnant puddle, they thought wrathful gods had to be appeased before they would send rain? Or if an approaching fleet of Roman warships was spotted, did they believe that only the most heartbreaking sacrifices could prevent the destruction of Carthage? It is unfathomable to us, but the Carthaginians must have had utter and unquestionable faith that the gods would look after them—but only if they sacrificed that which was most precious.

From the top of Byrsa Hill, I often looked at modern Carthage below. Among cypress trees, date palms, and garden greenery, the white houses lay scattered like sugar cubes. Our house was down there somewhere, but I could never figure out which one it was.

I thought of Salammbô, the fictional daughter of Hamilcar that Flaubert created. In his novel, Flaubert described what she might have seen as, in the evening, standing on the terrace of Hamilcar's palace, she gazed out over Carthage … *at the base of Malqua, the sailors' and dyers' quarters, fishermen's nets stretched from house to house, like gigantic bats spreading their wings.* She swayed as she inhaled and caught … *whiffs of fumes from a still burning sacrifice that drifted through bronze tiles … and the exhalations from sun-warmed walls.* In a trance, she raised her head and stared in the distance … *as the moon spread its glow upon the gulf, the mountains and upon the lake of Tunis, where amid sand banks, flamingoes formed long rosy lines, and below the cata-combs, the great salt lagoon shimmered like an immense silver coin.*

Near the coast, crumbling ruins of Roman times could still be found, but the panorama of Carthage that Salammbô observed, so poetically reconstructed by Flaubert, could only be imagined. From the top of Byrsa Hill, I could see the ancient ports in the distance, once crowded with Carthage's fabled war fleet but long since silted up. Beyond the ports, on cloudless days, the massive peaks of Bou Kornine rose up across the gulf, and the immense expanse of the Mediterranean sparkled in myriad shades of greens and blues. Only the sea and the mountain remained as they had been millennia ago.

CAIRO

ON ONE OF his routine visits to the medical unit at the American
Embassy in Egypt, Stuart asked me and the children to accompany
him. Our friend Fay invited us to stay at her spacious apartment in
Garden City, a residential section of Cairo. We had first met Fay in
Ethiopia. Twenty years younger than her husband, she was beautiful in a classic Grace Kelly way—tall, long blond hair in a French
twist. Lovely in a silk dress and heels, she joined us for breakfast
each morning. Charming and formal at the same time. An experienced and gracious hostess, Fay was attentive to our needs without
hovering, a skill that, over years, wives of senior diplomats acquire.
She planned each day of our visit.

Her husband Nick, as director of the Sinai Field Mission, spent
most of his time in this desert peninsula, cut off from the rest of
Egypt by the Suez Canal. After the Six-Day War in 1967, Israel
occupied the desolate territory, but in the constant turmoil of the
region, nothing stayed fixed for long. Even in 1976, at the time of
our visit to Cairo, boundaries were still in flux. After clearing land
mines, the United States monitored the strategic Gidi and Mitla
Passes in the Sinai. E-Systems, the Texas-based aerospace company,
built a base camp, watch stations, and sensor fields to detect unau-

thorized activities by either Israel or Egypt. Nick, in charge of such a crucial mission, rarely had time to be with Fay in Cairo.

The day after we arrived, Fay invited us to join her for a horse-back ride at the pyramids.

"But I must warn you," she said. "I go at dawn, before it gets too hot."

Before Stuart or I had a chance to think about it, Jen and our Nick were already nodding yes in excitement. Fay had her own saddle and was an experienced rider. The kids had never been on a horse. We would slow her down and probably ruin her morning ride, but she insisted we come along.

The following morning, saddled horses waited at the pyramid stables. Abdul, the Egyptian guide, helped us mount. He showed the kids how to hold the reins and told them their horses' names. When everyone was all set, he motioned for us to follow. Fay, on a fine Arabian, cantered ahead. With Abdul in the lead, his long white djellaba flapping and billowing, we followed at a modest pace.

Across soft sand, the horses trotted without a sound. As far as the horizon, nothing in front of us but a vast stretch of desert. Utter stillness. Through a thick haze, barely perceptible contours of the pyramids gradually appeared. In the half-light, they looked black, even ominous, giving the illusion they were rising from the sand. As if emerging from the depths of buried time.

The layers of silvery gauze dissipated, revealing an enormous red sun. With the sun came an intense dry heat that beat down like an oppressive weight. Every breath seared my lungs.

The first pyramid loomed ahead—no longer black but the color of sand. The horses slowed to a walk. As we approached, I could make out the individual blocks of the pyramid. Each hewn stone higher than my horse and just as wide. An uncountable number of them stacked up to a vertiginous height. The immense structure dwarfed us. Riders and horses looked like toy figures scattered in front.

I tried to imagine the crushing heaviness of each massive block of stone. Their dimensions and weight had been documented, but how to measure the grueling effort of the men who, stone by stone, constructed this astounding monument? In awe, I gazed up to the very top, and felt its grandeur press down on me. I ached with the knowledge that I, myself, would not leave anything enduring upon this earth.

The odor of the sweating horse mingled with the smell of the leather saddle. The overwhelming heat drained me, dry air parched my mouth. Up ahead, Abdul had turned his horse to head back and waved for us to follow. Impatient for the water pails in their stalls, the horses sped up. I tugged on the reins to slow down my horse, but he would not be held back. As it raced on, I grabbed the horse's mane for balance. Young Nick, fearless as usual, raced ahead. Jen too, face flushed with excitement, pigtails flying, her body moving in an easy, fluid motion with that of the horse.

～

That evening as the cook served dinner, Fay laid out plans for the following day.

"Horseback riding at the pyramids again?" Jen asked.

"No, Jen. Something else. Stuart, do you remember Jack and Lucia Mansfield?" Fay asked.

"Yes, of course." Stuart remembered Jack from his days in Libya.

Colonel Jack Mansfield, fluent in Arabic, had been the Public Affairs Officer at Wheelus Air Force Base in Libya, but Stuart had never met his wife, Lucia. Jack was now working for E-Systems in the Sinai with Nick. Lucia taught English to Queen Fatima, the wife of King Idris of Libya. The royal couple, exiled after the country's military coup in 1969, lived in Cairo.

Fay had told Lucia about our visit, and Lucia, during the English lesson, had mentioned it to Queen Fatima. When the king heard that an American doctor from Wheelus was visiting Cairo, he insisted a visit be arranged.

"The king would like a medical consultation with the American doctor," Queen Fatima had said.

"I can't imagine the king remembers me," Stuart said.

"No, in fact, he doesn't but he believes American doctors are the best in the world," Fay said. "And, by the way, the whole family is invited for tea."

Although King Idris had received all his medical care at the Wheelus hospital, Stuart had only met him once. When the king came to the hospital for dental treatment, Stuart had been asked to attend in case a medical problem arose.

The next day, a car arrived to drive us to the exiled king's residence on the outskirts of Cairo.

"Will the king be wearing a crown?" Nick asked as we got into the car.

Our laughter relieved the tension of the excitement we were feeling. Leaning back into the seat of the luxurious sedan, I tried to recall what King Idris looked like. I calculated he must be in his eighties now, and the queen probably in her sixties. It had been more than a decade since we had left Tripoli where I had only seen the king in official portraits hung in government buildings and schools. On my way into Tripoli, I had often glimpsed the royal palace, set back in formal gardens with tall flagpoles in front. I remembered the palace, a white squarish structure with a large gold dome in the center and four smaller ones, also gold, in each corner.

Palm trees on either side of the imposing entrance. Even the two guardhouses at the gate were topped with gold domes.

Arriving at the gated villa of the king's mansion, we were led past the Egyptian security guards through a foyer into a small side room with a grand piano by a window hung with dark velvet drapes.

It suddenly occurred to me that I didn't know the proper protocol for this meeting. Were we supposed to bow? Kneel? Kiss the king's hand? I wished we had discussed it with Fay. In the silent house, we waited. Jen wandered over to the grand piano. Just then King Idris entered, followed by Queen Fatima.

The king, wearing a simple long brown robe and sandals, came over and shook my hand. The simplicity of his attire surprised me. I had imagined something more regal. The handshake was a reassuring gesture that no display of royal protocol was necessary. The king appeared fragile, not much taller than I, with stooped shoulders. A white beard on a narrow face with smooth, almost transparent skin. Behind round wire-rimmed glasses, his pale blue eyes were a startling feature. He greeted us in Arabic in a high rasping voice.

Noticing Jen by the piano, he motioned to her and said something in Arabic. Queen Fatima translated that the king would like to hear her play. Jen was surprised and hesitated for a moment, wondering if she should. When we nodded our agreement, she sat down and played the first part of the Mozart piece she had just learned. The king and queen smiled.

Queen Fatima told Stuart the king had some questions about his health and would like a brief medical consultation.

While King Idris and Stuart were gone, the queen invited us to sit down. She was not veiled and wore a tailored suit. I needn't have worried about the inappropriateness of my orange sleeveless dress, although I appreciated that at the last moment, Fay had handed me a silk scarf to wrap around my bare arms. Queen Fatima, who spoke English well, inquired about our visit to Cairo and what we had seen so far. She had a charming way with the children, asking their ages and about their school.

When the king and Stuart returned, a cake was brought in and tea served. Stuart remarked that he had recently returned from Libya, where he had been on a regional medical trip to the American Embassy. As Queen Fatima translated, King Idris interrupted her. He looked upset, and his voice had an angry tone. Startled by this sudden change, the kids stopped eating their cake and looked at him with alarm.

When the king finished his long tirade, the queen calmly translated. "The king said he does not wish to hear anything about Tripoli, nor Libya."

A heavy silence settled on the room. Trying to restore the friendly atmosphere, Queen Fatima smiled and urged the children to eat more cake. I, who prided myself in being able to initiate conversations in awkward situations, couldn't think of anything to say. The queen broke the uncomfortable tension by asking the children what they liked best about Cairo. Stuart told her how excited the kids were about the felucca excursion on the Nile planned for the following day.

The mood in the room had changed, though. The king sat in stony silence, shrunken in his heavy robe. When a servant entered to clear the table, it seemed appropriate to end our visit. Stuart rose and thanked the queen for her gracious hospitality. Both the king and queen bade us good-bye with warm handshakes.

In the car on our way back to Fay's apartment, I thought about King Idris's irate outburst. Why would he not want to hear news about his country? But then after reflecting on it for a few moments, I began to understand his anger. After Libya became an independent country in 1951, the king had ruled Libya's two million citizens for nearly two decades. With the discovery of significant oil reserves, he had envisioned better opportunities for his people, who were at the time among the poorest in the world. But a military coup that put Mu'ammar Gadhafi in a leadership role ended the king's reign. Instead of being able to guide his country to prosperity, he lived in Egypt in exile.

He did not want to hear about Gadhafi and his despotic leadership. It was not what the king had planned for his country. He obviously suffered knowing what was happening to his people. No, powerless and embittered, he did not want to hear about Libya. It was too painful.

HORSEBACK RIDE

BACK IN TUNIS after our Cairo trip, Jen begged for riding lessons. I shared her enthusiasm and decided to take lessons myself. Jen's skills improved, and she joined the school's more advanced rider program. Nathalie, the French riding instructor, organized a riding excursion to a nearby beach for the dozen or so riders. She asked me to come along.

Arriving at La Soukra stables that morning, our little group was disappointed to find out that Nathalie would not be taking the group as planned. Mahmoud, a rather formal and demanding Tunisian instructor, would lead us instead. The kids groaned in protest. Mahmoud was stern, strict, sometimes even harsh. The kids were wary of him. His archaic methods of instruction included peculiar exercises, such as having the riders dismount from their horse with a backward somersault. To make the rider more skilled at falling off a horse? I wondered.

Mahmoud, with short salt-and-pepper hair, a sweater draped over his wide shoulders, strode up. Tapping a riding crop against his boot, he assigned horses to the riders. Pointing his crop at me, he said, "Alezan."

"Alezan? No, please," I said. "I've never ridden Alezan. I don't think I can handle him. How about Zarifa? "

"Why you always want slow horse? Alezan is good horse, you take him." Mahmoud's annoying swagger made it clear he was in charge. Under thick black brows, his dark gaze was unsettling. I turned away.

In single file, we rode out of the stables onto the narrow road. As the only adult along on the excursion and needing to keep an eye on the kids, I took my place at the back of the line. I immediately regretted not having insisted on riding Zarifa. As I had feared, Alezan was skittish and hard to control. He didn't want to be last in line and kept trying to overtake the other horses. Shaking his head from side to side, he pulled on the reins and took annoying sideways steps. When a dog ran out into the road, Alezan stopped so suddenly I nearly toppled off. After regaining my balance, I urged him on past the dog to catch up with the others.

Gradually, the horse settled down and accepted our position in the back. Reassured by his now steady gait, I relaxed. Jen, directly in front of me, rode as well as the older kids. She would be a fine equestrian soon if she continued riding.

The clear spring morning air refreshed. From atop my horse, I peered over high walls into the courtyards of whitewashed houses with blue nail-studded doors. We trotted past orchards of lemon trees and almond trees abloom in pink profusion. Beyond a stretch of olive groves, prickly pear hedges enclosed more modest houses.

As we neared the beach, I breathed its damp saltiness. Catching the scent, the horses sped up. I couldn't hold Alezan back. Raising myself up in the stirrups, I leaned forward and let him race with the others until the sea appeared. A perfect deep blue against a washed-out sky. We had the beach to ourselves as it was too early in the spring for bathers. Alezan slowed to a gentle canter, his stride so smooth, so even and comfortable that I almost regretted my earlier reluctance to take him.

Breathless, our little group gathered at the shore to cool off the horses. The kids loosened the reins and let the horses wade into the sea. Mahmoud saw my hesitation. Waving his crop, he motioned for me to join the others. I urged the horse to the edge of the water. "Deeper, deeper," Mahmoud shouted. "Alezan needs to cool off." Obeying, I guided Alezan into the sea. As the water rippled against the horse's flanks, he suddenly rolled. Not realizing what was happening, I lost my balance and fell into the water. I tried to get up, gasping and spitting out water, and dropped my riding crop. Ducking into the water again, I groped for it around my feet until I could grab it. With my boots filled with water, I sloshed back to the shore. My thin white cotton shirt, now soaked, had become see-through and clung to me. I plopped myself down in the sand and pulled off my riding boots to pour out the water. Mahmoud guided Alezan onto the shore. Giggling, the kids gathered around me.

"Mahmoud did it on purpose," a girl whispered in my ear.

"Alezan always rolls in the water," another said.

The kids all laughed. They obviously knew something I hadn't known.

So, Mahmoud had set me up for this.

The riders got back in their saddles. I stood up and tried to brush off the wet sand that was sticking to everything. Taking Alezan's reins, I tried to mount. The horse sensed my agitation and wouldn't keep still. He backed up and pranced about. I couldn't control him. The horse was too powerful for me. The group, already in their saddles, watched and waited.

I was furious with Mahmoud but now needed his help to mount. He watched me struggle. Then, with exaggerated ceremony, he got down from his horse and strode over to hold Alezan so I could get back into the saddle. The smug smile on Mahmoud's face was fleeting but perceptible.

As we rode back, the taste of saltwater still in my mouth, I wondered why Mahmoud had done that. But maybe for him it had just been a harmless prank. The kids had laughed. It was funny. The last thing I wanted was to let Mahmoud see how upset I had been. We led the horses back to their stalls and took off our riding hats. As our little group gathered to leave, I smiled and waved to Mahmoud.

◈

That evening, Stuart and I strolled along a busy street in Carthage. A young woman in jeans and a T-shirt, carrying a vegetable-filled *panier* hurried along in front of us. Hair loose around her shoulders. We approached a crowded café, and as the woman strode past, the old men swiveled around to watch her. They stared and shook their heads in disapproval.

As we continued on past the café, I told Stuart what had happened at the beach, how upset I had been. Then Stuart talked about his day at the medical unit. As I listened to him, my own incident faded in significance. Perhaps I was overdramatizing. Still, I wanted to know.

"Why do you suppose Mahmoud did that?" I asked.

"Why?" Stuart had a habit of repeating my questions. We walked in silence as he mulled it over.

"Hard to say. How old is Mahmoud?"

"I don't know, maybe in his fifties or so."

"Like those old guys at that café, rubbernecking the pretty girl?" He motioned with his head toward the café we had passed. "You know, they want women covered up. Certainly not riding a horse."

I nodded. "Notice, no women at the café."

"Never is."

We stepped aside to let a group of loud teenagers, puffing on cigarettes, pass us.

"I don't know why," Stuart continued. "Maybe, you know, power. A man thing."

He was probably right. Mahmoud was of the older generation of men who might be nostalgic for the past when their women stayed at home and didn't venture out in the street uncovered. But now that more and more women were abandoning not only the *sefsari* but other traditions, men no longer had the control over them they once had. I could imagine the men's frustration seeing their power erode.

Up ahead, at the supermarket, last-minute shoppers hurried out with bags full of groceries. Among them were a few men, but mostly women in casual dress, dragging tired children. There was, though, the occasional woman covered by a *sefsari*.

I watched the crowd walking down the street, and it struck me that a covered-up woman looked pretty much like any other covered-up woman, anonymous, unidentifiable. How much we revealed about ourselves by our appearance, our choice of clothing, the way we wore our hair—of who we are.

Seeing me bareheaded on a horse may have seemed disrespectful, even an affront to Mahmoud. He had demonstrated his disapproval. He was in charge, had control over me.

"You know, Stuart, Mahmoud was right about one thing."

"And what could that possibly be?"

"I'd be a better rider if I didn't always take the slowest horse in the stable."

THE BARON

EDWINA D'ERLANGER ASKED the American ambassador in Tunisia whether the embassy doctor would be kind enough to come to Sidi Bou Said to pay a house call on her ailing husband, Baron Leo d'Erlanger. Not far from Carthage, built on a cliff overlooking the Mediterranean Sea, the village of Sidi Bou Said was a spectacular site. On weekends, we met friends there to lunch on *brik* à *l'oeuf.* The deep-fried savory pastries were on the menu of most Tunisian restaurants, but at Dar Zarrouk they were memorable. As you cut into the crackling, thin flaky crust, the egg yolk oozed into the spicy ground lamb and parsley filling. From the terrace high above the sparkling water, we watched the bustling port scene far below.

I often went to a Sidi Bou Said bakery for its thick-crusted baguettes redolent with olive oil. Approaching the village, I was struck by the austere lines of its architecture, white cubes huddled on the green hill. A steep incline led to the village square. From a café, tables spilled out onto the sidewalk and neighborhood men gathered to relax. They waited for glasses of hot mint tea or tiny cups of strong coffee, savoring unhurried moments when time slowed down and daily pressures disappeared, a ritual that anchored and gave their life a pattern.

Next to the café, I would pass an old man, face shriveled and leathery, kneeling on a rush mat with a raffia tray of jasmine flowers. The thick, sweet scent followed me down the narrow centuries-old cobblestone streets, the stones worn to a slippery sheen. Behind imposing entrances, houses surrounded inner courtyards with hibiscus and oleander, or a few gnarled olive trees. In places, I heard the trickle of an invisible fountain—on a hot afternoon, a refreshing sound. To complement the white of the houses, their nail-studded doors, the latticed woodwork around windows, and the wrought-iron grillwork were painted the same shade of blue as the patterns of the decorative tiles embedded in the walls. Here and there an errant bougainvillea tumbled over a wall in a pink or purple cascade, disrupting the blue and white harmony. At the end of an alleyway, framed by high white walls, I would catch an unexpected and breathtaking glimpse of the Mediterranean.

∽

Following up on Edwina d'Erlanger's request, Stuart, with his black medical bag on the passenger seat, drove up to Sidi Bou Said to make a house call on the baron. To refer to it as a "house" call was a huge understatement, he found out.

As he turned off the main road, the roof and dome of Ennejma Ezzahra came into view. The d'Erlanger residence had been described to him as "quite a place," but he had not expected a palace. At the entrance, Edwina waited in the shade of an archway. Stuart followed her through the opulent salon, down hallways hung with portraits and landscapes in carved frames, to the ornate bedroom where, on a bed built into an alcove under a gilded dome, the baron was resting.

In his late seventies, he looked frail and complained of a dry cough and fatigue. Stuart did a thorough medical examination. When he checked the baron's ears, he saw a large buildup of wax and promised to return later with equipment to wash out his ears. The baron's hearing would improve considerably, Stuart told him.

"Oh, don't bother, young man. You know, once, because I did not hear something, I made an immense amount of money."

Startled by the confession, Stuart was curious to know more but dared not ask for an explanation.

The baron was suffering from a mild respiratory ailment—nothing serious.

◈

After the baron's recovery, Edwina invited us to tea. Arriving at the front gate, we walked through formal gardens of mountain laurel, borders of oleander, and pittosporum hedges. Between parallel rows of cypress trees, the walkway led to a terrace overlooking the sea. Bright geraniums spilled over the rims of Roman urns.

In the shade of tall trees, a table was set with dainty teacups on a white lace tablecloth. Elegant in a dove-gray linen dress and a long string of slate-colored pearls, Edwina welcomed us. She must have once been stunning. Already in her sixties, she still moved with the poise of a young dancer. The baron, a handsome man with white hair brushed back from the high forehead of his patrician face, invited us to the table.

While the butler poured tea and passed platters of dates and cucumber sandwiches, I contemplated the immense façade of the palace, blindingly white in the sun. A row of a dozen or so simple arches supported by Roman columns set off its otherwise stark architecture, its almost modern spareness. The chalk-white walls intensified the blue of carved lattices covering the windows and the iron grillwork.

"Who built this palace?" I asked, accepting a tiny honey-soaked cake from the butler.

"The baron's father, Rodolphe," Edwina said. "An extraordinary man."

Rodolphe came from a distinguished German banking family living in France. He decided not to pursue a career in the family bank and became a painter.

"He was fascinated by Arab cultures," Edwina said. "I'll show you his paintings. You will see how his passion for Arab themes is reflected in them."

At the turn of the century, seeking a warmer climate for health reasons, Rodolphe bought fifteen acres in Sidi Bou Said, designed and built Ennejma Ezzahra on land carved out of the cliffs. He transformed the barren rock into luxuriant terraced gardens.

"I'm sure he chose this site because of its history," Edwina said. "This is where Hamilcar Barca's palace once stood. Just imagine." She pointed out over the sea. "Hamilcar, in this very spot, scanning the horizon for enemy ships of the Roman Empire."

I followed Edwina's gaze past the terrace, across the bay, to the sailboats in the distance, a dazzling white against an indigo sea.

After tea, Edwina and the baron led us through a courtyard shaded by Seville orange trees. From a birdcage suspended between two columns, the warbling of two lemon-colored finches followed us as we entered the palace. I had expected the same restrained simplicity of the exterior architecture and was stunned by the grandeur before me. It was as if I had walked into Alhambra, the architectural gem of Andalusian Spain, which I once visited. With rows of marble columns and carved stucco arches on both sides, the resemblance to Alhambra was striking. Not an inch of any surface had been left unadorned.

Edwina explained that the most talented artisans in the Arab world had created the exquisite mosaics of colored glass, the carved wood paneling and beamed ceilings that glinted with gold. Just like in Alhambra, the central feature was a fountain. A narrow canal embedded in the middle of the marble floor connected the fountain to a reflecting pool outside. Water flowed along the canal with a lapping sound.

Walking across Persian carpets, ancient and threadbare, covering the marble floor, we entered a room with antique musical instruments. Exotic plucking ones similar to lutes and lyres, reed flutes and pipes, odd-looking drums. Edwina picked up an instrument that resembled a violin, but with only two strings, and pointed out a misshapen bagpipe. I tried to imagine the sounds these strange instruments could produce.

"Are you fond of Arabic music?" she asked.

"Well, yes." Stuart hesitated. "But mostly just Fairouz and Oum Kalthoum," he admitted lamely.

"The baron's father was intrigued by Arabic music," Edwina said. "Became an expert in its history."

Rodolphe had invited Arab musicians to the palace and studied their instruments. As he researched classical Arabic music, he realized how quickly it was becoming corrupted because the repertoire was not written down. Western instruments, which couldn't play the quarter-note tones, the essence of classical Arabic music, were replacing the more traditional ones like the *oud, kissar,* or *mizwad.*

"The nuanced microtonalities and melismatic melodies of Arabic music can be mesmerizing," the baron, who had been silent up to then, added rather cryptically. I had no idea what he meant but found the alliteration rather poetic.

I would later understand the baron's words. Arabic music could be mesmerizing.

At first, it was precisely those microtonalities that made the music disorienting and elusive for me, as it wasn't based on a twelve half-tone scale like Western music, but on a scale with many more tones—quarter tones and ones of even smaller intervals that create a melodic line of incredible subtlety, with a barely perceptible progression. With complex rhythmic patterns, it required careful listening and produced in me an almost trancelike state, an emotional response that was quite different from listening to Western music.

⁓⑤

The baron's health remained fragile and Stuart continued his visits. Edwina invited us for dinner.

That evening, we left our car outside the massive door that led to the palace grounds. At dusk, the white flower garden—calla lilies, roses, oleander—seemed to glow with a luminosity, as if lit from within. I inhaled the citrus scent of orange blossoms. In an eerie silence, we walked through silvery pools of moonlight with only the crunch of gravel underfoot. Across the metallic shimmer of the bay, the soot-black Mount Bou Kornine loomed, a silent witness.

From the terrace, the butler escorted us through the candlelit salon to an alcove of banquettes with faded satin cushions. Flickering candles cast distorted shadows of columns onto marble walls. Bowls of olives and fresh almonds had been set out on tables inlaid with mother-of-pearl. The butler served drinks and Edwina, in a delphinium-blue silk ensemble and white gloves, and the baron, dignified in a dark suit, joined us. For this evening, we had chosen the very finest from our own wardrobes.

Sipping sherry, I listened to the barely perceptible sound of water flowing from the fountain.

"So soothing," I said.

"The soldiers used to trip on it. No, not the water, the canal." Edwina pointed to the narrow canal in the marble floor. "You see," she went on, "Ennejma Ezzahra was occupied during the war. A dreadful time."

In a subdued voice, she explained that Sidi Bou Said was spared from bombing during World War II. But a general from Rommel's Afrika Korps had moved into the palace with his staff. When the occupiers left, the d'Erlanger family found that many of their precious possessions were gone.

Later, when the Allied troops took over Tunisia, Ennejma Ezzahra was again used to house soldiers. They were extremely careless and vandalized the palace.

"You can imagine what an enormous undertaking it was to restore everything." Edwina's voice trailed off into a long moment of painful silence. She sat there with a sad gaze, as if reliving the anguish she must have experienced at the palace's destruction.

The butler appeared to announce dinner.

Like in an Arabian Nights mise-en-scène, we entered a dining room with walls of pink marble and filigreed plasterwork. Near the domed ceiling, traceries of carved wood gleamed with gilding.

Edwina indicated our places at the round table set with gold-rimmed plates and antique silverware. The meal itself was of utmost simplicity: succulent pieces of young lamb surrounded by pumpkin, peppers, and squash in a splendid collage of orange, red, and green, served on a huge blue ceramic platter. The harissa sauce, passed separately, burned the tongue, brought tears to my eyes. Fresh figs poached in red wine followed. While strong sweet coffee in demitasse cups was served, the baron leaned over and whispered with a conspiratorial air.

"My dear, I would very much like it if you would invite me to tea one day," he said.

I promised him that I would. I didn't. I couldn't imagine inviting the baron, couldn't picture him in our house. Compared to the magical aura of his palace, tea in our living room would have been plain.

I regret it now.

Had the baron come to tea, perhaps he would have spoken about his own career. We knew of his father's brilliant achievements, yet the baron never mentioned his own distinguished career and accomplishments. I found out about them later.

Ironically, just as his father had given up the banking world to pursue the arts, the baron left behind his father's artistic realms to return to the Erlanger Bank. He became its senior partner; and in addition, served as chairman of British Airways. Ennejma Ezzahra, his father's embellished monument, conceived to please all the senses, became only an infrequent holiday destination for Edwina and the baron.

In 1994, hundreds of journalists gathered for the opening of the Channel Tunnel. One of the press releases cited that Baron Leo d'Erlanger, who had died in 1978, had specified in his will that his coffin be on the first train through the channel. The baron had served as chairman of the Channel Tunnel Company and had been a longtime supporter of the ambitious project. He had always believed that England and France would one day become linked by a tunnel—perhaps a subconscious and symbolic yearning to connect his own divergent roots in distant countries.

⁓

After three years in Tunisia, Stuart was assigned to Bangkok. I had already started making arrangements for our departure when, as I was leaving the house one afternoon, I saw the baron standing outside our gate. I apologized that I couldn't invite him in for tea because I was on my way to pick up Jen and Nick at school.

He had brought presents: a blue silk caftan and two long strands of hammered gold. One with a hand of Fatima on it—a symbol of good luck, abundance, and patience.

When I see the necklace in my jewelry chest, I think of Ennejma Ezzahra but our vivid moments there have become blurred by time.

Ennejma Ezzahra, or Star of Venus in English, has become a luminous abstraction—a palace built in equilibrium with the landscape, a place of accumulated history and dramatic events. I do remember clearly, though, the graciousness of Edwina and the baron and the strange alchemy of an exquisite evening.

KHUN YING'S HOUSE

UPON ARRIVING IN Bangkok, I was appalled by it. The trip, by way of San Francisco and Hong Kong, had been long and exhausting. From the airport, the taxi, with infernal stops and starts, crawled along the sweltering traffic-snarled streets.

Trapped in the suffocating taxi, I breathed air devoid of oxygen. Perspiration trickled down my temples. I felt like I was melting into the sticky plastic seat. Gusts of hot air from the open windows brought off-putting ripe smells I couldn't identify. Motor scooters careened wildly in and out of clogged lanes. Three-wheeled *tuk-tuks,* crammed with passengers, trailed exhaust fumes. Amid endless blocks of derelict shop houses and tangled power lines, high-rises and luxury hotels rose up in a confusing sprawl, the old haphazardly mixed with the new.

At that moment, the thought crossed my mind that it had been a horrible mistake to come to Bangkok.

Most American families lived in air-conditioned apartments in secure buildings with swimming pools, near the American Embassy and the International School Bangkok. Although a pool would have been nice for the children, apartment living didn't appeal to us.

During our search for a house, we learned that Udom Satravut, Commander in the Thai Navy, wanted to rent his home while on assignment in Washington, DC. If we decided to rent it, his wife, known as Khun Ying for the title of honor bestowed upon her by King Bhumibol, would like us to hire their gardener. Also, could we care for their two dogs during their absence?

The house, in Hua Mak, was a long ride away. When, following directions, we finally turned off the main street onto Soi Thongpras-ert, I thought we had gone astray. Small wooden houses on stilts lined the narrow street. Chickens scratched in the dirt underneath. Scraggly dogs and children scampered about. We barely avoided hit-ting an errant duck.

This can't be right, I thought, but we continued on. The number 108 on an entrance gate confirmed Khun Ying's residence. Behind a wall, we glimpsed the modern, nondescript house surrounded by thick vegetation. Thanom, the gardener, with the two dogs not far behind, greeted us with a *wai* and led us, past two reflecting pools filled with waterlilies, to the front door.

Downstairs, the living room, a study, and the dining room were small. The kitchen, bare except for a sink and a wooden cupboard whose legs stood in glasses filled with water to keep ants from crawl-ing up. No stove, just a charcoal brazier outside the kitchen door.

Upstairs, three bedrooms, a bathroom, and a string of tiny rooms used for visiting up-country relatives. In the spirit room, incense sticks and faded flower garlands surrounded a Buddha. On the shrine, a crackled celadon urn contained the ashes of Khun Ying's mother.

We rented the house. Naively, we had not taken into account that doing errands and getting the kids to afterschool activities meant I would spend many hours every day navigating Bangkok's bottlenecked streets.

After moving in, we noticed the paste marks—white dabs on windows and doors—that remained from Khun Ying's own moving-in ceremony. Following Thai custom, on an auspicious day her family had carried in their Buddha images, and monks had stretched a white thread around the house to keep out evil spirits. By candlelight, more thread was stretched from monk to monk, along which vibrations of prayers spread to protect the house and bring good luck. After kneeling and sprinkling holy water, monks applied the clusters of white blotches on each window and door. The house was blessed.

But perhaps it wasn't blessed for us. Not long after we moved in, geckos sabotaged the security system. To the delight of Jen and Nick, at dusk, a pale gray gecko often ventured from behind a picture frame, its hiding place during the day. Sticking to the wall with tiny suction disks on splayed toes, it stayed motionless. Through its nearly transparent skin, you could see the pulsating filigree of blood vessels. Suddenly, with lightning-fast thrusts of its long sticky tongue, it would catch a mosquito, an ant, or a fly. Lively at night, the geckos scurrying across the walls set off the alarm of the security system Stuart had installed. The motion detector had to remain deactivated, and we had no warning one night when an intruder scaled the wall, stole garden tools and a metal toolbox from the garage, and started to break into the house. Thanom, awakened by the noise, scared him away.

We got a refrigerator and a stove, but it was on the charcoal brazier that Somsri, our cook, prepared spicy Thai dishes. Each morning, returning from the market, cloth bags bulging, she spread out a bewildering array of devilishly hot chilies wrapped in a piece of newspaper, jars of tamarind juice and mysterious condiments, little plastic sacks of dried prawn paste, palm sugar, stalks of lemongrass, lily buds, and rambutans. From these, with a bit of chicken, pork, or crabmeat, she cooked our meals, each platter garnished with a hibiscus bloom or orchid.

In Bangkok's hothouse climate, with no cold spell to interrupt vigorous growth, our garden was a mass of lush chaos. Cutting, pruning, slashing, Thanom had a full-time job keeping plants from encroaching. Bamboo threatened to cover one side of the house and already partly blocked the back gate, which led to a path along a rice paddy to a *klong*. In its muddy waters, women and children bathed as long-tailed boats sped by.

With giant foliage of elephant plants swaying near red spikes of ginger flowers and clumps of banana plants, it felt like we were living in a jungle. Palm tree fronds brushed against windowpanes. After heavy rains, a pond would form under the mango tree.

In the evening, from outside the steamy dining room with its sea-grass rug and wood-louvered windows, came the myriad sounds of tropical nights. Often the peculiar call of the nocturnal tokay lizard echoed from high up in a tree.

∾

Neither Thanom nor Somsri spoke a word of English. We communicated by hand gestures and mime. Fortunately, they both had an innate sense of what needed to be done but my lack of even the most basic Thai was frustrating. I hoped that knowing a bit of the language would also help me better understand the culture, so I enrolled in a Thai-language class at the American University. I quickly discovered that the language was beyond difficult and impossible to master in just a couple of years. The writing runs from left to right, but that's where any similarity to English ends. As if an alphabet of forty-four consonants and thirty vowel sounds was not challenging enough, when written, there are no spaces between words and no punctuation. However, the biggest nightmare was that Thai is a tonal language with five different tones. Changing the tone of a word completely changes its meaning.

I did learn that even in English, conversations with Thais could be tricky, for words themselves played only a minor part in a dialogue. Context and body language conveyed more meaning than words. This always left me wondering what was being read into my facial expressions, my posture, or even the position of my hands. And so easy to lose face by displaying any emotion. Despite what you may be feeling, you were expected to show only positive feelings. Conflicts or disagreements had to be resolved with a smile.

When the American nurse at the medical unit was transferred to South America, we promised to care for her two miniature dachshunds until she got settled at her new post. Nitnoy's sweet disposition contrasted sharply with Sonny's aggressiveness. He growled when we tried to pick him up, and was happiest in the garden chasing lizards.

After harvest, the nearby rice paddies were set on fire and smoldered for days. Not dissipating in the humid air, the smoke settled, forming a thick cloud. To get away from the irritating fumes, Stuart suggested catching a flight to Chiang Mai for a few days, perhaps visit a hill tribe village in the cool mountains in the north. Tribes still lived in isolated villages along forest-covered hills where they cultivated opium poppies.

A few miles north of Chiang Mai, we trudged up a hillside to wander among the earth-colored thatched huts. Along the path, children waved and ran to greet us. Girls wearing hammered silver necklaces lined up to be photographed. A bare-bottomed toddler with a boar's tusk necklace squeezed in between them. I reached out to pat his head but quickly pulled back, remembering that Thais disliked having their heads touched. To them, the head was sacred.

Women went about their daily tasks. One woman, a baby slung on her back, looped out yards of indigo-dyed cloth to dry along bamboo poles while a pig scavenged behind her hut. An older girl with a head ornament of silver coins dipped a gourd into a hollowed-out tree trunk, scooping out rainwater. Her necklaces and anklets of bells jangled as she walked. Using round flat baskets, women winnowed rice. All around us, hills and forests. Behind the nearest hills, more hills, like giant blue waves of an ocean. I breathed in the cool air and realized it had been a long time since I had inhaled so deeply. For a moment, I envied this simple way of life, the tranquility. Rush mats, baskets, earthen jars—nothing that was not handmade, nothing that was not useful.

༅

Nick and Stuart in Chiang Mai, 1979.

Back in Chiang Mai, a few days was not enough to visit the hundreds of temples with their massive carved doors, gilded façades, and gorgeous murals. Taking off our shoes, we stepped into the bluish haze from burning incense that wafted around immense golden Buddhas. The sharp aroma of the incense mingled with the sweet muskiness of overripe fruit and wilting orchids left as offerings. Silence—except the sound of bare feet on stone, the occasional silvery tinkle of stupa bells, the muted chanting of monks.

Orange robes draped across thin shoulders, head and eyebrows shaved, barefoot monks radiated a calmness that struck me. At lectures on Theravada Buddhism, I had learned that through meditation and an ascetic regimen, monks achieved detachment from daily concerns. Their serenity came from the knowledge that everything in this world was connected and interrelated, even at death.

That existence on this earth was a fluid state, like water flowing in a river. To try to control it—a futile illusion. At funerals, in a lovely ceremony, a white thread was extended to the coffin so that prayers and merit could pass from the living to the deceased.

Before leaving Chiang Mai, we bought a decorative piece salvaged from an ancient temple. Even teak, the durable wood, eventually decomposed and temples collapsed. Their carved fragments were sold in shops nearby. Our five-foot-high weathered wooden *naga* head had once adorned the roof of an ancient temple and had the clean lines of a Brancusi sculpture. The stylized carving of a cobra poised to strike is a Buddhist symbol that links the earth to the heavens and is believed to ward off evil.

When we returned to Bangkok, the monsoon season had started with torrential downpours that flooded the poorly draining streets. Shoes in hand, people waded through calf-deep water.

Arriving home, we were relieved to see that the smoke from the burning fields was gone. Our pond had filled up. At the entrance gate, solemn-faced Thanom awaited us, carrying Sonny. Ten-year-old Nick ran to greet the dog. Sonny was dead. Right away, Nick noticed the two tiny puncture holes on Sonny's neck—a snake's fangs. Apparently, Sonny had been too aggressive with a venomous one.

That evening after dinner, I heard Somsri's shouts outside. I ran to see. There on the wet pavement near the kitchen door was a cobra. Hood flared, ready to strike. Fleeing the burning rice paddy, it had taken refuge in our garden. I quickly ran back inside. A few moments later, Thanom appeared with the limp length of the cobra dangling from his arm. He must have had misgivings killing it, for Thais believed that harming a snake brought bad luck. I shuddered at the thought that the cobra had been in our garden. Nick often waded into the shallow pond to float his yellow wooden boat.

HO CHI MINH CITY

ABOUT A YEAR after we arrived in Bangkok, Stuart received a cable from the State Department requesting him to go to Vietnam.

"They tell me I'll be the first official American to go to Saigon since the war ended," Stuart said. "Of course, it's now Ho Chi Minh City."

"Why you?" I asked. "Maybe the political officer should go, or the ambassador."

"It's got to do with medical examinations."

In order to get a visa to the United States, the Vietnamese needed to pass a medical exam and prove they didn't have certain diseases, like tuberculosis. By 1979, there was a huge backlog of applicants waiting for visas because the Vietnamese government didn't have the resources to do the diagnostic screening tests required by U.S. immigration authorities. Stuart's assignment was to find out why the medical examinations were delaying the issuing of visas and how the process could be speeded up.

"How do you feel about going?" I asked him.

"I've no clue what to expect. Might be interesting, though."

"When are you leaving?"

"As soon as I get a visa."

"What's the rush?"

"It's the piracy issue."

Since the Vietnamese couldn't get visas and leave legally, large numbers of them were leaving as "boat people," escaping in dangerous, rickety vessels that sometimes capsized. If they were lucky and made it to shore, they ended up in refugee camps in Hong Kong, Thailand, Malaysia, or the Philippines. Frequently, the boats were attacked by Thai pirates on the South China Sea or on tiny isolated islands where the boats washed up. The overcrowded boats were easy targets for the ruthless pirates, who knew that the Vietnamese often carried gold from selling their possessions.

Stuart's visa came quickly.

"The visa is for just one week," he told me. "So, I'll be back in a week, if not sooner."

The week dragged for me. I was worried. It seemed like a weird assignment. The United States had no diplomatic relations with Vietnam. Was it safe to go?

Stuart did return in a week. That evening we sat down for dinner, and Somsri had prepared green curry over jasmine rice, a dish she knew he liked. There was also chicken with cashew nuts and a glass noodle dish that both Nick and Jen loved. A shredded green papaya salad with dried shrimp and crushed peanuts was something she had not served before. The curry was spicy, as always, but not spicy enough for me. I craved the saltiness of the nam pla sauce with searing-hot green chilies added to it. The kids hated the smell of nam pla, so Somsri put the little bowl of it next to my plate, and I could dribble little spoonfuls.

I was anxious to hear about Ho Chi Minh City. But first Nick wanted to tell his dad about the blue and green uniforms his softball team was getting. Jen waited her turn to ask if she could go to the riding camp in Kanchanaburi.

"Where's that?" Nick asked.

"I don't know. But I'd like to go," Jen said.

"Kanchanaburi is near the Burmese border," Stuart said. "Must be a hundred miles from Bangkok. Let's talk about it tomorrow, Jen."

After mangoes with sticky rice, the kids went upstairs. We lingered, and I heard about Stuart's visit.

He had taken the weekly Thursday Air France Boeing 747 flight, which originated in Paris, stopped in Bangkok to pick up passengers, and continued on to Ho Chi Min City. On the nearly empty plane, he met two Canadians with similar missions in Vietnam—a physician and an immigration officer from the Canadian Embassy in Singapore. When they landed, Stuart was met by a Vietnamese official who handled the red tape, and by Hedi, the Algerian representative of UNHCR, the UN refugee agency. He was driven to the Doc Lap Hotel in the downtown section.

"There were these green plastic letters of the hotel's new name tacked to the façade," Stuart said, "but I could see traces of old lettering, like pentimenti, of the Caravelle Hotel."

"Where the wartime journalists stayed?" I asked.

"The same one."

The Vietnamese escort told Stuart that officials from the Ministry of Health would be contacting him with instructions. Later that day, Hedi briefed Stuart about life in the city and arranged a visit to the main hospital—the Cho Ray Hospital—in an old colonial building sadly lacking even the most basic equipment, medicines, and supplies. The two Canadians came along to the hospital, and the four of them spent a lot of time together after that.

"Days passed and no word from the Vietnamese officials." Stuart continued. "I spent my days wandering around the city."

He noticed the beautiful colonial buildings marred by patches of greenish discoloration that had spread over the walls like mold.

The boulevards were crowded with bicycles and scooters but very few cars. Store windows strangely bare, sidewalks unkempt and cracking. Groups of schoolchildren in neat school uniforms marching in disciplined rows. Women carrying coconuts and unidentifiable vegetables—a long pole across the shoulders with a basket hanging from each end. Having to balance the ungainly loads forced them to walk with odd mincing steps. Grim street kids selling American cigarettes—not the whole pack, just individual cigarettes.

"Hedi told me not to go to Cholon, the crowded Chinese section. Too dangerous."

Somsri came in to clear the dinner dishes, and Stuart stopped for a moment. When the table had been cleared, he continued.

"Days passed and no one contacted me. I was getting worried."

"Why didn't you contact them?"

"I'd been told not to contact anyone—to wait."

As Stuart waited, he explored different parts of the city. The two Canadians, Hedi, and he went to the coastal town of Vũng Tàu and walked along the beach, past small wooden fishing boats that had been dragged up on the sand. They had lunch in a thatched hut—four freshly caught mackerel lying in a basket by the door became their meal—simple fare. They saw the offshore oil rigs. Hedi explained that with the aid of Italians and other Europeans, the rigs were once again producing oil.

"The French Consul General invited me to lunch. I had to struggle with my French. God, I hate that. They wanted to know all about our upcoming presidential election."

The Air France manager and his Hanoi-born wife invited Stuart to their home. There were never many passengers on the weekly flights from Paris, but apparently, the cargo more than made up for any lack of passengers. The Frenchman pointed to the ripened cheeses, fine wines, platters of charcuterie on the sideboard in the dining room from which they had been served. Part of the cargo from France, he explained.

Hedi arranged a dinner for Stuart and the two Canadians at a small restaurant in a private colonial residence—La Bibliotheque—run by a former professor and his wife. Dinner was served in their library. Afterwards, they all went to the thieves' market.

"Oh, almost forgot," Stuart said. "Be right back. Want to say good night to the kids."

I went to the kitchen for more wine and ice. In Bangkok's heat, we had adopted the habit of diluting the Australian white wine with ice. Somsri had finished the dishes and retired to her room in the back.

I turned off the window air conditioner in the dining room and opened the wood louvered windows. Breathing in the hot steamy night air heavy with a wet-leaf smell, I listened to the whirring high-frequency insect sounds outside.

Stuart returned and handed me a small parcel wrapped in yellowing newspaper. "I got it at the market."

I unwrapped the antique blue and white porcelain vase, its globular base just large enough to fit in the palm of my hand. The blue decoration was a stylized phoenix in flight.

"It's exquisite."

"At the market, Hedi's wife bargained, or rather haggled, over it. So embarrassing," Stuart said. "I paid all of ten dollars for it."

Stuart continued to wait for word from the Vietnamese. Over the weekend, he wandered the shady paths of Tao Dan Park, where local people went for their morning exercise. He slurped pho at a street food stall. On a busy street, women wearing conical hats made from bamboo shouted for him to buy one of their freshly baked baguettes stacked on trays. He whiled away the evenings sipping cold beer with his new Canadian colleagues in a rooftop bar overlooking the city.

"On Monday, still no word from them." Stuart said. "So infuriating, all this waiting. Only two days left before my visa expired. I couldn't just leave without getting anything done. What a waste."

"But there was nothing you could do," I said.

"Finally. On Tuesday, they contacted me."

Stuart was driven back to the Cho Ray Hospital. Six Vietnamese officials, all dressed in dark trousers and crisp white short-sleeved shirts, almost like a uniform, stood as he entered the conference room.

"I'm not that tall but I towered over the Vietnamese. Very thin, black hair combed straight back. We sat around a huge table. One of the officials, in pretty good English, explained the visa problems."

The Vietnamese government wanted to comply with U.S. immigration requirements. They were concerned that the delays were causing more tragedies. But they did not have what they needed to do the medical screening of the visa applicants for diseases that might disqualify them from getting visas. Once diagnosed, the positive TB cases had to be treated. After treatment, new X-rays had to be presented, proving they were no longer contagious before the visa application could go forward. The whole immigration process was pretty much at a standstill for lack of equipment and supplies.

"What were you supposed to do about it?" I asked.

Stuart had been instructed by the State Department to find out what was causing the delays and what was needed.

"I assured them that the U.S. would send whatever was required. They seemed pleased."

The men nodded in gratitude. They said they needed time to work out a plan to itemize their requirements and asked Stuart to return to the hospital the following day.

"Getting close to your visa expiring," I said.

"It was tight. I had to be out of the country by Thursday."

On Wednesday, when Stuart returned to the hospital, the Vietnamese officials looked haggard. They had apparently spent the whole night figuring out what to request from the United States. Stuart had no idea what he was authorized to promise them. They handed him a long typewritten list of diagnostic materials and medication for treatment of TB—X-ray machines and film, chemical supplies, slides, drugs for tuberculosis, bacteriological stains, sputum containers, and on and on. The items seemed perfectly reasonable.

"When I finished looking at the list, I told them that I was confident that the U.S. government was prepared to provide the requested assistance."

The officials conferred among themselves for a few minutes. The room became silent. Finally, one of the Vietnamese spoke, struggling with his English, saying there was another item needed in order to carry out the program.

"I waited to find out what they had forgotten to put on the list. 'A helicopter,' the official said."

Stuart shook his head. "I couldn't believe it. Trying not to show my amusement at this surprising and absurd request, I told them to put it on the list and I would see what I could do."

Not long after the visit, the requested supplies were sent to Vietnam. Stuart's talks with the Vietnamese government helped lay the foundation of what would eventually be called the Orderly Departure Program, part of a UN initiative to have people leave Vietnam with visas in their hands, legally, rather than escaping on boats. Ultimately, half a million refugees were able to get visas to the United States.

"But," Stuart told me later, "I doubt if a helicopter was provided."

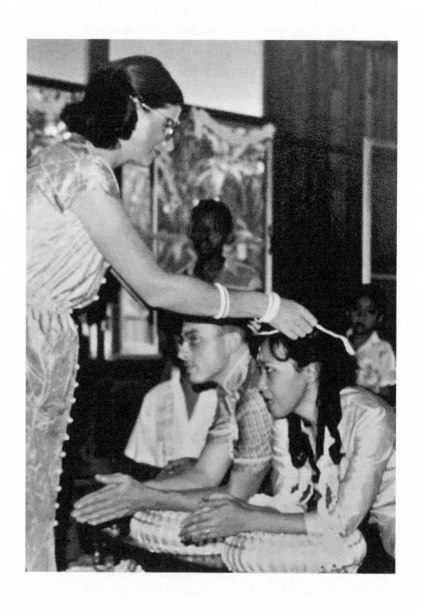

WHITE THREAD CEREMONY

ON LONG WEEKENDS, we often headed for the coast. Only a two-hour drive away was Pattaya, the crowded sea resort of palm-fringed beaches and luxurious air-conditioned hotels. The lively neon-lit night scene promised sequined dancers in gaudy nightclubs. Bars touting "beer and sexy lady show" upheld its reputation as a city of sleaze—a magnet for European package tours. Sunburned, sweating tourists swilling beer shuffled along the beach. Deafening motorboats and Jet Skis skimmed along.

Preferring a more tranquil setting, we usually bypassed Pattaya and continued farther south to Wang Kaew, not far from the Cambodian border, where we rented a small wooden house near a pristine shoreline.

Past Pattaya, the eye-cleansing citrus-green patchwork of rice fields stretched for miles on both sides. In a fishing village, shrimp drying on a wharf formed rosy carpets. As we approached Rayong, an unpleasant rotting smell announced its cottage industry of nam pla, the ubiquitous Thai fish sauce, extracted from barrels of decomposing salted fish.

That last stretch eastward toward Cambodia always brought chilling thoughts and a sense of dread in me. Just the previous week, I had experienced that same disturbing feeling when Stuart came home one evening and told me about the gray boxes with rope handles that had been delivered to the embassy medical unit.

"The size of a breadbox," he said.

They contained the unidentified remains of American soldiers who died in Vietnam. Even though the war had ended in 1975, several years earlier, remains of soldiers were still being stored until the military could transport them back to the United States.

"Why in the medical unit?" I had asked.

"We've got the only cold storage at the embassy. For medical supplies."

That was a reminder of a different war, but here so close to Cambodia, I couldn't help but think of what was happening in that country, what lay beyond the border. Pol Pot of the Khmer Rouge had driven most of the population from their city homes and forced them to work in the fields in the countryside. Press photos of Pol Pot's killing fields, with gruesome piles of skulls, were too ghastly to forget.

Cocooned in my own safe life, I felt appalled when I read about the tragic events. I couldn't imagine such atrocities. Numb from a mixture of guilt and helplessness, I was afraid of becoming immune to the violence and chaos of such nightmares. It was as if this brutality were taking place far away, perhaps on another planet, not a mere fifty miles away. As if these horrors that were causing so much suffering had taken place during some long-ago dark and barbaric era, not occurring now on this beautiful sunny day when we were on our way to the beach.

That weekend in Wang Kaew would turn out to be our last one there. Skittering, squabbling monkeys in the trees just outside the window of our beach house woke me at dawn. Even with the fan turned on full blast, the heat was oppressive. Getting up from damp sheets, I put on a bikini and hurried to follow Nick and Jen, already running along the path to the dock. Arms full of beach towels and a blanket, I trailed behind Stuart, juggling our picnic hamper and snorkeling gear. My white cotton shirt, drenched, clung annoyingly to my back.

On the dock in the evening, a humble seaside restaurant prepared spicy seafood on small charcoal braziers. That morning, the tables and chairs were stacked away, braziers filled with cold ashes. Only faint smells of fried squid, ginger, and garlic still hovered.

The fishing boat tied to the dock waited to take us to an uninhabited island. Two painfully thin barefoot men greeted us with a *wai*. The boat, its turquoise paint flaking, was filled with wet nets in tangles. Plastic buckets in the hull rolled from side to side as we stepped aboard. The boat skimmed along, and a breeze lifted the torpor of the morning. I inhaled the sea-fresh fish smell and listened to the soothing lap of waves against the boat. From time to time, a silver flying fish arched over the calm surface, then quickly disappeared into glassy depths.

Eventually, a row of palm trees came into view. Beyond the curve of the beach, gnarled roots twisted through dense vegetation. Holding the picnic hamper, snorkeling gear, towels, and blanket above our heads, we splashed through the sparkling waist-high water toward the shore. The boat would return for us in late afternoon.

On a dazzling expanse of white sand, in a shaded patch under coconut palms, we spread the blanket. The engine whir gradually diminished as the boat sped away. Only the rustle of palm fronds overhead broke the silence.

I swam far out in the transparent warm water, and the noisy chaos of Bangkok seemed far away. As I absorbed the languid rhythm of the day, accumulated anxieties began to dissolve.

Walking along the beach later, I picked up shells, mostly fragments with the lustrous outer part worn away. What remained were perfectly formed miniature coils, worn down by water, abraded by sand. Eventually, the tiny inner helixes that I held in my hand would also wear away and disappear.

Stretched out on the blanket, I half dozed. Soft breezes dispersed the heaviness of the afternoon. I didn't know how much time had gone by, but when I sat up, far in the distance and barely visible in the glare of the shimmering sea, a boat appeared.

"Why are they back for us already?" I asked.

"No idea." Stuart shrugged. Sitting a few feet away on the trunk of a fallen tree, he traced patterns in the sand with a palm frond. I watched the boat.

"That's not our boat," I said.

Stuart looked up. "No, ours isn't black."

The boat approached. Near the shore, an anchor was tossed out. Four men, then three more, followed by a couple stragglers—nine men waded onto our beach. Some of them crouched in the sand, others squatted on their heels. They were quarreling. What language was it? Could be Thai. Maybe Vietnamese or even Khmer. Were those languages tonal too?

"Who are they? Why have they stopped here?" I asked.

One of the men spotted us and pointed in our direction. They all turned to look.

A terrifying thought occurred to me. "Are they Thai pirates?"

From the look on his face, I could see Stuart was wondering the same thing. Every week, the *Bangkok Post* carried stories about Thai pirates, destitute fishermen turned to piracy, who attacked boat people fleeing Vietnam in makeshift boats. The pirates robbed the poor people of the money and valuables they often carried. I had read of instances when, in senseless brutality, they threw men and children overboard and raped women.

"What if they are pirates?" I said.

I suddenly felt cold. Our fishing boat wouldn't return for hours. I watched the strange wiry men in dark shirts. What were they doing here?

As if in a surreal dream, I saw Nick and Jen near the water's edge. Stooping down, Nick examined a jellyfish washed up on the beach. He prodded its transparent gelatinous roundness, lifting the inert tentacles with a stick. Jen was dropping shells into a plastic cup.

The men turned again and watched us. They noticed our kids. Stuart dropped the palm frond.

My stomach churned. How incredibly stupid it was to come to this island, I thought.

One of the men lit a cigarette. I smelled the smoke. They stopped talking.

Shallow waves washed up on the beach in a rhythmic swoosh. It occurred to me that no one would ever find out what happened to us.

Jen walked over to look at Nick's jellyfish. Stuart sat frozen on the tree trunk. I was trying not to move, not to breathe. I had the irrational thought that my slightest movement could trigger something.

One of the men stood up, picked up a coconut, and tossed it far into the sea. He turned around and said something to the other men. They all laughed.

The kids must be getting sunburned, I thought. I should tell them to put on their T-shirts, but I couldn't move. I sat paralyzed with my arms locked tight around my drawn-up knees. My heart was pounding. It throbbed in my temples.

The men lay sprawled in the sand.

Nick and Jen looked up and noticed the men. With worried looks on their faces, they came toward us, leaving pails and shovels behind.

The men got up, brushing sand off their clothing. Overhead, a gull hovered and emitted a long screech—like a warning. The tightness in my throat hurt.

A tiny crab scurried across the sand near the blanket. The men watched us. Then, one by one, they waded into the water. Moments later, they were at the boat clambering aboard. I saw the anchor being lifted. Slowly, the boat departed in the direction from which it came. We watched it recede and disappear.

By late afternoon the sky clouded over, turning the water a neutral gray, choppy. After what seemed like endless hours, our turquoise boat appeared. Sandy, sunburned, and salty, we scrambled to gather up our blanket, scattered masks, and flippers and splashed through the water. The fishermen must have wondered why such a hurry.

The flying fish were gone. A red sun, near the horizon, bled its reflections into the opaque water. The afternoon heat still persisted, but I wrapped myself in the blanket. My mind continued to conjure up dreadful scenes of what might have happened.

Often after that, when I remembered the men, my heart would pound again. I would visualize them crouching in the white sand, and my imagination distorted the figures. Their contours would dissolve and reform so that, rather than men, they became huge vulture-like shapes that cast elongated shadows. In stony silence, perfectly still, they waited. A strange scene, yet somehow familiar. Panic would grip me, and it would be amplified, become more crushing than what I had felt that day on the beach.

༄

I took part in a white thread ceremony. Porntip, the receptionist at the embassy medical unit, invited me to be the guest of honor at her simple wedding held in her home. The bride in a long jade-green silk dress and the groom, both with fragrant jasmine garlands draped around their necks, kneeled with elbows on embroidered cushions, hands in a *wai*. After the monks' blessings, I, as honored guest, removed the twin loops of white thread that had been placed on their heads. The thread, a symbol of connectivity, not only joined the couple but linked them to everything around them, connected them to a larger whole.

As I held the thread in my hands, trying to imagine a spark of mystical current flowing through it, I became aware of an absence of connecting threads in my own life. Or if they had ever been there, I had severed them time and time again. Perhaps my thread resembled more the fine filament that a silkworm secretes. Rather than connecting, it isolates. In an uninterrupted circular motion, the silkworm spins its mile-long length of silk around itself. Around and around, until it forms a protective cocoon.

⮝

Our two years in Bangkok passed quickly. In this city, hidden within a carapace of ugliness, unexpected delights had appeared in unexpected places.

Klongs provided tranquil boat trips. At edges of canals, from the murky brown water, among dense growths of leaves, pure white lotus blossoms rose atop long stalks. Touched by the sun's rays, the tight buds slowly unfurled, petal by petal.

So, bit by bit, the treasures of Thailand revealed themselves to me. The seemingly contradictory concepts of connectivity and detachment. The charm of its strange juxtapositions.

Along a congested road, a giant gilded Buddha suddenly looms on a hill. Sitting on a busy sidewalk under a garish movie billboard, an old woman strings jasmine garlands. Past the skyline, orange and green-tiled temple roofs glitter in the sunlight. Even the haze of the city smog can't dim the dazzle of the golden spires of the palace grounds. Smiling schoolgirls in immaculate white blouses and navy-blue skirts march along in pairs. In markets, sprays of orchids sit next to dried squid. Unidentifiable fruits spiral in floral patterns alongside brooms, exquisitely crafted. At night, streetlights transform Bangkok into quite a different place. People stroll, lingering at food carts for bowls of rice noodles and sweets wrapped in banana leaves.

When it came time to leave Thailand, I had the sense that its mystery had not yet been revealed to me. That I had missed the essence of it. Had I penetrated its meaning, it could have changed my life. Perhaps imperceptibly, it had already changed—I just could not yet know it.

NAIROBI

IN THE DARK, there was no panoramic view of the hills or the lay of the land. The plane began its descent. Far below, the light-strewn carpet was Nairobi at night, where Stuart and I would spend the next four years. With us was Jen, taking a semester off from college. After the fatiguing arrival procedures, we emerged into the red haze of dawn. An embassy van waited. As we drove along the airport road, the Kenyan driver pointed to a forested area on the left, the Nairobi National Park. In faultless English, he explained that the game reserve, enclosed on the city side, opened up on the south so that wildlife could wander freely across the Athi Plains. With a tilt of his head in the opposite direction, he indicated the distant cluster of white high-rise buildings of Nairobi. The downtown skyscrapers had sprung up in less than two decades, he told us. It occurred to me that it might take less time than that before Nairobi sprawled over the open space and drove out its wildlife heritage.

Beyond the downtown grid of streets, the congested roads branched haphazardly. Even at this early hour, the sun's glare dispersed the morning's freshness. Crowds hurried alongside frenzied traffic. Cars passed in a reckless manner, barely avoiding oncoming vehicles. I had the disorienting illusion of being in a mirror-image world. The insane traffic on the left side of the road, British style, felt sickeningly wrong. Overloaded trucks looked about to overturn.

We passed modest concrete-block houses, protected by iron grillwork on every window. Churned up from the dry clay soil, red dust hovered. Here and there along the road, a jacaranda tree bloomed, its lavender blossoms almost lurid in this setting.

Nairobi's streets contrasted, in a disheartening way, with those of Vienna, where—steeped in culture—we had just spent three years. Proud of their grand heritage, Austrians have preserved historic Vienna. Its copper domes, gothic spires, and baroque façades link it to a past that anchors and defines it. Grand gold-leafed palaces line the wide boulevards of this nostalgia-filled city on the Danube. Formal gardens of precise hedges and meticulous flowerbeds in harmonious arabesques reflect a culture that values decorative flourishes.

In Vienna, above all, a passion for order reigns.

In the summer, we had wandered in the shaded parks, studded with monuments to Strauss, Mozart, and Schubert—pedestaled icons of Vienna's gilded age. Like the Viennese, on Sunday afternoons we strolled along dappled paths in the ancient woods surrounding the city. In vineyards on nearby hills, sitting at long wooden tables under grapevine-trailing arbors, we sampled the latest vintage of their crisp white wines.

~

The driver took us to the house just off Waiyaki Way where the previous embassy doctor had lived—spacious and well-built, we had been told. As we pulled up in front, I saw that the large nondescript house was untouched by any trace of charm. The only whimsical, but at the same time distracting, detail was the grillwork on the windows—little iron circles welded together, painted white. Inside, too much standard-issue embassy furniture cluttered the rooms. I hadn't expected the crystal chandeliers and parquet floors we had in Vienna, but this house was dismal.

Wearing an immaculate white shirt, tan slacks, and heavy black boots, Maurice, the Kenyan cook, greeted us. A tall, handsome man with a square jaw and chiseled features. With his muscular build, he seemed to fill the room. In perfect English, he instructed that his name was pronounced *Morris*, in British fashion. He asked us to hire him. I thought of graceful Somsri, our cook in Bangkok, who spoke not a single word of English. When she had come looking for a job, I had hired her simply because of the red hibiscus flower in her long black hair. Going about her chores barefoot, she had walked through the house without a sound, invisible.

We hired Maurice and moved into the house on Waiyaki Way. It was the main road to the Ugandan border, and the rumble of diesel trucks could be heard day and night. With no trash pickup service in the area, people in nearby houses burned their garbage. The acrid stench lingered. There were days when we had no phone, no power, and no water. We decided to look for a house in another part of the city with fewer utility disruptions.

Stuart started work at the medical unit in the American Embassy, a five-story building in downtown Nairobi. A decade later, in July of 1998, truck-bomb explosions would crumble it into a pile of rubble, kill more than two hundred people, and injure thousands more, many of them in adjacent buildings or walking in the street. Investigations would link the attack to the Egyptian Islamic Jihad and Osama bin Laden. Even in 1987, when we arrived, there were strict security measures in place.

Jen and I went to the orientation meeting for newly arrived

embassy families. Before we could drive into the basement parking area, security guards searched our car. Later, seated in the embassy conference room, we listened to the security officer's unsettling presentation.

The downtown area, especially at night, was to be visited with caution. Recently a young American woman's five-year-old son had been grabbed from her side as she was leaving the Hilton Hotel. Our house would be provided with a day guard and another one for the night shift. We needed to create a "safe" room in the house where we could lock ourselves in during a robbery. Since telephones were frequently out of order, a two-way radio would be installed in our home for emergencies. If involved in an accident, we should drive away quickly from the scene and report the accident to the embassy. If a Kenyan was injured, there could be violence. Jen and I left the meeting a little shaken.

Things were not going smoothly at the medical unit. The last embassy doctor had traveled a great deal and had relied on Suzie, the contract nurse, to run the clinic. When Stuart arrived, she was not about to relinquish control. Instead of a nurse's uniform, she wore a white doctor's coat with a stethoscope draped around her neck. Conway Twitty and Dolly Parton were being piped into the waiting room. Stuart would have preferred Telemann and Purcell.

Suzie often invited us to gatherings at her home. Witty and pretty, with curly blond hair and an easy laugh, she was the life of the party. A flirt. She served hot chili and cold beer while in the background, country-western music twanged. After dinner, guests crowded into the living room for videos of football games. These simulated tailgate parties, a slice of Americana, seemed more alien to us than dinners at the homes of Indian doctors, who frequently invited us.

Evenings in the Indian doctors' homes began with generous

tumblers of Scotch, a luxury item in Kenya, served to honor us. In the kitchen, wives prepared elaborate dishes with pungent aromas. Often it was nearing midnight when they finally emerged in a procession of gold-flecked silk saris, jangling bracelets, red dots on their foreheads, carrying plates of pakoras, dals, tandooris, and steaming bowls of white rice. Serving after serving, our plates were mounded. We continued eating late into the night, for it was impolite to refuse a host's generosity.

✑

After a couple of months' search, we found a smaller house on a quiet road in the residential area of Runda. The plumbing needed to be fixed, and cracked vinyl floor tiles in the bathrooms would have to be replaced. It was the garden that charmed us. We would attend to the plumbing and bathroom floors later.

High-ceilinged rooms led onto a terra-cotta-tiled terrace enclosed by grillwork—decorative but also for security. Vigorous bougainvillea twined around the wrought iron, blocking out sunlight. Atop a tall ladder, our gardener, Thomas, pruned its twisted vines and restored our garden view. Tall hedges, like a green wall, surrounded a lawn which at the far end sloped down to clumps of tall grasses in a ravine that heavy rains turned into a shallow stream. Across this bit of wetland, neat rows of a coffee plantation's bushes covered the side of a hill. In the evenings, the garden would be a peaceful place to sit under the acacia tree and watch the crested hoopoes as they looped from tree to tree, echoing their low dove-like call. But we had only moved in a couple of weeks ago and were a long way from feeling settled.

THERE ARE LIONS

THAT MORNING, A damp chill woke me. Getting up to close the window, I flipped the light switch. Nothing. The power was out. Must be from the storm. All night, gusts of wind and driving rain had interrupted my sleep.

In the hallway, I groped for the phone. Dead. But I wasn't expecting any calls, nor did I need to reach anyone. A meager light seeped into the room. As if through a dull glaze of yellowing varnish, familiar outlines formed barely visible dark shapes. The monochromatic world of a bleak dawn. I hadn't been feeling well for the past few weeks. Unease unfurled in me like the petals of a malevolent bloom. The malaise, churning insides, and metallic taste in my mouth were the first symptoms of amebic dysentery. But that morning I believed I was suffering from existential angst, not from a minute protozoan parasite embedded and multiplying in my gut. When Stuart returned, he would diagnose and treat it.

"Mom, can we have breakfast?" Already dressed, Jen stood in the doorway.

"The phone's out, Jen."

"Again?"

In the house on Waiyaki Way, it had been out for three weeks while Stuart was traveling in Madagascar. Now he was in Rwanda.

"Maybe if Dad was here, he could fix it," Jen said.

We reminisced how in Tunisia, after heavy rains, the phone there too was frequently out, sometimes for days. Worrying that patients with urgent medical problems might be trying to reach him, Stuart would take matters into his own hands. Driving up and down the streets of Carthage, he scrutinized the telephone lines. Noticing where the lines were twisted, entwined from the wind, he stopped, climbed on top of our car, and undid the tangles with a long broom handle. Back in the car, he would drive on, looking for the next trouble spot. This crude fix usually worked if the problem was a local one.

"But he's in Rwanda now," I said, "and his method might not even work here."

That Sunday, it was just Jen and I. Maurice and William, cook and new gardener, had the day off. I was still saddened by what had happened to Thomas, our previous gardener. During the week, he stayed in a small room at the back of the house. He had left for the weekend but never returned. A relative came for his belongings—a couple of work shirts and a cooking pot. Maurice explained that Thomas's body had been found hanging in a tree in the nearby forest. We didn't know what happened, but I was plagued with the question of whether his death was related to his working for us.

William, our new gardener, was tall and well-built like Maurice. Alone in the house with Jen, I appreciated having these big men on the property during the week.

Later in the morning, at the makeshift booth at our garden entrance, the day guard would come to replace the night guard. A two-way radio for emergencies had been placed in our bedroom, but I hadn't figured out how it worked.

I had to think about breakfast for Jen. I wasn't hungry these days. The kitchen cupboards were still bare, and the butter I had bought the day before was rancid. We shared a small can of corned beef and stale crackers.

"What are we going to do today, Mom?" To make the most of her stay in Kenya, Jen wanted to spend the day exploring.

I had dreaded that question. Boxes still needed to be unpacked. The plumbers were supposed to return the following day to correct the water-pressure problem. It could be that the roots of the trees surrounding the house had twisted around and were obstructing the water pipes. The landlord wanted to cut down the trees; we wanted plumbers to find other solutions. A pile of papers on my desk needed to be sorted, letters to be answered. Perhaps Jen wanted to get me out of the house, to distract me. We decided to go to the Nairobi National Park.

Our new four-wheel-drive vehicle had arrived. With the Nissan's steering wheel on the right, navigating the roundabouts, of which there were many in Nairobi, was especially confusing. And it had been years since I had last driven a stick shift.

"Never mind, we'll manage," I reassured my daughter.

The park, a forty-four square-mile game reserve, was just a few miles outside Nairobi. Its open plains, forested areas, rocky valleys, and gorges were home to hundreds of species of mammals, hundreds of species of birds. At the entrance, we laughed at the sign in huge letters. "DANGER!!! STAY IN YOUR VEHICLE AT ALL TIMES."

The only large mammal not to be found in the reserve was the elephant. During our wildlife-conservation course at Nairobi's National Museum, Jen and I had learned about the fate of elephants in Kenya. At the time of the country's independence in 1963, the elephant population was thriving. Now, twenty-four years later, even after the ban of ivory trade in the seventies, poaching by organized gangs with automatic weapons continued. The number of elephants had dwindled, with a real possibility of total extinction in the near future. As we drove into the reserve, we saw an enormous mound of elephant tusks by the side of the road, the jumbled heap rising over twenty feet. Pathetic remnants of the magnificent animal. I visualized phantom gray forms ambling across Kenya's open grasslands, emitting a low rumble as they moved with dignity and a rhythmic sway of the trunk and flap of immense ears.

This pile had been confiscated from poachers. Richard Leaky, of the family known for exploration of the origins of man, was head of the Kenyan Wildlife Service. He had ordered the burning of the tusks as a warning to poachers that he would enforce the international ban. The ivory would be torched. A spectacular bonfire would reduce the millions of dollars' worth of ivory to a pile of ash.

Leaving this sad site, we drove through a thick forest and headed to the rolling grassland plains. The occasional feathery acacia tree with nesting weaver birds dotted the landscape. Driving here was straightforward—no other cars in sight.

"Can I drive, Mom?" Jen asked. "I'd like to practice using a manual shift."

"Sure, Jen, good place to do it.

We quickly changed seats.

The equatorial sun scorched, and the rarefied air seemed to shimmer and distort. Tall straw-colored grasses swayed. In the distance, dainty gazelles bounded in leaps with innate grace. A herd of wildebeest, ungainly in contrast, grunted and bleated as we drove past. Here and there, we crossed patches where, despite the previous night's rain, the bare earth resembled crackled pottery. Ostriches with their bald heads of wrinkled crimson skin strutted across the road. Clouds of red dust swirled behind us. A herd of watchful zebra stood still, their contoured black and white stripes stark against the sunbaked colors of the plains.

On the side of the road, the white glistening curve of a rib cage jutted up. Only shreds of hide remained.

"How sad," Jen said. "A hartebeest maybe? They've got odd shaped horns like that." A morbid cluster of black vultures pecked out the remaining bloody morsels from hidden crevices of the carcass.

Continuing south, we passed muddy pools where placid hippos, giant inflated hulks, bobbed in the water. One opened its enormous jaws, revealing yellow tusks in the delicate pink flesh of its huge mouth. We knew that the lethargy of the bloated bodies was misleading. They could suddenly explode and charge lethally on their stumpy legs.

Abruptly, the landscape gave way to a deep gorge and rocky ridges with scrub brush. Passing Kingfisher Gorge, we drove into a more remote area that a sign identified as Lion Corner. In between tall trees, the road crossed a shallow river. Because of the rain, the water level was higher than usual. To get to the other side, we had to drive over large, uneven outcroppings of the river bed. As Jen maneuvered over the irregular surface, the Nissan veered uncontrollably over the slick algae-covered boulders. The steering wheel spun out of her hands. The right front wheel skidded and wedged between two boulders. Stuck, the vehicle leaned perilously at a thirty-degree angle. To my horror, Jen opened the door and jumped out.

"Get back in. There are lions!" I screamed.

"No, the car's going to turn over!" she screamed back.

Jen scrambled up the bank to stand near a tree. I slid behind the wheel.

Don't panic, I told myself. This is a four-wheel drive. I can get it out. Just need to ease it back and forth. Like when you're stuck in snow.

Sweat dripped down my neck and arms. Changing gears clumsily with my left hand while keeping an eye on Jen, I started to maneuver. Back and forth. I gripped the wheel to stop my hands from shaking. Back and forth, back and forth. Over and over again.

It wasn't working.

I tried to calm myself and kept an eye on Jen under the tree. She shouldn't be out there.

I rolled down the window. "Get back in," I shouted. She shook her head.

I needed help. But I knew another vehicle might not pass for days. We could be stranded for a long time. I couldn't let Jen stand out there. It was crazy. If Stuart were here, he would know how to get this damn thing out. Once it got dark, it would be even more dangerous.

Back and forth. Back and forth. I must be doing something wrong, but I couldn't think of anything else to do. Back and forth. The engine produced a weird sound. What if it breaks down? I turned the engine off and waited. I should get out and force Jen to get in. A tipped-over Nissan was safer than being out there with God knows what kind of wildlife roaming about.

I restarted the engine. Back and forth. The vehicle lurched. Mud swooshed and spattered. The car swerved and slid over the boulders into deeper water. It sloshed to where the bank was only a few feet away. If we slid any more, we would end up in deeper water. I straightened the wheel and eased the Nissan up on the other side. In the rearview mirror, I watched Jen dash down the steep bank and hop across the slippery boulders. I reached over and opened the door for her. Limp, I slumped against the steering wheel.

"Mom, do you know how to get out?" Jen was breathing hard from the sprint across the riverbed. "It's getting dark."

By the time we found our way out of the reserve, the sun had set. Neither one of us wanted to go back to the empty cupboards in the kitchen. The power was probably still out anyway. We stopped at the Horseman, where the rotund polo-loving Swiss chef concocted his famous prawns in Pernod and other exotic fare. Inside was formal dining, but a more casual atmosphere prevailed at the tables outside. As we drove up, we noticed the outdoor section was flooded from last night's storm, but, oddly, the restaurant was open. A couple of waiters, wading through the ankle-deep water, brought platters of food to the few diners already there. Jen and I took off our shoes and rolled up our jeans.

The murky water rippled and lapped about our ankles as we savored spoonfuls of scalding soup with chunks of fresh fish in a curry of coconut and hot chilies. Feeling nourished, we began to relax.

I was thankful Jen had been in Nairobi with us since we arrived. But in a couple of months, she would return to the States. Nick was away at college, too. With Stuart frequently gone, I would be mostly by myself. Whereas Stuart was anchored by his work at the medical unit and his demanding travel schedule throughout East Africa, I would be living outside any tangible context. With Maurice and William taking care of the house and garden, what would my day-to-day routine be? I would be adrift.

As we dawdled over coffee, a new thought occurred to me. When Jen returned to Boston, when the plumbing was fixed, when the house was in order, I too would leave. Perhaps the intensity of trying to right the tilting vehicle had dispersed my mental malaise, had snapped me out of my muddled thoughts. With new focus, I had to admit that adjusting to life in Nairobi was going to be difficult.

I would try to get my job back at the International Atomic Energy Agency in Vienna, where I had worked before coming to Kenya. Career opportunities for Foreign Service wives living overseas were rare. I had not been optimistic about getting hired when I sent my application to the IAEA when we first arrived in Vienna. As in all UN organizations, the application process was cumbersome, filled with bureaucratic hurdles. Job vacancies were posted worldwide and drew a large number of applicants. When the call came for an interview, I was thrilled. The position was in the budget office, which prepared the agency's $250 million annual budget.

I worked with colleagues from Austria, Sri Lanka, Malaysia, Germany, and Turkey, a truly international group. My office in the IAEA headquarters was on the sixth floor of one of the slick skyscrapers that housed the United Nations organizations. From my desk, I looked out over the Danube and the iconic giant Ferris wheel. The job gave me a new identity and a circle of friends outside the embassy. I was not just the doctor's wife. Had I stayed in Vienna, the job could have been the beginning of a new career for me.

On the way back to our house, Jen told me how excited she was to be returning to college. She had already selected the French and German literature courses for the coming semester. She wanted to go on some more excursions before leaving—perhaps even a horseback safari.

In my head, I was outlining a plan to get my job back.

SAFARI

... a landscape that had not its like anywhere in the world. There was no fat on it and no luxuriance anywhere; it was Africa distilled up six thousand feet, like the strong and refined essence of a continent. The colours were dry and burnt, like the colours in pottery.

Isak Dinesen

SEVERAL TIMES EACH week Jen and I went riding at the stable run by Liza Burrell, a tough expat Brit who grew up in Kenya. Her close-cropped gray hair, tanned leathery skin, and trim muscled body spoke of years leading horseback safaris. She had provided horses for the 1985 film *Out of Africa.*

I was a cautious rider, but Liza coaxed me over low jumps, insisted I try a different horse each time, and never took no for an answer. One morning she brought out Rubani, a horse I had not ridden.

"Ride him gently," Liza warned. "He's a good horse, just needs a light touch. Otherwise, he'll probably throw you—like he did Robert Redford."

I took the reins from Liza and eased myself up into the saddle.

Leaning against the stable door, she lit a cigarette and watched. I walked the horse into the riding ring, expecting at any moment to end up on the ground, and waited for the others to get saddled up for our morning hack.

Every week, Liza took a group of us out across the open fields around her stables near the town of Karen. We cantered across stretches of the grassy terrain where Karen Blixen, the Danish author also known as Isak Dinesen, had planted six hundred acres of coffee on a six-thousand-acre farm. She wrote about her sixteen years in Kenya in her memoir, upon which the film *Out of Africa* was based.

The high altitude of the farm was not suited for growing coffee. Droughts and fluctuating coffee prices forced her to abandon it and return to Denmark. I sensed her nostalgia for the farm as I read in her memoir:

> ... *a coffee plantation is a thing that gets hold of you and does not let you go. There are times of great beauty on a coffee farm. When the plantation flowered in the beginning of the rains, it was a radiant sight, like a cloud of chalk in the mist and drizzling rain.*

As my riding improved, Liza proposed a three-day horseback safari. Kenya is synonymous with safari. The word conjures excitement, exotic wildlife, adventure. My safaris up to that point had been mundane experiences, as they typically are. In game reserves, crowded in a stifling Land Rover, we rode for hours on bumpy roads with windows closed against dust. The guide would promise to take us to the best places to spot "the elusive five." More often, it was the cluster of other vehicles that signaled something of interest. Through the open sunroof, we took photos of lions sprawled in tall grass—indifferent and unafraid, staring up with sad, amber-colored eyes. We were the caged ones. The lions—free to roam.

Never having spent an entire day, and certainly not three, on horseback, I had misgivings about my riding abilities, but the chance to see Kenya from the back of a horse instead of through a dusty windshield was too tempting.

It was my only chance for that experience since, in November, I would be leaving Kenya, returning to Vienna and my job at the International Atomic Energy Agency. It had been several months since I applied, and I had almost given up hope when the acceptance letter finally arrived. Knowing how much the job meant to me, Stuart supported my decision and offered to come to Vienna with me to help find an apartment.

"Mom, let's go on the safari," Jen said, hardly able to contain her excitement. "Let's do it."

Of the eight riders, all were young except Liza and me. Geert and Doortje, a young Dutch couple on their honeymoon. Helga, a German, and Kate from Ireland, both in their thirties and experienced riders. Even younger than the rest, a teenage jockey from the Nairobi Racetrack would be joining us, riding her own powerful mount, Princess L.

The Sunday before the safari, the group met on the shady porch of Liza's stone bungalow, next to the stables with their smells of freshly cut hay and horses. Maps spread out on the wicker table, Liza plotted our trek, marking the two campsites. Her stable hands would truck in water and feed for the horses. I had persuaded Stuart and our son Nick to participate in our escapade. In our all-terrain Nissan, they would bring tents and food and set up camp. Nick was spending a college work semester in Kenya and would help navigate the rough back roads. For the past two months, on night drives, he had been assisting a Dutch scientist track and set traps for jackal, genet, and other wildlife for a research project at the National Museum of Kenya.

Stubbing out her cigarette, Liza turned to Stuart and Nick.

"We'll be counting on you guys to be there with the gear. Before sundown. If you're not there …" She let the sentence hang, leaving us to imagine our own versions of dire consequences.

"What about lunch?" Helga asked.

"Hard-boiled eggs and bread. In the saddlebags, everything else gets macerated. And plenty of water, of course."

The maps folded away, Liza brought out a pot of tea and a plate of McVitie's biscuits. From time to time, we heard whinnying from the paddock behind the stables, as if the horses too wanted a voice in the planning.

"By the way, no riding helmets." Liza paused to whisk away flies hovering over the saucer of brown sugar cubes. "It's too hot. Wear a wide-brimmed hat."

For a moment, we nibbled biscuits in silence while Liza's pet mongoose scurried around our legs, scavenging for fallen crumbs.

"No riding helmets? Is this not dangerous?" Doortje asked.

Jen looked at me as if to ask what I thought. I shrugged, but thought riding without helmets was probably not wise.

At dawn, our group set out. Forest, my large black horse, plodded along.

"I know he's a bit slow," Liza said. "But he won't buck."

Jen had skittish Breeze, a lovely but nervous horse. In single file, we trotted through small neighboring shambas with plots of maize, banana plants, and the occasional grazing cow. Barefoot children chased the horses, clucking chickens scattered.

Leaves and grasses dripped with the previous night's rain. The high-altitude air here has been described as having the sparkle of champagne, but I had that euphoric feeling as if I had drunk a glass of it. I breathed in the morning's green freshness and settled into Forest's steady gait. Ahead of me, the horses' glossy coats gleamed. Liza led the way, followed by the jockey and the Dutch couple in close tandem. Helga, with camera slung around her neck, trailed behind Kate. In front of me, Jen rode with confidence, her long fair hair blowing back in the wind. The apprehension I had felt evaporated.

In a canter, Liza led us across fields to a stream of clear water trickling over pebbles. Forest balked at crossing even though the water was shallow. With firm heels, I nudged him across and hurried to catch up with the others, disappearing among the trees of the Oloolua Forest. Thick vines twisted around trunks of ancient old-growth trees. Perched on branches in the canopy, colonies of gray monkeys screeched and chattered. The horses trod through tangles of exposed tree roots. From the damp shade, we emerged onto the lush foothills of the Ngong Hills, four mounded peaks, like humps in the otherwise flat landscape. The horses took the gentle slope at a trot and, nearing the crest, lengthened their strides with a burst of energy.

Abruptly, the fertile green was gone. From the top of the hill, I looked out at the dry land on the other side. A monotonous landscape of scrub brush and patches of bare red clay that stretched endlessly. An acacia tree here and there. Where were the landmarks?

How would Stuart and Nick find where to set up camp? Did Liza know the way through this vast, featureless plateau? If this parched and desolate terrain was what we would be riding through, it was going to be a grueling three days. My apprehension returned.

As we made our way down the steep two-thousand-foot descent, loose stones slipped and rolled underfoot. Forest stumbled. If he lost his footing, we would go tumbling down the precarious slope. Liza motioned for us to dismount and lead the horses. In the furnace-hot air, swarms of flies buzzed around the horses' ears. By the time we reached the bottom of the hill, the sun was directly above us. The hot air vibrated with a shrill insect drone. Walking in riding boots, I skidded on the smooth stones on the uneven ground. At the bottom of the hill, it was good to get back in the saddle.

Overhead, turkey vultures soared. Dry grasses swished against the horses' legs. Liza waved for us to gather around.

"Watch out for cracks in the ground. Stepping in one, a horse can break a leg."

We set off again, scanning the ground for treacherous cracks. Ahead of me, Jen was trying to rein in Breeze, startled by something in the brush ahead. A pair of giraffes, browsing on leaves of the upper branches of a tree. On tiny heads, their ears flicked as they bounded away, long necks rocking in fluid motion, tufted tail curled up over their backs.

Liza waited under an acacia tree. Its tiny lacelike leaves on horizontal branches provided only a bit of shade. Above her, weaver bird nests dangled like strange limp fruit.

Liza dismounted. "Let the horses rest. Grab some lunch."

Mouth parched, I reached in the saddlebag for water. Eating our hard-boiled eggs and bread, we watched a herd of gazelle bounce across the plain with elegant leaps, as if on springs.

Back in our saddles, we reached a patch of dense thickets

blocking our way, their stiff branches covered with two-inch-long needle-like thorns. Guiding Forest through the branches, jutting out at impossible angles, I felt a tug on my shirt and heard the sound of ripping cloth—my shirtsleeve tearing open. Blood trickled down my right arm. I pushed Forest on to catch up to the others, already far ahead. Helga had stopped to take photos of a herd of impala, but we had gotten too close to them. With high leaps, they disappeared through the brush. I rolled up my tattered sleeve and examined the gash. From the dry heat, the blood had already crusted.

Liza set off again. I squinted against the blinding sun. Hot air seared my lungs. Kate took off her canvas hat and wrapped a long scarf around her head, Lawrence-of-Arabia style. The Dutch couple lagged behind. The young jockey rode hunched over. The wildlife that had earlier been a distraction from my aching legs and dry mouth had disappeared. Forest settled into an even trot, and I let him carry me along. The afternoon dragged unbearably. I lost track of time.

Eventually, tall silky grasses swayed in a breeze. The harsh light softened to a glow. Horses and riders cast elongated shadows. I searched for signs of a track or road, afraid that Stuart and Nick might get lost in this unending flat plain. And what if we didn't find the camp?

As the sun began to sink, Liza pushed us from canter into gallop. Rising up from her saddle, she searched the horizon for signs of the camp. Here, close to the equator, twilight was brief. After dark, we wouldn't find the camp.

Temples throbbing and heart pounding, I struggled to keep up. Light faded rapidly.

In the distance, against the darkening crimson sky, the black outlines of tents appeared. Stuart and Nick were clearing brush with their pangas. The stable hands stretched a long rope between tree trunks. After we had tethered our horses to the rope, Stuart and Nick passed out drinks. Iced beer had never tasted so good.

Nick ready to clear brush with panga.

"Did Stuart bring whiskey?" Liza asked.

"Um, I don't think so."

She reached for a beer, and from the disappointed look on her face, I could tell she had hoped for a nice stiff drink.

In the cool air, the campfire crackled. From somewhere out in the dark came the unnerving, hysterical whooping of hyenas. After dinner, exhausted, we crept into our tents. The campfire, kept burning at night, would keep wildlife away.

Jen with Breeze.

❧

In the bracing early-morning air, we saddled the horses.

"Our jockey's sick," Liza said. "Spiked a fever last night. She'll go back in the truck with the stable hands."

Princess L., her horse, stayed with us. Without her rider, the nervous horse pranced about. We would have to take turns leading her. My aching muscles protested as I hoisted myself into the saddle. Stuart and Nick, taking down the tents, waved as we rode off.

Eroded gullies and sparse vegetation—a drab palette of copper and ochre. In a plain studded with teeming bare-earth termite mounds, hundreds of hartebeest made grunting noises as we rode by.

Above the tops of grasses, a row of upright tails scampered, leaving a trail of barnyard smell. Warthogs. On their large heads, out of proportion to their stocky rumps, mean-looking tusks curved upward over a long snout.

The sun blinded. Hot, dry wind blew. The air quivered with shimmering mirages. I tried to ignore the dust on my face, the sore muscles, the dry mouth, the throbbing temples. Ahead, as if posing, zebra stood perfectly still. A troop of baboons, their young clinging to the adults' bellies, skittered away, barking.

Helga spotted an eland, its horns twisted in a screw-like spiral. Fawn-colored with thin white stripes, it grazed unperturbed and stately.

"It looks like someone dribbled white paint down its back," Jen said as she rode up next to me. "I'm worried about Breeze," she added. "She didn't touch her oats last night. Water, either."

"Well, Jen, she's high-strung. She'll devour her oats tonight."

Through the afternoon, we trudged on, tiny figures in the vast desolate plateau of more sky than land. In places of bare ground, whorls of dust drifted. Hours and minutes seemed to dissolve rather than progress.

Gradually, it cooled off. It would soon be dusk. Again, the camp was nowhere in sight. Having to lead Princess L. had slowed us down. Liza picked up the pace, and I urged Forest to keep up.

With upraised hand, Liza brought us to a halt. Now what? Why are we stopping? We need to keep going.

Then I saw it.

Up ahead, a huge buffalo. Massive. Head lowered. Utterly still, black, as if cast in iron. A surge of cold dread washed over me. Solitary males can charge. With a swipe of its deadly up-curved horns, it could slice open a horse. Liza up front, as if frozen, stared at the threatening hulk that loomed as if rooted in the ground. Why was Liza just standing there? My heart pounded, and I felt the quivering of Forest's muscles, sensed his fear. He started to back up. Afraid he might bolt, I tightened the reins.

Beside me, frightened Princess L. yanked on the lead; Kate tried to hold on to her. The long scarf of her turban came undone, dropped down on her shoulders. On my right, Helga swiveled her horse around to get away.

"No, Helga!" I tried to shout but no sound came out of my mouth.

In slow motion, Liza eased her horse around. As if drained by the effort, in a sluggish slow-motion gait, she retraced her steps away from the menacing buffalo. One by one, we urged our horses around and followed her. For endless minutes, we walked at a maddening slow pace in a wide circle away from the buffalo. I brought Forest up alongside Jen to ride close to her, all the while imagining the thuds of charging hoofbeats behind us.

We had lost precious time. It was getting dark. Once again, the race against the setting sun began. I scanned the plain. The red sky turned purple. By making the detour, had Liza lost her bearings? What if we didn't find the camp? Stuart and Nick must be anxious.

In the ever-diminishing light, we stayed in close formation, afraid to stray. I plodded on, unsettled by the strange night sounds. An incessant insect drone. The call from an invisible bird. Unidentifiable grunts, growls, yelps. The first stars appeared.

Far in the distance, I spotted the coiling plume of bluish smoke—the campfire.

By the time we unsaddled and tethered the horses, it was dark. Liza measured out the horses' oats. I picked up a pail and went to feed Forest.

All of a sudden, I was struck by a hard blow that knocked me down. In agonizing pain, I sprawled on the ground and struggled for breath.

Stuart ran up. "What happened?"

"I can't move my arm. It's broken." I gasped.

"Don't get up," he said. "I'll get something cool. Keep it from swelling."

Despite the excruciating pain, it was good to just lie there. To not move. To let my tensed muscles relax. Soothed by the cool air, I looked up at the night sky. Around me came the reassuring sounds of metal pails clanking, horses chomping oats, the soft flapping of a tent's loose panel.

As I inhaled the resinous campfire smell, I felt the prickly stubble under me. It occurred to me that if I couldn't move my arm, I couldn't ride. In the morning, I would have to drive back to Nairobi. I tried to lift my arm. It was heavy, as if a weight had been attached to it. But I could move it. I wouldn't have to quit.

Cradling my arm, I raised myself up. Liza, on her knees, scooped up handfuls of the precious oats that had spilled when I dropped the pail. In the flickering light of the campfire, I read annoyance on her face. In the dark, I had walked too close to one of the horses and been kicked.

Dawn came too early. The hurting arm had kept me awake most of the night. I ached all over. My legs wobbled. I didn't think I could get up into the saddle. Struggling against the pain, I hoisted myself up.

"Mom, look how thin she looks," Jen complained as she mounted her horse. Once again, Breeze had refused oats. The horse looked gaunt but hadn't slowed down. Jen had to hold her back from racing ahead.

The rhythm of Forest's gait lulled and distracted me from my aching arm. In a hypnotic daze, I watched the unending processions of graceful gazelle, jackal, and strutting ostrich. Soaring vultures and clusters of marabou stork. More giraffe, termite mounds, and sweet-smelling grasses. A carcass of bones picked clean.

Up ahead, a slight figure in her red plaid shirt, Liza sat ramrod straight in the saddle. The rest of us slouched from exhaustion. I realized that even though Jen and I went to the stables several times a week, I didn't know anything about Liza. I thought of her harsh life—making a living with a dozen or so horses on her small parcel of land with only a couple of stable hands to help. Yet, it had given her independence and an enviable freedom that I suspected I wouldn't have the guts or confidence to pursue.

᷍

I held on to Forest's mane and let his energy carry me through the interminable afternoon. As if in a trance, I watched us, horses and riders, insignificant in the vast tableau of which we had become a part. The incessant insect drone and blinding glare of the sun melted time. Nothing around me reminded of the twentieth century. Mile after mile, we rode through land that was untouched by the ugliness man so easily creates. And yet, man had existed here and wandered across these plains. After all, East Africa was the cradle of mankind. The artificial borders of Kenya and the neighboring countries, which interrupted and cut across tribal boundaries, had been created less than a century ago.

Not far away was a geological wonder, the Great Rift Valley, an enormous, deep trench that ran north and south for thousands of miles across much of the continent. Up to a hundred miles wide in places, it was edged with dramatic escarpments and a repository of fossils that traced man's evolution. For millions of years, man's ancestors lived here. They took from the land only what they needed. They built no spires or domes with their illusions of permanence but left the land unspoiled, unmarked. Their legacy was this pristine wilderness.

Not long ago, a hominid thighbone was discovered not far from here, and it might have belonged to that early man who first walked upright. I imagined how, as he stood up, his perception of the world must have shifted, his vision expanded. With the full sweep of the horizon, viewing the immensity of the sky, he must have perceived the possibility of new dimensions. On clear nights, observing the phases of the moon may have fed the seed of a thought in that nascent brain, the notion that there might be an underlying order in the universe.

⋖⋗

Under a violet sky, in the coolness of dusk, our little group of riders slowed down. The sun had set, and the last stretch of the trek was in darkness. It didn't matter. There was no hurry now. From here, the horses knew their way to the stables.

Layered with dust, sunburned, swollen arm throbbing—I had been on a safari.

PART FIVE

VIENNA-NAIROBI LETTERS

IF THIS WERE a film, the opening scene would be a panoramic view of Vienna's gothic spires, copper-clad domes, tree-lined boulevards, and meandering inner-city streets.

Scene 1

To the east, the camera tracks the calm expanse of the Danube and gradually zooms in on futuristic concrete and glass buildings surrounding a rotunda. Inside, the camera lingers on the color medley of the ten flags of the United Nations organizations that are headquartered here. It pans the early-morning crowd crossing the immense marble lobby to rest on its focal point—me.

Wearing a trim navy suit, I'm entering through the revolving door of the front entrance. After a year of casual attire—light cotton shirts and khaki shorts—I feel constrained in the narrow skirt, wobbly in high heels. At the front desk, I retrieve my ID badge and pass through security. An elevator takes me to the sixth floor of the International Atomic Energy Agency building. My spacious office, with windows sealed shut and climate-control panel on the wall, overlooks the river. Muted silvery-gray walls, neutral wool carpeting, and a serious over-sized desk—an austere and functional, if antiseptic, workspace.

I have returned.

Austrian, German, Russian, Malaysian, Sri Lankan, and Turk-ish colleagues welcome me back. We will be starting the preparation of the agency's $250 million annual budget.

Abruptly, the scene shifts to an empty apartment. After spend-ing a month in Vienna helping me find an apartment, Stuart has returned to Nairobi. I have just moved in. I write.

Vienna, November 1, 1988

I'm sorry you had such a hassle getting back to Nairobi—all the charm has gone out of air travel. Saturday was a gloomy day for me—you having left and then it rained all day long.

The airfreight came so I moved in even though the rest of the household goods won't come for another two weeks. I sleep on the floor—the ironing board is my only piece of furniture. Set at two feet off the floor, it is my dining room table and my desk where I am now writing this letter to you. It is dark in the evenings, no lights in the apartment except for the one lamp I bought to carry around and light whatever room I'm in.

Vienna is terrible without you. –D

Scene 2

The scene switches from fog-shrouded Vienna to the blinding midday African sun. The terrain is hilly with steep cultivated slopes. Small family plots, probably bananas, sweet potatoes, and cassava, surround clusters of huts. From a huge roundabout, curving roads lead outward so that, from the air, the appearance is that of an enormous gray spider. It's the center of Kigali. Just to the west, in an area devoid of any green, a concentration of rust-colored tin rooftops comes into view through a haze of red dust—a crowded shantytown. Stuart is on a routine regional trip to Rwanda. He writes.

Kigali

Things are <u>*very*</u> *relaxed here all green hills and the view from my hotel room (Milles Collines) is lovely. A very small quiet town. 1 Bata store (very few shoes), 1 grocery, 1 gas station.*

But there are Belgian commandos with their red berets manning a machine gun nest not too far from the hotel—the peace and calm are illusory. The perennial Hutu-Tutsi tribal conflict, never-ending.

Last night I went to the ambassador's residence—a reception for a small group of Americans. An ABC TV team and some foundation types, all very nice. They are making a one-hour documentary on mountain gorillas. There are some 250 left—that's all.

Today I give a health talk to newcomers at this very small post. The usual precautions of living in Africa, food handling practices, malaria—my standard spiel.

Very restful, no-stress trip. Saturday I fly twenty minutes to Bujumbura then back to Nairobi. Kampala trip postponed so I'm in Nairobi until the Madagascar trip. The patient the nurse was to take to the U.S. this week died at Nairobi Hospital—heart—yesterday evening.

Consulting the notebook you filled up with recipes and menus, Maurice makes sure that I'm well fed. William putters in the garden. The dogs are fine.

I play and replay Mozart's Requiem—to remind me of you and Wien. –S

Scene 3

My job is coordinating the budget preparation of several of the IAEA's divisions—the Office of the Director General, the Legal Division, Nuclear Power, Nuclear Fuel Cycle, Radiation & Waste Safety. Elevators take me to consultations with staff of each division. An express elevator goes directly to the twenty-eighth floor, the office of Hans Blix, the Director General.

The division's programs have to be matched to appropriate resources: staffing and funding. Member states—the United States in particular—scrutinize the budget process, ask for transparency. The agency's budget is in U.S. dollars, but a huge complicating factor is that most of the expenses are in other currencies, which are in constant flux against the dollar.

I spend endless hours at the computer performing rigorous analyses on a morass of data. The printer spews charts, graphs, complex number-crunching spreadsheets.

Vienna

I miss our garden in Nairobi—all those birds with their bird-noises flitting about. When I look out my apartment window, I see the silvery observatory dome in the park across the street. Against an opaque grayness, in dark trees that have lost almost all their leaves, there are crows and they sit in the bare branches like big black raisins.

The apartment feels empty—as it is—and sounds echo off the walls. But I suppose when the furniture does come (in a week or two) I will wonder whether I need all that stuff.

The shopping here is a welcome change from the bare and drab shelves of grocery stores in Nairobi. I feel guilty when I think of what you have to contend with from day to day with shortages of even the most basic foods. I love the fruit and vegetable place on the corner here—everything available and of the finest quality. The fish store is excellent as well and there is even a small butcher specializing in game.

Early in the morning, when I go past the butcher to catch the Strassenbahn, there are carts outside full of dead rabbits. I suppose someone shot them before dawn and they all bled from the mouth. Their gray furry bodies are all stretched out and the white fluffy ball of a tail is still intact. There are also freshly killed pheasants hanging from a hook with their long sweeping feathers trailing down. They must be really beautiful to see in the woods—the iridescence of some of the feathers catching light.

Miss you very, very much. –D

Scene 4

From Nairobi, which has the largest American Embassy in East Africa, Stuart travels to several other embassies in the region—Rwanda, Burundi, Uganda, Madagascar, the Comoro Islands, and the Seychelles—all relatively small hardship posts with tours of duty limited to two years, with extra pay. There is a high risk for food-and-water-borne diseases—bacterial diarrhea, hepatitis A, typhoid fever, and malaria. Added to that are the psychological factors and security issues of living in countries amidst political turmoil, with hazardous driving conditions and high incidence of crime. Serious illnesses require medical evacuations to Nairobi, U.S. military hospitals in Germany, or a return to the United States, usually accompanied by the doctor. At these embassies, staffed by State Department, CIA, USIS, USAID, and U.S. military employees and their families, the doctor's visits are eagerly awaited.

"I do a lot of hand-holding," Stuart might say.

He is on his way to Burundi. As the small plane approaches the airport, he peers down at the deep blue waters of Lake Tanganyika. Bujumbura, the capital, on the eastern coastline, is surrounded by terraced hills of coffee and tea plantations, which look as if they're covered with quilts made of patches of varying greens and browns. Wide boulevards and imposing public buildings at the city's center date from the colonial era.

Bujumbura

From the Hotel Source du Nile, I can usually see the Mitumba Mountains of eastern Zaire smoky-blue on a cloudy day—like a Chinese painting—across the northern tip of Lake Tanganyika.

So, this time I brought the camera, fresh film, got a room with a great view over the lake and as I sit on the balcony, the 10,000 ft. mountains in Zaire are invisible! It is the rainy season here but still plenty of sun and actually pleasant most of the time.

The food? I certainly can survive without bread—in Rwanda and Burundi all the "rolls" served with meals can only be described as hamburger buns! Perhaps some sort of Belgian ex-colonial revenge.

As I was packing for the trip the doorbell rang. It was Maurice. He and William were outside wondering about the appearance of the moon. Maurice suspected it was an eclipse. I got out the binoculars and gave a nice astronomy lesson on lunar eclipses as well as solar ones.

Much love. —S

Vienna

I think about you a lot and worry about your safety in all your East African travels. I do hope you're not suffering too much from stomach upsets, headaches, insomnia, etc. I know, no one in Kenya is exempt from the periodic gastric ailments. My health is 100% better since I came back to Vienna. I even brew myself strong black coffee in the morning.

The apartment still has that sharp acrid carpet-glue smell and I'm hoping the smell of coffee brewing and my spicy cooking will counteract it. I think that once our furniture arrives, with all the hidden dead elephant smells, it will smell more like home.

I miss the piano. From the downstairs apartment I hear Für Elise being played over and over and over again—and badly too, the same mistakes every time. Right now I would play Bach's preludes and fugues.

Tomorrow the furniture will be delivered and I hope it's not too hectic trying to orchestrate what goes in the apartment and what goes into the storage area in the basement without having to unpack the boxes. The elevator is so tiny nearly everything will have to be brought up the stairs.

It has not been all that bad sleeping on the floor, etc. Mostly it is just boring being in an empty apartment by myself. This apartment is so quiet—you don't hear any traffic or outside noise. I really hope that we can somehow get you to Vienna soon, soon.

Take extra good care of yourself and the puppies. Try real hard to find a patient to Medevac back to the U.S. so you can stop in Vienna on your way back.

I miss your energetic hustle and bustle. —D

Nairobi

Don't worry about the furniture it will get fixed, moved, etc. eventually. I just finished sunning and reading out with the doggies. Another "f***ing beautiful" day. I am at the desk looking out—so lovely.

I dug out our better stationery—enough of the lined office paper.

Thanksgiving dinner at Pam and Jerry Blake's was pleasant. Much food, of course, quite good (changed pens— dug out the pens also!) It was all very enjoyable until almost everyone went inside to watch an American football game on video. Jerry has tons of stuff, e.g., video laser discs, compact discs, tapes, records, video cassettes, 2 TVs, etc. Between that and his love of cars his brain must be full up. They've had a landscape gardener put in all kinds of tropical plants in the garden—looks ok, as we know, not a great house. There was a TENT! Outside next to the terrace I think it must be permanent. I noticed shiny copper tubing running along the wall outside the house—a long length of it and then it went into the wall. I jokingly said to Pam, "Looks like a gas pipe." She said, "Yes, that's what it is. I couldn't live without a gas stove and if I'm expected to entertain and with possible power failures I had to have it." What about everyone else? Jesus.

Talking about tents. The Martins had a dinner, one of those affairs set up in a huge tent with about twenty card tables and lots of folding chairs. The Embassy General Services staff set the whole thing up and on Monday they usually come to take the tent and all the tables and chairs back to the warehouse. On Sunday while the Martins were out and the servants off for the day, a truck came and picked up all the tables and chairs. The guard thought the Embassy had sent them. Then on Monday when the real Embassy truck came to pick up the stuff everyone had a bit of a shock.

The felt tips are dying. There is one Medevac coming up, but unfortunately no escort will be needed. Damn!

The house feels empty without you ... –S

LIVING APART

Scene 5

FROM THE AIR, the most conspicuous features of Madagascar are its rugged highlands, running north and south like a giant backbone of the island. To create land for farms and grazing for zebu, Madagascar has been almost entirely denuded. What is left of the forest covering, which once harbored the world's most varied and exotic fauna, can be seen as a narrow dark-green ribbon along the east coast and some small patches scattered here and there. Serious erosion problems mar Madagascar's landscape. Rivers running down from the highlands appear like ruddy-tinted tentacles that lead into huge deltas, then flow carrying rust-colored silt, spreading an immense café-au-lait stain far out into the Indian Ocean.

Madagascar

Had a great train trip up-country, rugged terrain, stayed in the Railway Hotel, a very primitive inn. In the rain forest saw lemurs, jumping from tree to tree. Bright green chameleons, like jewels.

I got up at 6 am today for my scheduled tennis time at 6:30 am but the court was too wet from last night's rain. When I said things were inexpensive here I didn't know that tennis costs $1.40 an hour for the trainer and 70 cents for the ball boy!

Later in the morning went to the incredible hugely crowded central market in Antananarivo. Was warned of incidents of pockets being slit, wallets stolen, etc. I will get all the Christmas presents I can, if not all of them. I will pack and send them. Madagascar has lots of embroidered tablecloths, stone things, inlaid wood boxes, fossils, minerals, medicinal plants, dried fish, orchids, you name it. Vanilla beans sold everywhere. Do you need some?

Visited the Institute Pasteur where they are studying malaria in lemurs—cages full of them, long black and white striped tails. Went to the ambassador's for dinner—lots of Malagash guests—throughout the evening had to struggle with my French.

Tomorrow I will finish Christmas shopping. So far I have for your sisters tablecloths with eight or twelve napkins— beautifully embroidered with flowers. One set poinsettia, one hibiscus, one daisies/cornflowers. They also have lilacs, etc., etc. I have the sisal bags in Nairobi for the girls—now have to find things for men, boys, parents, my office—also Nick & Jen.

Much love. –S

Vienna

Madagascar sounds great. I would like to go there with you one of these days. It is Sunday morning and I have just finished breakfast—Turkish bread and Danish Esrom cheese. The apartment is getting to be comfortable—I enjoy seeing it in the daytime—which is only on the weekends now. The curtains are finished but the light fixture situation still has to be improved. I dug out the old Tunisian light and think it might be nice for the entrance.

I'm making progress in the storage area but I can only do so much on one weekend as I don't want to overload our trash area too much with packing materials—you know how meticulously this building is kept. The recycling is so organized—bottles separated by the color of the glass! And poor Nairobi where trash burns right there on the street—the overpowering reek of the smoke permeating everything. Kenya is a really beautiful country, but even when the purple jacarandas and orange and red flame trees bloom, Nairobi is not a pretty city.

I'm sorry that Jen had to spend Thanksgiving by herself. How far apart our little family is now! Love. —D

Nairobi

By the time you get this you'll have 3 more weeks before your Christmas trip to Nairobi. Counting the days.

Monday Dec 12th is the 25th Anniversary of Kenya's Independence. I return from Madagascar Sunday the 11th about midnight. I plan to stay home and guard the house. By the way, I am very careful and drive very carefully. I am panicked that some lunatic will cause problems.

Elaine was driving on Waiyaki Way toward St. Austen's and some driver came out from the left and smashed the left side of the BMW. She was not injured but is some annoyed.

And in today's paper (enclosed) terrible—an International School teacher, a Danish fellow murdered in Mombasa area at holiday cottages—bows and arrows. Tourism will never survive much more of this.

We have a new night guard—maybe he started before you left—very bright & cheerful. I gave him his first KS 200 today for November. Maurice and William are due next to be paid December 20. How much extra should I give them?

Trip to Kampala coming up.

Oh, I put in a work order before my last trip to fix the goddam washing machine. When I returned Maurice told me it works fine—all they did was change that hot/cold valve thing in the machine. It seems that the crook Raschid kept replacing it with broken ones. The hot and cold water runs in now and the machine cycles all by itself.

With that bit of housekeeping silliness I now profess my undying love for you. —S

Scene 6

From Kenya, the flight to Uganda is across the huge freshwater Lake Victoria. In the distance, shifting veils of mist obscure, then reveal, the snow-capped peaks of the Ruwenzori Mountains. Near the shore, in unruffled shallow waters, men in dugout canoes fish for Nile perch and tilapia. Approaching Entebbe Airport, as the plane descends, a cloud of smoke appears as if arising above the water. Closer observation solves the mystery of the smoke—it is an immense swarm of insects. Through green hills, the road leads to Kampala.

Kampala

Marabou storks walk (if that's what they do) all over the grass next to the hotel and kites and crows soar overhead. It is very green but warmer than Nairobi. The plane was two hours late but that is now normal for travel in East Africa. Things may be getting a little more stable here. The "road blocks" on the way from the airport seem less forbidding. The Embassy van does not have to stop, but this trip instead of soldiers in jungle fatigues with automatic weapons, there are men in blue-gray slacks and light-blue shirts and no guns to be seen. Progress.

Visited the local hospital. At the height of the AIDS epidemic and the Ugandan lab technicians are <u>not wearing gloves</u>!

At the DCM's house for dinner, power outage, caused the generator to kick in. I guess this happens so often that all the Americans have back-up generators. After dinner sitting on the balcony overlooking the valley I was startled by rounds of machine gunfire close by. "That's a sound you hear all the time," unperturbed, the DCM explained. "Everyone here has AK47s, even young kids."

My big chore when I get back to Nairobi is to wrap and send all the gifts.

Missing you very much. –S

Vienna

Yesterday, during lunch hour I went and picked up your glasses. They are great—only hope the prescription is ok. I got a sleek hard case for them—too bad I can't give them to you <u>now</u>. You won't believe this—frames have a year and a half guarantee *but they must be "serviced" after six months for the guarantee to be valid. Only in Austria!*

Friday night went riding with the UN Riding Club. In the chilly damp riding school I rode a huge, old horse that needed a lot of prodding to get it to do anything—my hands and feet were numb from the cold. I felt nostalgic about riding in Kenya with Jen. The crisp high-altitude air, the horses needing no urging or prodding—horse and rider, as one, cantering through tall fragrant grasses—nothing between us and the wide horizon but the Athi Plains—as if it were the first day of creation.

The people in the club are extremely friendly and we always go to an Italian restaurant afterwards. The restaurant people don't seem to mind all the riders coming in as the garlic smell overpowers any lingering smells of the stable.

Last Sunday morning I walked in the Vienna Woods again. Off the main path, on damp mossy trails I strolled up the hill in the dappled shade of oak trees—thick dark trunks encrusted with lacework of lichens. Down a steeper slope, across a meadow I went to "Agnesbrunnel"—a sprawling outdoor restaurant. In front, neatly chalked on a blackboard was the special lunch menu. It was Beuschel, that wonderful Austrian delicacy prepared from heart and lung of pig—undoubtedly a relic of war years. I suppose the scarcity of meat forced cooks to improvise dishes from previously untried cuts. I skipped lunch.

Next to it was a funny sort of farm with animals wandering all about—ducks under cars, three giant mottled boars penned in a muddy enclosure, donkeys and ponies grazing under apple trees, chickens and geese everywhere, staccato-pecking in the strewn-about straw. I loved the place, so rundown. I lingered a moment to absorb its raw barnyard smells. Next to the grunting, snorting boars were three black goats, just like Billy Goats Gruff. At the edge of their wire cage, blue hyacinths in bloom. What an alarming smell—hyacinths and goats.

Vienna is getting all decorated for Christmas, which means I will soon be in Nairobi.

Missing you. —D

Nairobi

My travel makes time go by very fast. I am looking for a Medevac both in Nairobi and all over the region. Had to make a quick trip to Mogadishu—not a nice place now—has a very beautiful beach and everyone used to enjoy it. But a few months ago they built a meat-packaging factory right on the beach that is attracting large numbers of sharks. There have been deaths because of the sharks and now no one goes to the beach any longer.

When I got home I found that Maurice had put his big bag of green stuff in the refrigerator so next day I had him make me some. It's called "Sukuma Week." I had Maurice write the name for me. It was delicious I'll get the "recipe"—he puts something in it but I forgot to ask him. Small amount of tomato or onion?

I'm off to the Sarit center for some vegetables then out in the garden to read in the sun. I will be very tan when you see me—a whole new me. I miss you a lot. —S

Vienna

This morning when I got up we had one of those incredible Kenya-like blue skies. But now as I sit in my office I can't see two feet in front of the window—the fog is so thick.

Work is very hellish now but that's ok—makes the time go by faster.

So looking forward to all of us spending Christmas in Nairobi with you. Am glad Jen will be coming to Vienna first and we can travel together.

It is a treat to come home in the evening, and it has been cold, wet, rainy, slushy, to open my mailbox and find one of your letters. The little gray mailbox vibrates with the dazzling stamps on the letters—bright spotted butterflies, and other exotic creatures.

Love you. –D

TOGETHER BRIEFLY

Scene 7

JEN, NICK, AND I have spent Christmas in Nairobi. After a short camping trip in the Aberdares, our holiday has come to an end. In our garden, enclosed on either side by tall, clipped hedges, the air is alive with the wing flutter of twittering birds, the incessant high-frequency whirring of insects. Gold and magenta bougainvillea twine around the iron grillwork of the veranda. We sit in the shade of eucalyptus trees; the leaves rustle as a breeze plays through the branches. Strange raucous calls announce the flight of hadada ibis. They glide overhead, necks extended, long legs trailing. On the hills across the valley, bent-over workers tend the bushes of the coffee plantation.

Nick and I will leave tomorrow, Jen a few days later. Once again, we will each go our own ways. The dogs, unaware of the approaching departures, romp around us playfully, weaving a thread of joy through the afternoon.

Vienna

I'm trying out some new word processing software that is called Multi-Mate—sounds like a Playboy bunny. Almost finished P. J. O'Rourke's book, Nick's present, along with the one by Hunter S. Thompson. It is the funniest book I have ever read. I will mail it to you.

At the apartment your letter from Kampala was waiting, also the little post-it "Choklit" scribbled by Jen, on the inside of the front door so we would not forget your Godivas (in the fridge) when we departed for Nairobi at around 5 am.

The only event during my absence was that the two kohlrabies which I left on the kitchen window sill had sprouted leaves.

To counteract what I ate on Kenya Airways I made myself some very hot curried squid using my lovely Indian spices. The only person who could possibly have enjoyed a lunch like that with me is Calvin (Calvin & Hobbs).

The time spent in Kenya was really lovely and much, much too brief. I do consider it a miracle that all of us actually got there. Jen and Nick seem to be thriving. It seems so incredibly gray here now—looking out the window I can hardly see anything there is so much fog.

Love ya. –D

Nairobi

I think Jen had a good time after you and Nick left—much riding with a fine jumping class. Her departure went smoothly but so sad (me). I spent a while with her at the airport lounge but had to get home for some sleep at the empty house—Jen ended up with a nice tan.

On Jen's last day of riding, we had arrived early and were seated under the trees—very strange weather, dark and misty. Suddenly a dark catlike animal darted over to Jennifer, gave a grunt groan, and jumped into her lap startling her; then he jumped into my lap, curled up, closed his eyes and sucked its thumb! It was a mongoose. Liza told us later her daughter had found the newborn marsh mongoose in the Mara and had reared it on formula. They have hairless feet with "fingers" with claws. It just curls up in your lap and sucks away at one finger, very friendly and funny. I enjoyed my hack—just Jen and me, no syce. I cantered quite a bit across the fields.

The telephone wire got knocked down again yesterday—hope to get it fixed soon.

My travels begin soon to Moroni, then the Seychelles, then Bujumbura/Kigali. I must find a trip to Europe. Soon.

Our Medical Conference this spring will be in Lisbon. Perhaps you would like to come. I will certainly come to Vienna after the conference.

I'm getting rambly, illegible and tired. There has been <u>much</u> rain lately—unseasonable. Dogs are great.

Much love. —S

P.S. Big fat ticket enclosed—just save it (or use it!) good for a year—convertible to other itineraries.

Vienna

My work is interesting at the moment as I am doing a few studies and analyses and that takes me out of the office and I get to meet more people and work independently.

Riding last night was fun except for some reason the horses were unsettled and jumped around a bit. For a moment it looked like a rodeo as several of them started to buck. Fortunately, no one fell off. Afterwards as usual we went to the Italian restaurant and ate dishes which were all laced with big chunks of chopped garlic. Healthy for the heart but I'm sure I still reek this morning. Anyway, after dinner out came a few bottles of Dom Perignon (The UN Commissary, of course) to celebrate the occasion and it was a late night. I'm not used to this.

Heard from Jen and she had enclosed a letter from Tufts University informing us that she had been placed on the Dean's List for the fall semester (with an A in calculus). Wow! Jen writes that she just read Jonathan Carroll's new book and you're in it—"Dr. Scheer with his mustache." Love. —D

Scene 8

Surrounded by the intense blue of the Indian Ocean, from the air the volcanic Comoro Islands look like moonscapes—bleak lava fields. In the center of the largest island, a huge crater appears like a vigilant eye. Radiating from the barren crater, ridges of lava flows that have solidified—the last eruption well within memory of the island's older inhabitants.

Moroni

Moroni is quiet and restful and Victoria should be the same. I will stay with the ambassador there but I will not try roasted fruit bat for lunch as Nick did when we were in the Seychelles.

Am not sure why we have an embassy in this backwater— former French colony. They imported the island's exotic fragrant oils—ylang-ylang, citronella, jasmine.

The most prevalent malady here is boredom.

Went for lunch on the beach—rocky. Slab of freshly caught tuna grilled on hot coals at an open-fronted shack of a restaurant.

Near these islands, coelacanths (thought to be extinct) can still be found—live nearby at 600 feet down—sometimes coming up to 150 feet. Every so often a live one is caught and studied by fish biologists who come and go in teams. The New York Aquarium team wants to take one back to New York! They have a pressurized tank on the island—none of the coelacanths have lived more than a few days. They should leave them in peace.

When I come we can trade books. Nick keeps us amused with P. J. O'Rourke & Hunter S Thompson—all I have to send him is an occasional copy of the local paper.

Jen called after I spoke with you—she really is wonderful. Nick was coming over to dinner that night.

I'm glad you drink the Dom Perignon after riding. Drive carefully—.

Miss you very, very much. –S

Vienna

Dear Stuart, Jen & Nick,

I hope you don't mind that I will write my 3 in 1 letter again as time has slipped by quickly during these last two weeks. Anyway, I like addressing you all at once—it's as if we're all sitting outside in our garden in Nairobi waiting for dinner. As it's only 5:30 pm we still have to wait an hour until Maurice serves and he won't serve before that because in that little spiral notebook of recipes I have written Dinner: 6:30 pm. And we're all starving, smelling the cooking smells wafting about. And there are all those noises of clattering pans, onions being chopped, dogs' food being prepared, hot oil sizzling, etc. Usually Maurice glides about the house like a shadow but when he gets into the kitchen there is a whole unbelievable orchestra of kitchen sounds. I don't think you can hear anything when I cook—but maybe you can, you'll have to tell me.

Nick, I hope the database is not taking over your brain in favor of the wonderful quirky humor that usually resides there. Computers make you think in a straight line.

Zita, the last empress of the Austro-Hungarian monarchy, died. I think she was at least 97 years old. Her funeral was a very big event in Vienna. She lay in state in the Stephansdom for about three days and the lines of people waiting to pay their last respects reminded me of the lines we saw outside Lenin's Tomb.

My love to all of you. —D

Nairobi

I am sitting at our desk at 6:30 pm just having finished a nice parrot fish dinner. Now I have a bit of brandy in a Moser glass snifter. The garden scene is peaceful with sunlight still on the trunks of the trees. You complained that the mail was taking long—not so. Your letter dated the 25th was waiting for me at the embassy this morning. Just 6 days. It shows how our concept of time shrinks and expands.

I am busy with projects like redoing the health information book and organizing a scheme to supply many African posts with Hepatitis B vaccine. In the U.S. and Europe, 3 doses cost around $137. In Nairobi the Belgian-made vaccine costs $37 for 3 doses—the third-world price! Wrote to Washington and suggested we supply the region or Africa and save hundreds of thousands of dollars. We can pouch it anywhere—it is good out of the refrigerator for 30 days or more.

There has been no Paludrine, a critical malaria preventative, on the market for the past 3 months. We finally received a huge supply last week from Bonn—we were down to our last 100 tablets.

A few days ago someone called me from the Japanese AID and Volunteers office—90 volunteers in Kenya. They too were out of Paludrine and asked for help. A "delegation" of three people showed up—so nice and friendly. I gave them 2500 tablets ($25 worth!) plus advice on how to get some from Europe.

Later that day I told the DCM that I had helped out the Japanese AID people in case he was "thanked" at some reception or other. I explained that it only cost $25 and we now have tons of Paludrine. Then he asked if they were going to replace it. I told him that I did not want that. Jesus, these professional "managers." What fools.

Enough chatter. I feel quite mellow (mellow?) and look forward to a restful visit to Victoria. I am taking them a big supply of medicines, etc. and I always enjoy the ambassador's company.

Missing you. –S

Vienna

Got Nick's fall term evaluations—they're always such a pleasure to read. Want to share Rudolph Serra's comments on Nick's work in Sculpture. "Working in cardboard, Nick constructed a sculpture combining red and black planes. Much like the works of Alexander Calder, the sculpture drew in space as compositional form. It was excellent. For the final critique, working in wood, he presented a mechanical Kiddie Krusher. That is, an arm with sharp nails sprang forth upon contact. All in its path were destroyed. Painted pink & purple, the project was excellent and enjoyed by all in the class. Nick surely has creative potential."

I had a nuclear training course all of last week and now I know everything and more than I thought I would want to know about the nuclear fuel cycle, nuclear reactors, critical mass, etc. One presentation was done by an "expert" who worked on the atomic bomb at Los Alamos but now his efforts are directed toward peaceful purposes. One whole day was spent visiting the Atominstitut as well as Zwentendorf, which is in the process of being dismantled. We entered the steel containment area and the "core" of the reactor and could see how the fuel rods are assembled for fission.

Am reading Hunter S. Thompson's Generation of Swine. *I love the quotes he has chosen as occasional chapter headings. "And I will give him the morning star" from the Book of Revelation. (Stuart, your birthday is coming up and I thought that would be a most appropriate present—not a bible, a star.) Another quote from Revelations 13:18. "Here is wisdom. Let him that hath understanding count the number of the bears: for it is the number of a man; and his number is six hundred threescore and six." (And I was feeling so smart too after my nuclear course.) But I do love what HST says: "I have stolen more quotes and thoughts and purely elegant little starbursts of w r i t i n g from the Book of Revelation than anything else in the English language—and it is not because I am a biblical scholar, or because of any religious faith, but because I love the wild power of the language and the purity of the madness that governs it and makes it music." It is also because there is always a Gideon Bible in the hotel room where he is staying.*

I love you. —D

Nairobi

In Kigali with nothing left to read I picked up the Gideon Bible. (They are everywhere) and looked through it, especially Revelations. Must have been ESP.

Yesterday the nurse asked me to help out with a patient she was seeing. A USAID, middle aged (like me) guy with lower right back pain. She was thinking kidney but I helped her differentiate between renal and muscular back pain. (She often asks my help—I enjoy teaching this way.) The patient exercises—sit ups with knees unbent, runs, etc. Pain was <u>low</u> *back and with movement—easy case—told him hot, hot showers, no exercise, etc. As I was returning to my desk and paperwork the nurse drawled, "Doctor Sheeah, whatdya think a bein' gay?" Right in front of the patient—a nice USAID married guy, father and all. "Being gay," I said. "Yeh, bein' gay." My mouth did pop open but I pushed it shut quickly. Had this man just come out or something and she wanted me to give a quick AIDS lecture? On the third or fourth go-around I got it—Bengay. "Sure, it warms your skin and if it helps, fine," I said. "But don't forget the hot showers and heating pad."*

Thinking I should apply for the medical director job at the UN to be with you in Wien.

Much love. —S

P.S. They paved all the potholes on our street.

CRITICAL MASS

Scene 9

FACING UNREALISTIC DEADLINES, I compile budget data, estimate expenditures, calculate currency fluctuations, project price increases, produce complicated budget tables. The three-hundred-page budget document will be translated and printed in the six official UN languages. Every table, every calculation has to be checked, rechecked, and checked again. Taking my fatigued, computer-screen-riveted eyes off the blinking cursor, I am startled by the dazzling alchemy of ruby-magenta sunset veils transforming the Vienna sky. The red turns to purple, then to black.

Vienna

Saturday afternoon we had a storm. At three o'clock in the afternoon it suddenly got so dark that the street lights went on. It was very eerie, and then the downpour started. I had a little pot of black beans simmering on the stove and the smell was comforting. Recently I read in the International Herald Tribune that black food was all the rage in New York among the trendy and knowledgeable. So you see how fashionable we have been with our black beans all along. It's not easy to think of black things to eat aside from caviar. Nick could always do his Ramen in squid ink.

I was feeling rather nostalgic for Kenya and so started reading back issues of "Swara" and other Nairobilia. The primary and dominant topic these days seems to be poaching, and rightly so. In a letter to the editor, Daphne Sheldrick's comment brought it poignantly home—"You can replant forests, and even reclaim deserts in time, but no one, when the last elephant has gone, can make another." I once heard her lecture in Nairobi. When you see her—very matronly, lots of makeup, nail polish and hair as if she just stepped out of a salon, you can't imagine that this pampered-looking woman has spent the last 40 years of her life caring for baby elephants and rhinos that have been orphaned. Baby elephants have a very low survival rate and are exceedingly difficult to care for, demanding feedings every two hours and producing quantities of unspeakably foul diarrhea. And she did it all by herself.

I've started my German classes once again but I think that my problem is that my enthusiasm for that language is diminished and I get very irritated when the sentence structure is unnecessarily complicated.

Love –D

Nairobi

Your letter arrived yesterday—Black Food!

Another three day weekend—beautiful weather and I sit outside enjoying Satanic Verses*—excellent book. I'll bring it to Vienna. Enclosed is a picture of rock hyrax from Hells Gate Park.*

Read in the "Nation" that three German tourists and Kenyan driver were seriously injured when two bandits shot at their vehicles. Early this month, two German tourists were shot and wounded in the Tsavo National park by bandits. The Commissioner said that there was no cause for alarm.

I sleep with Nick's baseball bats next to the bed.

Much love. —S

Vienna

How are you? We have had some appalling weather and I often think of sitting in our garden in Nairobi at dusk.

With Nick in Israel for the semester work program, Jen in Boston, you in Kenya, and me in Vienna, I realize that our little family is on four different continents at the moment— well, four different geographical areas, anyway.

I don't think that either one of us realized that this living on two different continents would last two, perhaps even three years. This is much, much too long, especially since we have a great relationship and make a wonderful team. Don't you think? These next few months are going to be the most difficult ones but maybe some ideas will crystallize and we will realize what it is that we want to do next.

At work right now we are doing a five-year analysis of past programs and budgets. A lot of people are going on leave in August so the pace is quite leisurely and no impending deadlines until September. I'm supposed to be Acting Director of the Budget Section while the Director is gone. I'm not sure at this point that I want to carve out a career here and I cannot see myself doing this for any extended period. I crunch a lot of numbers, produce estimates and masses of tables that look rather impressive. But, really, of what benefit to anyone is all that? Frankly, I feel that I have accomplished more, ironing five or six of your cotton shirts.

One of the things that I am looking forward to doing in our next household (when we will be together) is cooking big pots of peasant food—the kind of cooking that I enjoy most like stews and couscous and roast goose, etc. even baking bread again—these things that are instantly gratifying.

Love. –D

Nairobi, February 8, 1991

After three days in hot and dry but amazingly green Bujumbura, I am happily enjoying the warmth of a blazing fire on this cold, gray drizzle of a weekend.

I have been reading Alice Walker's Temple *and halfway through I am already overwhelmed by the insights—women and men, blacks and whites—sharpened, I suppose, by our being in separate places and my living and traveling in Africa.*

The trip next week to Madagascar will be my last for a while. I'm living in great anticipation and impatience. I miss you a lot.

Get me out of here! –S

Scene 10

In the oldest part of Vienna, just a short seven-minute U-Bahn ride from my office, is St. Stephen's Cathedral. Crossing the uneven cobblestoned square, I enter through its immense doors. Inside, the cathedral is dark. Through stained-glass windows, a feeble winter light casts pale-colored lozenges on the stone floor. Flickering sacrificial candles emit a warm melted-wax scent. The camera scans the ornate gilded altars, the Byzantine icons, baptismal chapels, crypts, and marble tombs. I have come to immerse myself in the vastness of this echoing space, to absorb the cathedral's tranquility.

The deep and solemn cathedral bells start to ring. They mark each passing hour ... my passing hours. Each mournful sound of pealing bells weighs down, seems to sink into the damp atmosphere. Each stroke of the hour penetrates my very being.

It strikes me with sudden clarity and finality, the thought that has been eluding me, that I have tried to push aside. The thought that the people with whom I have surrounded myself here are not the ones I care about deeply. Those dearest to me are far away, very far away.

The fragile tableau of my lonely life in Vienna is no longer sustainable—it has reached critical mass.

Outside, the camera plays on the glazed tiles on the cathedral's steep roof. On the towers, it traces the gables, pinnacles, delicate finials. Briefly, it frames the twilight-lit rooftops of Vienna. Gradually fades out.

TIME BLOWN THROUGH A TRUMPET

"HOW WOULD YOU like to go to Barbados?" Stuart asked, calling from Nairobi. The American Embassy on the small Caribbean island could very well be his next assignment.

That February afternoon when he called, bruised clouds massed across the sky. A cold drizzle had turned to freezing sleet. It was a bleak winter day in Vienna.

Don't we all dream of living on a tropical isle with azure waters and swaying palm trees?

⊷

In a blast of humid oven-hot air, we walked down the rickety ramp of the small plane that had just landed in Bridgetown. Until we found a house, we would be staying at the Divi Southwinds Hotel on a white sand beach.

It was after dark that the island came alive. The high-frequency whistle of countless tiny tree frogs filled the air. But in the bar by the pool, their trilling flute-like sound was drowned out by the steel band's persistent beat. Sipping exotic rum concoctions, we dined on flying fish, fried plantains, and callaloo. The dancing continued long after we had gone to bed. Deep into the night, the calypso/reggae rhythms throbbed. Perhaps it was the beating of my heart that I heard—or the two had somehow synchronized. When the music ended, I listened to the soothing swoosh of waves on the beach.

"I've got to go away for a while," Stuart told me the next morning.

"What? We just got here."

"Must visit some embassies and consulates in the region—Grenada, Martinique, Trinidad and Tobago, Georgetown in Guyana, Paramaribo in Surinam, Caracas and Maracaibo in Venezuela."

"Doesn't sound like a hardship trip."

"Hardly. While I'm gone you could find us a house to rent."

Each morning, at about the time when I finished my early-morning jog along the curve of the beach, five Bajan men appeared. Leaving towels in the shade of a coconut palm, they walked down to the water's edge. The gray-haired men were unsteady on their feet, frail from infirmities of old age. I wondered if because of their dimmed vision they could even see the turquoise sea. In the waist-high water, holding hands, they formed a circle, reminding me of Matisse's painting, *The Dance*. But the angles of their stiff elbows interrupted the fluid lines of the circle, disrupted the undulating rhythm of arms and shoulders depicted by Matisse. Buoyed by the water, though, the men's arthritic knee and hip joints were, for the moment, made supple again.

I wondered whether their lives had been spent in back-breaking labor on sugar plantations. If, in dense tangled thickets, the wielding of machetes cutting cane had bent them over, had hunched their backs, diminished their stature. Their sons and daughters, no doubt grown by now, might have left the crowded island in search of a different life.

On those sun-drenched mornings, with the sun's warmth on their worn backs, the cares and sadness accrued over long lives melted away. They had no need for words, for they knew each other's stories well. With infectious, explosive gaiety, their bursts of laughter echoed down the beach.

It occurred to me that it might not be long before the circle of five was reduced to four. The cruel inevitability of their gradually diminishing circle was, I was sure, far from their thoughts at that moment.

As I swam in the glassy warm water, its surface barely ruffled by a breeze, I thought of my mother. She didn't have close friends with whom to share the simple pleasures of life, nor had she ever enjoyed frivolous, carefree moments. On beach outings, she never ventured into the water, not even to wet her feet. As my sisters and I swam with my father, she stayed on the blanket fully clothed, folds of her dress tucked around her outstretched legs. I couldn't remember her going for leisurely walks, nor digging in the damp earth to plant a bulb to bloom in the spring. Or pause to listen to a bird's melodic warble, except the one time a blue jay, in attack mode, swooped down on her as she was hanging wet laundry on the clothesline in our backyard. She seemed to prefer to remain indoors, protected by the walls of her comfortable home. I wondered if she ever looked at the stars.

Above wispy clouds, very high up, a large black bird with forked tail—a lone frigate bird—glided in wide circles. The enormous span of its wings kept it aloft a long while, rising and soaring in an aerial swirl. Floating on my back, I too felt suspended, as if poised at the top of a giant arc. An arc that might have already begun the imperceptible descent of its curve.

On those mornings, I wore a red bathing suit, a bright flame-red one that I had bought for my new island life. On the front of the suit, embroidered in metallic gold thread, was the American flag, and under it, large gold letters spelled out U*S*A—the stars separating the letters embroidered in silver. A flashy piece of clothing, flashier than anything I had ever bought before or have bought since. I still have it in a drawer with all my other bathing suits, the black ones. I am reluctant to get rid of the showy red one—it reminds me of a sparkling moment. It no longer fits.

With patient real estate agents, I crisscrossed the island searching for a house. If there had been highways cutting through the island, its paltry dimensions would have been more apparent. Instead, narrow, meandering roads led around and back again, making it easy to get lost. But this roundabout way created the feeling of having traveled and actually gone some distance. Past endless sugarcane fields, along stretches of road lined with scraggly casuarina trees. Past small plots of avocado trees, banana palms, and papaya plants, their clusters of green fruit hanging below lobed leaves.

When asked by the agents to describe the house I was searching for, it was hard for me to explain. I could hardly tell them I was looking for a house that would define me, that I was waiting for the house to find me.

One agent took me to the house where the previous embassy doctor had lived. On the rugged east coast, it was perched on craggy escarpments. The rough sea crashed on cliffs, sending up tall salty sprays. In the immense stone house, the empty rooms echoed eerily. A precarious wooden staircase built over large boulders led down to a stretch of pink-sand beach inundated by huge waves. Although gloomy and foreboding, the house was not without a certain drama, but maybe not for us.

Cut down to create sugar plantations, not many forests remained in Barbados. But in the middle of the island, in one of the remaining ones, was a house named Middle Earth. Surrounded by magnificent trees, in a shady haven from the tropical sun, the house was built around an ancient tree with rooms that spiraled up around its huge trunk. But it would be a long commute to Bridgetown, and how would we get our grand piano up that spiral staircase? During sweltering days, I visited dozens of other island houses with tiled floors, ceiling fans, louvered windows. Wooden porches looked out on walls with sprawling sun-bright allemande flowers and gardens of croton, the yellow and red mottled leaves garish against pink hibiscus.

Back from the trip, Stuart attended his first weekly staff meeting with the ambassador. The last item on the agenda was a newly arrived work of art, shipped to Barbados by the State Department as part of the Art in Embassies program—a blend of art, diplomacy, and culture. Galleries and museums lent works of American artists to be exhibited in ambassadors' residences.

At the meeting, the large, framed lithograph propped against the wall generated comments from the staff.

"Good God, what's that supposed to represent?"

"My six-year-old could do better."

"Those colors!"

"I wouldn't put it anywhere, Mr. Ambassador."

"Look, if we can't find a place for it, we'll just store it in the warehouse," the ambassador said, annoyed he had to deal with such trivial matters.

But Stuart had a solution. "If no one wants it, I'll take it for the medical unit."

Frank Stella's floor-to-ceiling work was hung on the bare white walls of the medical unit. *The Symphony* was a bravura work with a visual punch—an egg-yolk yellow form surged under a hovering black mass, and Life-Saver-colored flourishes surrounded a swooping white arabesque. In the aseptic setting of the waiting room, an optical feast.

The medical unit was a small operation, with just Muriel, the Bajan nurse, and Stuart. Health problems in Barbados were not as acute as in many of the other embassies where Stuart had worked. Most patients came in with minor medical problems, and psychological counseling was the most time-consuming part of his practice. The isolation of island living and the danger of crime were significant problems. Early on, Stuart noticed a strange and surprising phenomenon. For one reason or another, many embassy staff assigned to Barbados curtailed their assignments and left paradise island before their tour was completed.

Each overseas post presented unique medical problems and challenges, and Barbados was no different.

One evening over dinner, Stuart mentioned that Jim Todd, the young security officer, had come to see him. Jim was worried, almost embarrassed, and explained that there was something weird going on. Sitting on the examining table, Jim pointed to his bared right leg. On his thigh was a large mark in the shape of a hand. The blistering rash, angry red in the middle of the palm part of the handprint, gradually diminished to a pinkish color toward the fingertips, the thumb barely perceptible. Jim placed his hand over the rash to demonstrate that the shape matched his right hand exactly. Had Jim's own hand produced the rash? Stuart had never seen anything like it.

"It looks like contact dermatitis," Stuart told him. "Something you touched. Have you been working in the garden? There are toxic tropical plants in gardens here."

Jim seemed relieved to hear that there might be a plausible explanation, but said that he did not work in the garden. He had a gardener.

Stuart tried to get Jim to think back to whether he had inadvertently touched anything unusual. Jim shook his head and said he couldn't remember anything odd. Then, almost as an afterthought, he added, "This is silly, but the other day when I was on the beach with the kids, there were these little green apples strewn about in the sand under a big tree. I didn't think they were apples really, just looked like them. I picked one up and tossed it into the water."

"And then, you placed your hand on your thigh. Jim, that little apple-like fruit that you picked up was from the manchineel tree."

Everywhere in the Caribbean, growing on sandy beaches, were manchineel trees, forty or fifty feet tall, with lustrous elliptical green leaves that resembled those of an apple tree. These magnificent trees provide shade and a natural windbreak. Their roots stabilize the sand and prevent beach erosion. But everything about them is poisonous. The trees are marked with a red cross and a warning notice attached to the grayish bark of its trunk. Eating one of its sweet-smelling apple-like fruits can be fatal. During a storm, if you sought shelter under a tree, the rain passing through the leaves could cause painful blisters. Even burning the tree was dangerous; the smoke irritated the eyes.

But the tree had its uses. Cutting it released sap that Carib Indians once used for poison darts.

꩜

The real estate agents were just about ready to give up when one took me down a quiet lane on top of a high ridge on the west coast of the island. To the right, stretched the manicured grass fields of the Polo Club; to the left, along a white wall, a row of giant blue agaves. Past a wrought-iron gate, at the end of a long driveway shaded by the canopy of mahogany trees, stood Croeso House.

Its entrance led into a high-ceilinged great room that served as the living room and dining room. It was not really a room. By folding back the slatted wooden doors during the day, the entire wall opened onto a brick-paved courtyard. In the middle, a fountain with a trio of arching dolphins was surrounded by a shallow pool filled with lavender water hyacinths. From each side of the courtyard, doors led into two bedrooms, separated by a bathroom.

Through an archway overgrown with magenta bougainvillea, gardens extended to the ridge that dropped off to the Caribbean Sea. The house had been built to frame the exquisite setting.

✎

Shortly after moving into Croeso House, I was scheduled to return to Vienna to work for another three months. It was a promise I had made when I handed in my resignation at the IAEA. The director of the budget office asked me to come back during the hectic months of final budget preparation, and I had agreed. It was winter in Austria, so I packed my wool skirts and tweed blazers.

The evening before my departure, Stuart and I sat with glasses of wine in the shade of the flame tree, ablaze with orange blossoms and black pods hanging from the branches above us. Creamy flowers frothed over the hedges next to a profusion of red-spiked ginger flowers. A stone path led to a mango tree and elephant ear plants, along the edge of the ridge. The garden had never looked so lovely. This garden is where I want to stay, I thought.

"Maybe we don't have to leave," I said. "I mean, after I come back from Vienna."

"We've still got two years here," Stuart said.

"I know, but I would like to stay forever."

"You mean retire here?" He sipped his wine. "I could, you know."

At the end of our tour in Barbados, Stuart would have been in the Foreign Service for twenty-six years and eligible for retirement.

Mulling over the possibilities of that thought, we looked out over the Caribbean Sea, where the sky flared in golds and crimsons that faded to a lime-colored glow at the horizon. As if released by darkness, a sweet smell wafted from the frangipani tree. Palm fronds rustled.

At night, for security, we closed the folding doors of the great room and crossed the courtyard, past the trickling sound of the fountain, to our bedroom. We padlocked its iron gate. The windows, protected by decorative grillwork, could be left open to the breeze that billowed the sheer white curtains into the room, ruffled the mosquito netting draped over the bed. The soft rhythmic thwack of the ceiling fan accompanied the sounds from the water-hyacinth pool—the loud croaking of giant brown-speckled frogs.

My three winter months in Vienna were long days and dreary weekends. I spent hours in front of the computer, struggling to meet budget deadlines. I sifted through data, checked hundreds of financial tables, and counted the days until my return to Barbados.

A week after I returned, Nick called from New York.

"I've got some enlarged inguinal nodes," he said. "The doctor told me to have them biopsied. Still waiting for the reports. Don't worry. Just routine follow-up."

After graduating from college, Nick had found a job he loved at The Bettmann Archive and had just moved into an apartment on Manhattan's West Side.

"You would love my apartment, Mom," he said. "It's got wood floors."

A few days later, Nick called again. This time he had terrible news. The biopsies confirmed non-Hodgkin's lymphoma, stage four.

Nick in sculpture class at Bennington College, 1989.

We reeled from the shock of the unexpected and serious diagnosis. Nick would be undergoing grueling treatment for many months. As soon as packers could be scheduled, we would return to the States to be with him. Stuart and I were devastated, and walked around numb from nightmarish worry about Nick. Stuart spent the following days at the embassy organizing an immediate transfer back to Washington. Shrouded in a fog, I moved like a phantom through the house, getting ready to leave Barbados.

෯

Croeso House can be rented now. You can stay there for $1,500 a day. The tall mahogany trees still shade the driveway, but the house has been transformed. In the great room, the traditional dark tray ceiling has been painted white, and Versailles-style crystal chandeliers have replaced the cooling ceiling fans. The long louvered wall that once opened onto the courtyard is now closed off; large mirrors reflect the decorator-designed interior. A covered gazebo and an entertainment room bristle with self-important luxury.

The breathtaking setting has become an afterthought, the focus deflected from the garden and from the sea. A guard is on duty, and air-conditioning in the bedrooms shuts out the sounds of the tropical night. The water-hyacinth pool has been bricked over. The frogs' loud croaking can no longer be heard.

BUTTERFLY ENVELOPE

"THIS IS TIZETA." The voice on the phone had an odd accent. Not knowing any Tizetas, I was about to hang up.

"Askale," the woman said. "You remember her?"

Hearing her name startled me, and I thought I could not have heard right. Of course, I remembered Askale. How many years had it been since we left Ethiopia? Thirty? Maybe more. I could still picture how each morning, wearing a gauzy white *shamma* with embroidered hem, she arrived at our house in Addis Ababa. I remembered her bright smile as Nick and Jen ran to greet her.

"I am her daughter," Tizeta said. "Askale wants to see you."

When we left Ethiopia, I didn't think I would ever see Askale again. And now, was it possible we would meet after all these years? It surprised and pleased me that she had wanted to search for us. How did Tizeta find us?

"Where is Askale?" I asked.

"In Maryland, with me. I will bring her and when I come, you will meet my two sons," Tizeta said, and hung up. She called again a few days later, and we made arrangements for their visit.

❧

We were living in upstate New York when I received that call. In Ethiopia, Askale helped care for our young children. At the time, she was raising five children of her own, the first one born when she was only fourteen. While she was taking care of our children, I often wondered who was looking after hers. Jen and Nick adored her, and when we left Ethiopia for our next assignment, we were sad that we had to leave Askale. Now, thirty-six years later, I would see her again with her daughter and two grandsons.

◦৲

On a cold winter morning with a snowstorm blanching the landscape, I set the table for breakfast. Tizeta, driving during the night, planned to arrive early in the morning. The weather forecast was for continuing snow.

"I'm worried," I said to Stuart. "They're not used to snowstorms."

Addis Ababa's average daytime temperature is a balmy seventy degrees.

"Instead of breakfast, I think you better prepare lunch," he said.

I reset the table for lunch.

The heavy flakes, accumulating rapidly, had whited out landmarks. By late afternoon, drifts obliterated our long driveway. Maybe they weren't coming after all. The dangerous and slippery roads might have forced them to turn back.

I had looked forward to this visit. Of course, I wanted to see Askale, but I was also hoping she could provide insights for this exercise of self-examination I had begun—putting experience on paper, telling my stories. From unearthed scraps and fragments, an archeologist can extrapolate an entire culture. Unlike the archeologist's tangible clues, though, memories are amorphous and fleeting, filtered through viewpoints, perceptions, and misconceptions. I had hoped to capture some of Askale's recollections, get a backward glimpse that would help me interpret that encapsulated segment of time when we lived in Ethiopia. As seen from another culture, hers would be a fresh view, not unlike that of an anthropologist making observations on first encountering a primitive tribe. I had hoped to ask, "Askale, when you first came to work for us, what were your impressions?"

The path to the front door, shoveled just a while ago, had disappeared under more snow. We hadn't heard from our visitors, but in case they were still on the road, two herbed chickens were roasting in the oven. I set the table for dinner and lit the logs in the fireplace.

At dusk, the storm ended. Across the valley, flickering lights appeared. It was that moment when snow-covered fields appear to acquire a blueish tinge in the fading light.

Just when I thought they wouldn't be coming, their van pulled up in front of the house.

Would we meet with the slightly distant and respectful formality we had maintained in Ethiopia? Would Askale greet me with a slight bow of the head, hands clasped under her chin as she had done when she came to our home those long-ago mornings in Ethiopia?

I need not have worried. Tizeta, even though I had never met her, ran up the front steps to embrace me. Askale, helped by Yafet, her seventeen-year-old grandson, got out of the van and walked with careful steps up the snowy path. When she reached our front door, she threw her arms around me in a prolonged and tearful hug.

As Askale took off her coat and shawl, I saw her abundant hair was now gray and the years had added pounds to her once-slender figure. But the radiant smile and the sparkle in her eyes were the same.

She stood and looked around her for a moment, as if she expected the four-year-old Nick and six-year-old Jen to run in and greet her with a hug.

"They're big now," I said.

"I know," she sighed and fumbled for something in her coat pocket.

"This is how I found you." She handed me a blue envelope, worn and crumpled.

The envelope, decorated with four colorful butterflies, was addressed to Dr. Stuart C. Scheer, American Embassy, APO 09319, New York, NY—our mailing address in Ethiopia. Askale, fascinated by the bright butterflies on the Bonwit Teller envelope, which had probably contained an ad for a sale in the New York department store, had retrieved it from the trash when we still lived in Ethiopia.

"I will find the doctor for you," Yafet had told his grandmother when she showed him the faded butterfly envelope. She had kept it all those years in a small basket, along with her husband's military memorabilia and a handful of family photos. On the internet, it didn't take Yafet long to trace us, to match our name with a phone number.

At dinner, Askale's plate remained empty for she was fasting to observe Genna, the Ethiopian Christmas celebrated on January 7, according to the Julian calendar. Her fast could not be broken until the following day. The Ethiopian Orthodox Church had an astounding two hundred fasting days each year. It occurred to me that in a drought-plagued country with frequent famine, fasting may have served to conserve scarce food.

Askale had been studying English, but her Amharic accent made it hard to understand. Not to discourage her, I nodded from time to time as if I understood. Yafet was quick to recognize the problem and translated. I was touched by Yafet's attentiveness to his grandmother. At dinner, he pulled out the chair to help her get seated, and later went to get a shawl to wrap around her shoulders. Yafet's face reminded me of those I had seen on ancient Ethiopian church frescoes. Above a high forehead, black frizzed hair framed his solemn face like a halo. Under arched eyebrows, dark compelling eyes dominated his features, observing everything around him.

Michael, Tizeta's other son, a couple of years older than Yafet, didn't speak. He had been diagnosed with a poorly controlled seizure disorder, and his silence may have been due to medication. Tizeta told us that Michael loved to draw and spent hours copying portraits of Haile Selassie. Around his neck, Michael wore a scarf knitted in red, green, and yellow—colors of the Ethiopian flag—with the words "Lion of Judah" embroidered in black. The black onyx ring on his right hand bore a tiny stylized gold lion.

After dinner, we gathered in front of the fireplace. Bathed in the glow of the smoldering logs, Tizeta struggled to tell us what they had lived through.

We knew that in 1974, about a year after we left Addis Ababa, the Derg, a leftist military group, came into power. In a bloodbath called the Red Terror, the brutal Soviet-backed regime tortured and executed countless citizens. The king was deposed, probably murdered. Droughts led to famine. The country was ravaged and changed forever.

From Tizeta's recounting, we were able to piece together the circumstances that led to their leaving the country. Askale's husband had served in Haile Selassie's Imperial Guard. Perhaps because of this connection, the family's property was taken. They lived in fear of what might happen to them.

Tizeta's vocabulary in English was too limited to convey the hardships they had endured, but the anguish on her face revealed the suffering. Askale sat in silence. As Tizeta faltered midsentence, searching for a word, Yafet shifted uncomfortably in his chair. To the young man, sitting in front of a warm fire after a dinner of more food than they could eat, listening to the harrowing events in Ethiopia may have sounded unreal, belonging to another world, better forgotten. It could be that he doubted we could understand what his family had experienced.

The questions I had hoped to ask now seemed trivial and frivolous.

"Would you like to return to Ethiopia one day?" I asked instead.

Askale and Tizeta both shook their heads in an emphatic no. Yafet didn't but sat with a distant gaze. I suspected he would learn how to straddle the two cultures and probably return to Ethiopia one day.

With her two young sons, Tizeta had come to the United States fourteen years earlier, when she was granted political asylum. I wondered about the fate of Tizeta's husband, but did not want to ask.

She found a job as a security guard and, with her scant savings, brought her mother to Maryland four years ago. Askale had hoped her husband would join her, but he died before they could be reunited.

As if to interrupt the conversation with which he was visibly becoming impatient, Yafet stood up and wandered around the room. He examined the brass processional crosses we had displayed on a side table, looked at the framed parchment paintings in our dining room, the black Falasha pottery on the bookshelf, the reproductions of ancient frescoes of Lalibela's rock churches. He plucked the strings of the *begena*, the large Ethiopian musical instrument that stood in the corner of our living room.

"You have more Ethiopian things in your home than we have in ours," he remarked.

❧

Next morning, I set out bread baskets and jams for our visitors' breakfast. Stuart measured out coffee for the filter and poured in water when, as if he had suddenly thought of something, he stopped.

"Tulu Guya's artwork," he said.

I knew what he was talking about. We looked at each other and nodded. There was no need for discussion. We knew what we wanted to do.

Stuart dashed down to the basement and brought up the frayed portfolio, improvised from two large pieces of cardboard, fastened together by little cloth ties. Inside, sixteen large woodcut prints and half a dozen copies of each one, all numbered and dated 1969, were signed by Tulu Guya. The artwork depicted Ethiopian rural life—a woman milking a cow, grain being winnowed, men harvesting teff with scythes, water being poured from earthenware jugs, bent-over women carrying large gourds on their backs.

This collection of prints had come to us under somewhat mysterious circumstances. Shortly after we left Ethiopia, a friend from the American Embassy in Addis brought them to us in Washington, DC. He didn't explain how he got them, nor did he give instructions about what to do with them. Just that he didn't want to keep them any longer.

Respectful that the work in the portfolio represented an artist's considerable effort, we kept it for more than three decades. As we traveled from country to country, the portfolio was packed and unpacked with care each time. It couldn't be given away to someone who might not understand or value its meaning.

Recently, through the Addis Ababa School of Fine Arts, Stuart traced Tulu Guya and offered to return his artwork. Tulu responded by sending two new works—*Skinning a Goat* and *Gugs*, the latter portraying two warriors on horseback competing with shields and spears in an Ethiopian jousting game.

A correspondence followed that revealed a strange story.

"Every thing have its own history," Tulu's letter began. After graduating from art school in Addis, he got a job in another town and entrusted his entire artistic output to Lebna, a close friend. Several years later, when Tulu returned to Addis, he searched and searched but could locate neither Lebna nor his artwork. "Day by day I tried to forget my loss." What saddened Tulu the most was that he had not expected this from Lebna, "a friend as close to me as a brother," he wrote.

Tulu's letter continued: "Now after all these years a man whom I don't know searching me to give back my art work keeping as his life from dangerous things. This is a message of God not of man."

Tulu didn't want his work back—rather, he hoped it might be exhibited in a gallery somewhere. He sent another series of prints from more recent years.

The more recent prints, on thinner paper with narrower margins, perhaps for more efficient use of paper, were of similar rural scenes. But this new series was different. Gone were the subtle colors on cream-colored paper. The new work used black ink on stark white paper. The complex crosshatchings that had previously created depth and rich textures were subdued. Fluid compositions with interesting negative space had been replaced by rigidity. Voluptuous lines had frozen up, become arthritic, as if some fundamental academic training had been abandoned. My immediate reaction was to dismiss this work as inferior.

But my initial superficial judgment was misguided. In a country that had undergone such drastic changes, a difficult life had shifted Tulu's focus, taught him to eliminate the superficial, to suppress the decorative, the picturesque. Struggling to extract new meaning, to portray the truth of what he now saw, I suspect he must have thrown down his woodcutting tool in frustration from time to time, for he was trying to express the inexpressible. It could be that his hand had cramped on the carving tool, had refused to embellish raw reality. What he now confronted could no longer be expressed with romanticized artistic flourishes for purely visual pleasure. Tulu's attempt to convey something more elusive than rural workers going about their daily tasks had resulted in more direct, more powerful work.

The print collection, a record of an artist's painful experience and artistic evolution, was a cultural treasure.

Stuart opened the portfolio and, one by one, showed Askale and Tizeta the artwork. When finished, he put the woodcuts back in the portfolio and tied up the little cloth ties. "We want you to have this Ethiopian art," he said and handed Askale the portfolio. "When you look at it, you will think of Ethiopia."

Askale looked at Tizeta as if to ask her permission. Tizeta nodded. Tears ran down Askale's cheeks as she took it.

Stuart did, however, keep out one of each of the sixteen wood-cuts and mailed them back to the artist in Addis Ababa.

As Askale and her family left, I thought about the fragile but-terfly envelope and what it had made possible. I knew I would not see Askale again.

THE POND

IN 1991, AFTER the fall of the Soviet Union, Latvia once again became an independent country. My father, already in his eighties, was given the opportunity to reclaim our family's property in Riga. He declined to do so.

It could be that the war had taught him the ephemeral nature of property ownership. That rather than have it taken away from him again someday, he preferred to renounce his claim. The house, the garden, for him then would have been an empty stage-setting. The peaceful early decades of his life could not be recaptured. What he had lost could not be returned to him.

Father died in January of 1997. On the day of the funeral, a blizzard whited out Cleveland. Through snowdrifts obliterating the cemetery paths, shivering, we gathered at the gravesite for a brief eulogy. The somber words were muffled by the hiss of driving snow and wailing wind—nature's own raw requiem. The turbulence of the weather seemed to echo the turmoil of my father's life. As the storm continued unabated, the coffin could not be lowered into the grave. Numb from the arctic cold, we hurried away. The coffin remained there, blanketed with snow.

That sad winter day led me to reflect upon burial traditions in our family. My maternal grandmother who fled Riga with us died in the DP camp in Germany. At the time, I thought she was very old and had lived out her life. I am much older now, I realize, than she was when she died. She lies buried in a rustic graveyard just outside a town in Bavaria, in the shade of ancient oak trees. For the next forty-five years, Mother sent money and corresponded with Frau Hitze, who had promised to take care of Grandmother's grave.

In Ohio, my parents acquired two cemetery plots for themselves, side by side, many years before their deaths. They selected matching tombstones, and my mother once showed me the brand new satin shoes in her closet, still in the shoebox—her burial shoes. She had also bought a beige lace dress for the occasion—a dress more beautiful than any she ever wore during her lifetime.

Stuart's parents also followed tradition and purchased gravesites while they were still alive. They were buried in Riverside Cemetery, next to each other as they had wished, in a section set aside for the Scheer family.

When my sister Maija was widowed, we gathered in her house to mourn. Neighbors, friends, relatives brought food—casseroles ready for the oven, sugary spiral-cut hams, apple pies, homemade loaves of bread, cookies. We reminisced and we ate.

Stuart and I are going to break with tradition. He wants his ashes scattered over our pond. I understand. The deep clear pond nurtures us, as it does the wildlife it attracts. It is our communion with the progression of season's rhythms. In early spring at the edge of the pond, we contemplate the first frogs and toads, then swarms of tiny tadpoles. We wait for the pair of honking geese to arrive each year, the crested wood ducks that come next. Later, barn swallows loop in giant arcs, barely skimming the crystalline water. Dainty damsel flies, iridescent blue, rest briefly on a floating leaf. A great blue heron perches on the dock.

Our pond was dug some years ago in the middle of a field of

black-eyed Susans, Queen Anne's lace, and meadow grasses. After it was dug, I was dismayed by the immense, hideous twenty-eight-foot-deep hole. It looked like a dead crater. What had we done to our beautiful landscape?

Gradually, rain and underground streams filled the raw excavation. Sparse at first, vegetation grew in at the edges, thicker every year, creating refuge for wildlife. When cattails first appeared, we welcomed them, admiring the undulating stalks. In the spring, red-winged blackbirds built nests in the dense growth. Herons came for the tadpoles, frogs, and toads. Even an occasional snapping turtle appeared.

The invasiveness of the cattails surprised us. Their thick roots grew foot-long shoots from which new plants quickly sprouted and started to take over the pond. Advancing from near the dock, they spread deeper and deeper into the water.

We decided to eradicate some of them, pull them up one by one, gather them, and cart them away—a monumental undertaking.

As I waded into the pond, the disturbed water turned from clear to muddy. Tiny damsel flies rested on plaques of algae floating nearby. Reluctantly, I scooped up a handful of the algae, expecting it to be slimy. It wasn't. The soft warmth of it wrapped around my hand. I threw handfuls of it onto the edge of the pond.

"Check yourself for leeches," Stuart warned, already chest-deep in the water.

"Leeches?"

"There might be some near the cattails."

I grabbed a cattail stalk, a few inches below the surface of the water, and cut it with my Felco pruner.

"Don't do that! Don't cut it! Pull the whole plant up, root and all, so it can't continue spreading."

I tugged at the cattail. Firmly rooted, it didn't budge. "I can't do it—it won't come up."

"You have to yank several times at an angle to loosen it, to dis-lodge the root, then it comes right up. Look!" And he showed me one he had just pulled up—a mass of tangled root and an emerging succulent-looking white shoot.

I tried again, pulling harder, but in the waist-deep water there was not much traction. After several attempts, the root loosened from the clay and the cattail came up. It felt like something was crawling on my back. Startled, I slapped at it until I realized it was only the tips of the cattail I had pulled up, arching over my back.

As we progressed, all around us frogs plopped and splashed. Slogging through the now stirred-up murky water was hard work, the sun hot on my back. I thought of workers cutting sugarcane in the blistering summers of Barbados, bent over, sweating in an unending field of suffocating vegetation.

Why are we doing this? I wondered. We could hire someone to come in and do it for us.

My back was beginning to ache, and my arms would be sore tomorrow. We called it a day and climbed onto the dock.

"There's a leech on your foot," Stuart said.

I hurried to pull it off. Not easy. The sucker, firmly attached, adhered tenaciously, and the soft body slipped through my fingers. Stuart pulled it off and crushed it, leaving a patch of my blood on the weathered wood of the dock.

"It's been on your foot for a while," he said.

Yes, I promised myself, I will call someone tomorrow to do the rest of the cattails.

To cool off, I lowered myself into the pond. As I swam in large circles in the cool now-clear water, a heron flew overhead. Black and white dragonflies whirred about my head, swallows descended in giant swoops to skim the surface. I floated on my back, and near me on the calm surface, a few ghost shells of nymphs drifted—the translucent outer casings of the dragonflies' underwater phase. Their only imperfections, the tiny slits through which the dragonflies emerged—suddenly airborne and free.

The pond had many rhythms, many voices. I listened.

ఌ

When our lives end, why could we not be freed into another realm with the ease of an emerging dragonfly? We have funerals and burial traditions, wakes, tombstones, and ash-filled urns. Somber rhythms of funeral marches evoke grief and regret.

What do I imagine for myself? Well, first of all, no food, please. I couldn't bear to think of friends and relatives summoned to reflect briefly on the transience of life being distracted by food. Perhaps a glass of sparkling champagne. Echoing through the house might be the wrenching yet tender *Vier Letzte Lieder* by Richard Strauss. These poignant melodies convey the pain of heartbreak, the sorrow at life's twilight ... *the summer shudders ... the garden is in mourning.* Hermann Hesse's poetry set to haunting music.

And the soul unwatched
would soar in free flight,
till in the magic circle of night
it lives deeply and a thousandfold.

And my ashes? Well, I have just found out about Algordanza, a Swiss company. For €5,500 they could take my ashes and reduce them to about 500 grams of carbon. The retrieved carbon could be transformed into a sparkling blue diamond.

Now you lie revealed
in glitter and array,
bathed in light
like a miracle before me.

～

As I think about my experiences in the many countries where I have lived, I am reminded of a quote from the Scottish writer, Ernest Gordon.

I recall that when I was visiting the town of Paisley in Scot-
land I had been told how the old-time weavers, all the while
they were making their beautiful and intricate patterns, saw
no more than a tangle of colored threads. They never saw the
design until they took the finished fabric from their looms.

My memories of those years have often felt tangled like the threads of the cashmere paisley shawls from Scotland. Nothing more than fragments. Out of order. Collections of smells and sounds that evoked certain isolated moments. Bits and pieces, memory flashes. But now as I look back, I can see the intricate and rich pattern. I see the connecting threads.

ABOUT THE PHOTOS IN PART ONE

My father, an accomplished photographer, took countless photos of my three sisters and me when we were young. In his artful compositions, proof of his remarkable eye, he captured our childhood and our emerging personalities. As I looked through the photos for this book, I became aware that it is not readily apparent that they were taken against the backdrop of disruptions and deprivations of war. Editing out the drab and the miserable, my father focused his camera lens on us.

The photos reveal happy children being themselves, doing typical things—walking in the woods, dressing up, and playing musical instruments. My mother assembled the hundreds of photos in albums, and looking at them today opens up a vault of memories. My sisters and I can relive our childhood. Father's gift to us.

Made in United States
North Haven, CT
19 October 2021